THE WATER BATH & PRESSURE CANNING MASTER'S COOKBOOK

Your Complete Guide to Safe and Delicious
Home Canned Foods for Every Season. Preserve Nature's Best in a Jar
and Create the Pantry of Dreams

Sandrine Kelly

Table of Contents

HERE IS YOUR BONUS!

"Seasonal Canning Calendar"

Your Essential Printable Calendar to Capture the Bounty of Each Product

INSIDE YOU WILL FIND:

1. **Seasonal Sections**: The calendar is divided into four seasonal sections, each with its own introduction.

2. **Highlight of the Month's Seasonal Produce**: Each month is meticulously detailed with the specific fruits and vegetables that are at their peak. Use this information to plan your canning projects around these seasonal stars, ensuring you're working with the freshest, most flavorful produce.

3. **Recipe Inspiration**: Alongside each month's produce, you'll find recipe suggestions tailored to those ingredients. These are starting points to inspire your canning creations, allowing you to explore new flavors and techniques.

4. **Monthly Canning Tips**: Every month comes with its unique set of tips and advice. These nuggets of wisdom will help you in selecting the best produce, utilizing effective canning methods, and understanding the nuances of preserving different types of produce.

SCAN HERE TO DOWNLOAD IT

Introduction

Have you ever stood before a shelf, mesmerized by rows of gleaming jars filled with jewel-toned preserves? Those jars are not just containers of deliciousness, but vessels of history, brimming with the essence of ancient practices. But what lies behind that shimmering facade of preserved fruits and vegetables? What alchemy transforms perishable items into long-lasting delights?

Preservation is nothing more than an act of defiance against the relentless march of time, and historical records suggest that ancient civilizations had already mastered the art of salting meat or drying fruits.

For centuries, humankind has sought to exploit nature's abundance, turning ephemeral harvests into lasting sustenance. Our early ancestors led lives linked to the seasons, gathering what they could from the earth. The seasons regulated their movements, hunting and harvesting.

However, to ensure their survival in lean periods, our ancestors had to find ways to make what was abundant in one season last until the next season.

Regarding canning, often people mistakenly assume it is a modern-day marvel. However, as documented by Nicolas Appert, often lauded as the 'father of canning', this method found its footing in early 19th-century France. The technique? Simple, yet revolutionary. Place the food in a glass vessel, seal, boil, and voilà! Sailors and soldiers could now venture forth, armed not just with weapons but with jars of nutritious sustenance.

Canning, in essence, is akin to capturing a moment within a container. Picture this: a summer's day, sunlight dripping like golden honey, captured within a jar of apricot jam. By heating and subsequently cooling the sealed food, we're locking away that fleeting moment, ensuring that bacteria and molds remain mere spectators, unable to partake in the preserved feast.

Diving deeper, water bath canning and pressure canning are the two most used canning procedures. While the former bathes high-acid foods like pickles and jams in warmth, the latter pressurizes low-acid foods, ensuring they remain uncontaminated. But why does this matter in a world brimming with off-the-shelf conveniences?

In an era where the authenticity of our food sources is often shrouded in mystery, canning shines a beacon of transparency. As posited by "Taste" Magazine in an article on organic eating, understanding our food's journey allows us to make conscious, healthful decisions. Canning, therefore, is not just a culinary technique; it's a bridge to a past where food was simple, pure, and unadulterated.

So, the next time you pop open a jar of homemade preserves, remember: you're not just tasting fruit or vegetable; you're savoring a moment, a tradition, a history. Isn't it wondrous how a simple jar can be a time capsule of flavors and memories?

The History of Preservation

Long before refrigeration and modern food supply chains, preservation was born of necessity. Our ancestors, ever at the mercy of seasons, soon realized the bounty of summer could be harnessed to mitigate the scarcity of winter. It wasn't merely about survival but also a reflection of early societies' keen observation, respect for their environment, and the understanding of nature's rhythms. From the solar-dehydrated fruits of Mesopotamia to the fermented fish sauces of ancient Rome, preservation was a universal response to the same challenge - sustaining through scarcity.

Our earliest ancestors relied on nature's own methods. They dried fruits under the blazing sun and salted fish from the sea, creating simple but effective ways to extend the life of essential food resources. These rudimentary techniques, born of necessity and careful observation, were the precursors to a wide array of preservation methods that developed over time.

The transformative magic of microbes was soon harnessed by ancient civilizations, marking fermentation as a key method of preservation. In the vineyards of ancient Greece, grapes transformed into wine; in the markets of China, soy became savory sauces. Fermentation was celebrated not just for prolonging food's life but also for creating new, tantalizing flavors.

Another significant advancement was the art of sealing food in containers. Whether using clay pots submerged in cool waters or amphoras sealed with olive oil, this method protected food from external contaminants, allowing flavors to meld and mature over time. The Romans, with their vast trade networks, heavily utilized these methods to transport and enjoy a wide range of preserved foods from their empire.

The advent of canning in the 19th century heralded a new era. This innovative process, a brainchild of Nicolas Appert in France, was driven by Napoleon's need to feed his vast armies. Food sealed in glass jars and subjected to heat not only lasted longer but retained more of its nutritional value. This breakthrough revolutionized preservation, making it more accessible and efficient.

As the 20th century unfolded, refrigeration and freezing took center stage. While cold storage methods, like ice houses, had been in use for centuries, modern refrigeration allowed for more precise temperature control. Freezing food, in particular, became a popular method of preservation, offering a way to lock in freshness and nutrients with unprecedented efficiency.

Interestingly, as the 21st century unfolds, there's been a renewed interest in ancient methods. The global gastronomic community is embracing fermentation, pickling, and smoking with renewed vigor, celebrating their unique flavors and textures. This revival coincides with technological advancements in areas such as vacuum sealing and molecular gastronomy, reshaping the landscape of food preservation.

Chapter 1

The Essence of Canning and Preserving

The Science Behind Preservation: How It Works

From the moment fruits or vegetables are harvested, the decay process commences. Microorganisms, always on standby, become active, seeking to degrade the freshly harvested produce. The challenge, therefore, is to halt this process and retain the freshness.

The Pivotal Role of Heat

Heat emerges as one of the most critical elements in the preservation process. When subjected to the right amount of heat within a sealed environment, such as a jar, harmful bacteria, yeasts, and molds lose their vitality. Once the jar cools, a vacuum forms, effectively sealing the contents and keeping new microorganisms out.

Acidity and Salinity as Barriers

Beyond just enhancing flavor, sugar, salt, and vinegar play a crucial role in preservation. These agents alter the environment within the jar, making conditions inhospitable for harmful bacteria. For example, in fermented pickles, naturally produced lactic acid ensures both safety and that distinct sour flavor.

Osmosis in Preservation

Osmosis, a fundamental scientific principle, becomes a protective mechanism in the realm of preservation. In jams and jellies, sugar acts to extract water from microbial cells, incapacitating them. This high concentration of sugar ensures an environment where decay-causing microbes cannot thrive.

Texture and Flavor Dynamics

Beyond just preventing decay, the science of preservation also plays a significant role in determining the texture and taste of the preserved item. For instance, the crispness of preserved cucumbers isn't coincidental. It's the result of conditions that neutralize enzymes responsible for softening foods. Pectin, a naturally occurring substance, is vital for the gel-like consistency found in many jams.

In conclusion, each step of preservation, from heating to the addition of preserving agents, ensures that the taste, texture, and freshness of nature's produce can be enjoyed long after its typical expiration.

The Benefits of Preservation

A fresh peach or a crisp lettuce head might be a delight when freshly plucked, but their transience is their most defining characteristic. Despite the vibrancy and flavor they bring to the table, perishables come with an unspoken timer. Without intervention, their inevitable decay is not just a loss to our palettes but to the environment and our pockets.

Enter preservation. This age-old technique offers a lifeline to these fleeting flavors. Through preservation, the shelf life of food extends far beyond its natural expiration. This continuity allows to relish in nature's bounty long after harvest.

However, the extended shelf life brings with it an even more significant advantage: the drastic reduction in food waste. Globally, a staggering amount of food is discarded, much of which is due to spoilage. By harnessing the power of preservation, a large portion of this waste can be curbed. It's not just about enjoying a favorite fruit off-season; it's about conscious consumption, where every harvested produce sees its full potential.

Another benefit of extended shelf life through preservation is the democratization of food availability. Think of regions with harsh climates or cities far from agricultural hubs. For them, certain foods might be seasonal luxuries. Preservation bridges this gap. Whether it's a jar of pickles in a cold Arctic home or a can of preserved peaches in a city apartment, preservation ensures that geography and climate no longer dictate one's dietary choices.

On the economic front, extended shelf life paints an optimistic picture. With longer-lasting foods, households can make bulk purchases during peak seasons, translating to savings. Producers, too, benefit, as they can now cater to markets year-round without the constant pressure of rapid sales before spoilage.

Nutrient retention: maintaining the health benefits of food

When we speak of preserving food, our first thought might drift to the sheer convenience it brings, the ability to stretch the lifespan of our favorite fruits, vegetables, or meats. Yet, there's a subtler, equally crucial advantage to this age-old culinary tradition: the artful retention of nutrients. Deep within the sealed jars and tight lids, a battle ensues against nutrient degradation, ensuring that the health benefits of our cherished foods remain largely intact.

Every fresh product brings with it so many nutrients. Vitamins, minerals, fibers, and a plethora of other compounds coexist, promising a wealth of health benefits. But as time ticks on after harvest, essential vitamins like C and A begin to wane, diminishing the nutrient profile of the food. Yet, when we intervene with preservation, a transformative process unfolds. Techniques like canning, freezing, or drying, when executed correctly, act as shields. They slow down, and in some cases, nearly halt the process of nutrient degradation. Also minerals remain largely untouched in preserved foods, ensuring that our jars of pickles or canned beans are still potent sources of essential nutrients like iron, potassium, and magnesium.

Consider the canned tomato, for instance. Research has shown that the lycopene content—a powerful antioxidant—can be even higher in canned tomatoes than in their fresh counterparts, owing to the heat processing involved in canning. Moreover, in certain preservation methods like fermentation, we witness an enhancement in the nutrient profile. Fermented foods, rich in probiotics, become powerhouses of gut health, all while retaining most of their original nutritional content. This is a testament to the prowess of preservation in safeguarding the health treasures within our foods.

It's essential to recognize, however, that not all preservation methods are equal guardians of nutrition. The key is to choose the proper method for the right product. Freezing, for instance, is a stalwart protector of vitamin C, ensuring that those frozen berries or peas remain as nutritionally rich as they were on the day of freezing. On the other hand, drying might lead to some loss of this vitamin, yet, it's exceptional in preserving calorie-dense macronutrients, making dried fruits a powerhouse of energy.

Home-Canned Vs. Store-Bought Items

ASPECT	HOMEMADE CANNING	STORE-BOUGHT PRODUCTS
Nutritional Value	Higher due to fresher, peak-ripeness ingredients	May be lower due to pre-ripe harvesting
Additives and Preservatives	None or minimal, with full control over contents	Often include additives, preservatives, higher sugar/salt
Cooking Process	Shorter cooking times, less aggressive heat	Longer, more aggressive heat, potentially more nutrient loss
Consistency	Varies batch to batch	Standardized, consistent across batches
Flavor and Personalization	Personal touch, potentially better flavor	More uniform flavor, less personalization
Storage Medium	Often in natural juices or minimal additives	May use liquids that dilute nutrient content

Essential Vitamins and Minerals Retained in Various Foods Through Home Preservation

NUTRIENT TYPE	EXAMPLES OF FOODS	STABILITY IN HOME CANNING	BENEFITS
Vitamin C	Berries, Citrus Fruits, Bell Peppers	Partially diminishes due to heat, but better retained in immediate processing	Immune-boosting, antioxidant
B-Vitamins	Legumes, Green Leafy Vegetables	Stable during canning	Essential for energy production and cognitive function
Potassium	Tomatoes	Well retained, especially when preserved in own juice	Vital for heart health
Magnesium	Seeds and Nuts	Preserved effectively through dehydration	Important for muscle function and mood regulation
Phytonutrients (e.g., Lycopene)	Tomatoes	Can become more bioavailable through canning	Potent antioxidant, health benefits

How to ensure safety while avoiding harmful additives during home preservation

Each step in home preservation, from choosing the freshest ingredients to sealing the final product, must be executed with precision and care. Yet, as the modern connoisseur becomes increasingly discerning, the desire to sidestep harmful additives gains prominence.

Starting with the bedrock of preservation, the selection of ingredients is paramount. Freshness isn't just a desirable trait—it's non-negotiable. Fresh produce, free from blemishes and signs of decay, not only offers optimal taste but also ensures that harmful microbes are kept at bay from the onset.

When recipes call for water, make careful you use distilled or pre-boiled water. This simple step wards off unwanted minerals and potential contaminants.

Moving onto the preservation mediums, nature offers an exquisite range of options. Salt and its moisture-wicking prowess creates an environment where spoilage-causing microbes find it challenging to thrive. However, it's vital to opt for pure, non-iodized variants, avoiding those with anti-caking agents or other undesirable additives.

The vinegar acidic demeanor ensures most harmful pathogens are kept in check. Yet, not all vinegars are created equal. For preservation purposes, it's advisable to choose varieties with an acidity level of 5% or higher, guaranteeing an environment where safety and flavor are in harmonious balance.

Natural sugars, when used in concentrations, act as effective preservation agents. Their knack for binding water molecules means most bacteria are left dehydrated and dormant. But here too, the key lies in selection. Organic, unrefined sugars that have not been bleached or overly processed offer a twofold advantage: impeccable preservation and a depth of flavor that's truly unparalleled.

Heat processing, whether it's boiling, water bath canning, or pressure canning, is the shield against potential contaminants. It's the sentinel that ensures any lurking pathogens are promptly dealt with, rendering the preserved food not just delicious but also safe for prolonged storage. Following recommended processing times, based on the specific food type and jar size, is crucial.

Lastly, it's essential to be vigilant against cross-contamination. Tools, jars, and surfaces should be well cleaned. Sterilizing jars and lids, using dedicated utensils, and ensuring a clean workspace might seem tedious, but they are critical for safety.

Preserving for Special Diets and Health Conditions

With the rise of bespoke diets and increasing awareness of individual health requirements, there's a palpable demand for preserved foods tailored to specific needs: low-sodium, low-sugar, and allergen-free.

At first glance, one might ponder the feasibility of altering age-old preservation recipes without compromising on safety or flavor. But as any devoted chef will attest, the world of gastronomy thrives on innovation and adaptability. And so, with a pinch of creativity and a dash of knowledge, preserving for special diets becomes not just feasible but also a delightful exploration.

Consider the world of low-sodium diets. Salt, historically considered essential for its preservative prowess, might seem irreplaceable. And yet, there's a silver lining. By combining reduced sodium with other preserving agents, like vinegar or lemon juice, one can strike a delicate balance. While it's essential to remember that lowering salt may reduce the shelf life of some preserved items, storing these tailored goods in cooler environments or even refrigerating can be a worthy trade-off for heart health.

Sugar, beyond its sweetening charm, plays a vital role in texture and shelf-life, especially in jams, jellies, and certain pickled delights. Yet, with the dawn of natural sugar alternatives, like stevia or monk fruit, and the creative use of spices and herbs for added flavor, one can craft concoctions that please the palate without spiking glucose levels. To ensure safety, it's pivotal to use recipes designed for low-sugar preservation, as merely reducing sugar in traditional recipes might not yield safe results.

Then, there's the sensitive approach of allergen-free preservation. In an age where food allergies are increasingly prevalent, ensuring the absence of allergens like nuts, dairy, or gluten in preserved foods is more than a culinary trend—it's a necessity. The key here is twofold: impeccable ingredient sourcing and stringent cross-contamination prevention. Opting for certified allergen-free ingredients, thorough cleaning of all equipment, and designating specific tools for allergen-free preservation are steps that transform an ordinary kitchen into a safe haven for those with dietary restrictions.

Chapter 2

Safety First

The Role of pH in Preservation

In its simplest form, pH quantifies the acidity or alkalinity of a substance on a scale from 0 to 14. While pure water sits neutrally at a pH of 7, values below denote increasing acidity, and those above indicate rising alkalinity. Delving into its definition, the pH scale is a logarithmic measure that gauges the concentration of hydrogen ions in a solution. The scale's center, stationed at 7, is the benchmark of neutrality, epitomized by pure water. But how does this relate to our kitchen endeavors?

The answer lies in the invisible world of microbes. These tiny organisms, ever-present in our environment and on our food, can both enhance and deteriorate our edibles. While some lend to the rich tanginess of fermented foods, others can lead to spoilage or, worse, foodborne illnesses. Here, pH serves as a gatekeeper. Microbes, much like us, have specific environments in which they thrive. By controlling the pH levels of our preserved foods, we can inhibit the growth of unwanted bacteria and mold, ensuring not just the taste but also the safety of our dishes.

Consider the world of pickling, where the acidic environment acts as a natural barricade against many unwanted microbes. The tartness of a pickled cucumber or the zesty bite of pickled peppers isn't just for flavor—it creates an acidic environment where harmful bacteria struggle to survive. The same principle applies to jams, jellies, and marmalades, where the combined acidity of fruits and added citric acid plays a dual role in flavor and preservation. Beyond flavor, acidic environments play a pivotal role in preservation, creating hostile terrains where spoilage bacteria find it challenging to thrive. The increased concentration of hydrogen ions in acidic conditions disrupts the cellular processes of these microorganisms, effectively inhibiting their growth or killing them outright. This is why acidified foods like pickles or sauerkraut can be stored for extended periods without spoilage. This inherent protection mechanism has been harnessed for centuries, from pickling vegetables to crafting zingy chutneys.

Low acid foods, like many vegetables and meats, can also be preserved safely, but they demand a different approach. These often require the intervention of pressure canning to ensure all potential pathogens are annihilated. Yet, understanding their natural pH can inform decisions about additives or combinations with more acidic ingredients, creating a harmonious blend that's both safe and delectable.

The pH scale, with its gradient from acidity to alkalinity, is more than a scientific concept. It's a compass in the culinary landscape, guiding chefs and food enthusiasts alike in crafting dishes that resonate in flavor, texture, and nutritional values. Foods, when naturally aligned on the pH scale, contribute to our body's ability to maintain its optimal pH level, supporting overall health and well-being.

Furthermore, an understanding of pH is essential when experimenting in the kitchen. It informs decisions, from selecting the right preserving method to ensuring the proper rise in baked goods. It can transform flavors, textures, and even colors, making it a powerful tool in the hands of those who understand its intricacies.

The Common Types of Microorganisms in Food

Bacteria

Bacteria are ubiquitous, colonizing nearly every surface on Earth. In the context of food, they play a role that can be both benevolent and malevolent. Beneficial bacteria are the stars behind fermented foods like cheese, yogurt, and sauerkraut. Through their metabolic activities, they produce lactic acid, alcohol, and other compounds, transforming raw ingredients into culinary delights. Lactic acid bacteria, for instance, transform milk into cheese and cabbage into sauerkraut. Their metabolic prowess acidifies the environment, not only crafting unique flavors but also acting as a natural preservative against spoilage organisms.

Not all bacteria are friendly. Pathogenic bacteria such as Salmonella, E. coli, and Listeria can contaminate food, posing significant health risks. These harmful interlopers are the reason food safety and proper preservation techniques are paramount in the culinary world. Botulism, caused by the toxin of the bacteria Clostridium botulinum, stands as a stark reminder. Improper canning can create an environment where this bacteria thrives, producing a toxin that can lead to severe paralysis or even death. However, it's essential to note that the majority of microorganisms we encounter in our food are either beneficial or benign. Harmful microbes, though critical to be aware of, are the exception rather than the norm.

Mold

Molds, members of the fungi kingdom, decompose organic materials in the environment, acting as natural decomposers. On foods, they often appear as fuzzy patches, signaling decay. While they play a crucial role in nature, in the kitchen, they are generally unwelcome. Molds can produce mycotoxins, harmful substances that can cause health problems if consumed.

Yet, molds also have their celebrated place in gastronomy. The blue veins in Roquefort cheese or the white rind on Camembert are the handiwork of specific mold species, intentionally introduced to add unique flavors and textures.

Yeast

Yeast, another member of the fungi family, has been humanity's ally for millennia. Saccharomyces cerevisiae, a type of yeast, is the driving force behind bread's rise and the effervescence in beer and champagne. Yeasts feed on sugars, releasing alcohol and carbon dioxide in the process. This fermentation action is what gives bread its airy crumb and alcoholic beverages their kick.

However, unwanted yeasts can also be problematic. In certain foods, their uninvited fermentation can lead to spoilage, off-flavors, and textural changes, underscoring the importance of proper storage and preservation.

Sources of Contamination and How to Minimize Risk

Understanding the various sources of contamination in canning is paramount to ensure the safety and quality of preserved foods. With expertise and caution, one can effortlessly steer clear of these hidden pitfalls and secure the integrity of their preserved treasures.

Identifying Sources of Contamination

Raw Ingredients: At the very genesis of the canning process, the ingredients themselves might harbor microorganisms. Fresh produce, for instance, comes in contact with soil, water, and air, each a potential vector for harmful microbes.

Water Source: Water used in canning can be a stealthy source of contamination. Whether it's used to boil, blanch, or fill jars, impure water can introduce unwanted organisms.

Equipment and Utensils: The tools of the trade, if not properly cleaned and sterilized, can be inadvertent carriers of contaminants. This includes jars, lids, funnels, and even the surfaces where food preparation occurs.

Minimizing Contamination Risk

Thorough Cleaning: Washing raw produce under running water, using brushes where appropriate, can dislodge dirt and reduce the microbial load. Ensure that every tool, jar, and surface meets the highest standard of cleanliness.

Sterilization: This step takes cleaning to the next echelon. Boiling jars and lids for 10 minutes (adjusting for altitude) can effectively sterilize them, preparing a safe environment for food.

Acidity and Heating: Many harmful microbes despise acidic conditions. That's why many preserved foods, like pickles, have vinegar or lemon juice added. Additionally, proper heating, especially in pressure canning, kills off a vast majority of potential contaminants.

Seal Integrity: A well-sealed jar is akin to a fortress against contamination. Ensuring that jar rims are clean, free from chips, and that lids are appropriately tightened guarantees a vacuum seal, warding off unwanted invaders.

Storage: Once the work of canning is done, proper storage in a cool, dark place prolongs the life of the preserved goods and further reduces any risk.

Spoilage vs. Pathogenic Bacteria

Spoilage bacteria are often overshadowed by their more nefarious counterparts that pose direct health risks. However, despite not being pathogenic, these bacteria can undeniably play the role of antagonists in preservation. They may not jeopardize our health, but they can certainly rob our preserved delicacies of their taste, texture, and visual appeal.

Spoilage bacteria represent a diverse group that affects food quality. Unlike pathogens that can cause foodborne illnesses, spoilage bacteria focus their efforts on turning our preserved items into unappetizing, often inedible, versions of their former selves. Their presence signifies that conditions were ripe for bacterial growth, which raises questions about the food's overall safety and quality.

The Telltale Signs of Their Activity

Odor: One of the most unmistakable signs of bacterial spoilage is an off-putting smell. What once was a fragrant jar of tomato sauce or a delightful preserve might now exude an aroma that is anything but appetizing.

Texture: Spoilage bacteria can break down the fibers in food, leading to an unexpected and unpleasant mushiness. The crisp bite of a pickled cucumber might be replaced by a soft, almost slimy texture.

Appearance: Cloudy brine, discoloration, or the presence of gas bubbles can be attributed to these bacteria. Such visual cues often serve as the first warning sign for many home preservers.

Prevention

Temperature Control: Most spoilage bacteria thrive in the "danger zone" between 40°F and 140°F. Storing preserved foods outside this range, especially in cooler temperatures, can significantly inhibit their growth.

Sanitization: Ensuring that all equipment is cleaned and adequately sanitized before use removes potential hiding spots for these bacteria.

Proper Processing: Following recommended canning times and methods ensures that any spoilage bacteria present are effectively eradicated before sealing the jar.

Quality of Ingredients: Starting with fresh, high-quality ingredients decreases the initial bacterial load, offering a head start in the preservation process.

Pathogenic bacteria undoubtedly stand out as the most disconcerting. While food preservation offers the bounty of prolonged shelf life and delightful flavors, it also presents challenges in ensuring the safety of the end product. Pathogenic bacteria, in particular, are those bacteria that, when allowed to proliferate, can transform a culinary delight into a potential health hazard.

These bacteria can be naturally present in foods or introduced through contamination, and their harmful effects range from mild discomfort to severe foodborne illnesses. Some notorious members of this group include Salmonella, Listeria monocytogenes, E. coli, and Clostridium botulinum.

Symptoms and Impact

The severity and range of symptoms caused by pathogenic bacteria can vary based on the type of bacterium and the amount ingested. Common symptoms include fever, vomiting, stomach cramps, and diarrhea. In certain vulnerable populations, like the elderly, very young, or those with compromised immune systems, these bacteria can cause severe conditions or even prove fatal.

The Role of Preservation

Preservation techniques are designed not only to extend the life of foods but also to ensure their safety. Proper preservation methods can effectively inhibit or kill pathogenic bacteria.

Heat Processing: Both boiling water bath and pressure canning utilize heat to kill bacteria. While boiling is sufficient for acidic foods, pressure canning is essential for low-acid foods where harmful bacteria, especially Clostridium botulinum, might thrive.

Acidity: High acid environments are inhospitable for many pathogenic bacteria. By ensuring foods have sufficient acidity (either naturally or by adding vinegar, lemon juice, or citric acid), one can create an environment hostile to these bacteria.

Salinity: A high salt concentration can inhibit the growth of certain pathogens. While beneficial for preservation, it's crucial to strike a balance to ensure the end product isn't overly salty.

Thus, pickling, fermenting, and brining can serve as effective preservation methods.

Refrigeration and Freezing: While these methods do not kill bacteria, they slow their growth significantly, preventing them from reaching hazardous levels.

Prevention

Hygiene: Maintaining impeccable personal hygiene and ensuring that all equipment is thoroughly sanitized is crucial.

Temperature: Avoid keeping food in the danger zone (40°F to 140°F) for extended periods. This range is optimal for bacterial growth.

Vacuum Sealing: When canning, the process often results in a vacuum seal. This lack of oxygen is detrimental to aerobic bacteria, though it's worth noting that some pathogens, like Clostridium botulinum, are anaerobic and can thrive without oxygen.

Inspect and Respect Expiry: Always inspect canned foods for signs of spoilage, such as a bulging lid or an off smell. And even if everything seems perfect, respecting the shelf life is non-negotiable.

Stay Updated and Educated: Best practices and recommendations can evolve. Stay informed about the latest research and guidelines on home canning.

Common pathogens in food and how to prevent their growth

1. Salmonella: Commonly found in raw poultry, eggs, beef, and sometimes on unwashed fruit and vegetables.

2. E. coli: Typically associated with undercooked beef, this bacterium can also be found in apple cider and unpasteurized milk.

3. Listeria monocytogenes: It can be found in soil and water, and thus, vegetables can become contaminated. Deli meats, soft cheeses, and unpasteurized dairy are other potential carriers.

4. Clostridium botulinum: This anaerobic bacterium produces the botulism toxin in low-acid, low-oxygen environments, making it a significant concern in canning.

Botulism

As mentioned above, at the heart of botulism lies the bacterium Clostridium botulinum. This hardy microorganism is found in soil and water worldwide. The real concern with C. botulinum is not so much the bacteria itself, but the potent neurotoxin it produces under specific conditions: an environment devoid of oxygen, a certain temperature range, and a pH level above 4.6, which is on the less acidic side.

Manifestations and Telltale Signs

When someone ingests the botulinum toxin, the symptoms can begin anywhere from a few hours to several days post-consumption. Early signs often include dry mouth, slurred speech, muscle weakness, and blurred vision. As the toxin continues to affect the body's nervous system, symptoms can escalate to paralysis and even death.

Foodborne botulism, specifically linked to home canning, is the variant of most concern for those in the realm of preservation. If there's a silver lining, it's that the toxin is heat-sensitive. Boiling home-canned goods for 10 minutes can denature the toxin, rendering it harmless. Still, prevention is always preferable to after-the-fact measures.

The challenge with botulism is its elusive nature. Contaminated food might look, smell, and taste completely normal. However, there are a few signs that something might be amiss:

1. Bulging or damaged can lids.

2. A hissing sound when a jar is opened.

3. Contents that spurt out upon opening.

4. An unusual or off odor.

If any of these signs are present, it's best to discard the contents without tasting.

Minimizing Risk

The good news is that botulism is entirely preventable. The key lies in understanding the factors that allow C. botulinum to thrive and taking measures to counteract them. Here are some pivotal steps:

1. **Educate Yourself**: Before diving into home preservation, familiarize yourself with the latest guidelines. Organizations such as the USDA offer comprehensive guidelines on safe canning practices.

2. **Acidity is Crucial**: C. botulinum cannot produce toxins in highly acidic environments (pH below 4.6). That's why many jams, jellies, and pickled items are less susceptible. However, for low-acid foods like vegetables and meats, pressure canning is mandatory. This method reaches temperatures high enough to kill the spores.

3. **Stay Fresh**: Use only fresh, high-quality produce. Damaged or overripe fruits and vegetables might have higher bacterial loads, increasing the risk.

4. **Cleanliness is Paramount**: Sterilize jars, lids, and other equipment. Wash and clean your produce thoroughly, and always work in a clean environment.

5. **Follow Recipes to the Letter**: Use tried-and-true recipes from reliable sources. These recipes have been tested for safety. Altering ingredient ratios, especially when it comes to the balance of acidity, can jeopardize safety.

6. **Mind the Time**: Process jars for the recommended amount of time. Cutting corners might mean your food doesn't reach the temperatures required to neutralize harmful spores.

7. **Heat Processing**: Always adhere to recommended canning methods. This isn't a domain for improvisation.

8. **Storage**: Canned products should be stored in a cool, dark place and consume within the recommended timeframe. Before eating, check for any signs of spoilage like a bulging lid, leakage, or off odors. When in doubt, it's always better to discard the product.

9. **Heat Before Eating**: As an added precaution, especially with low-acid foods, boil the contents for 10 minutes before consumption. This can neutralize any botulinum toxin present.

In essence, while the dangers of botulism are real, with knowledge and careful adherence to guidelines, home preservation can be both a delightful and safe endeavor.

What to Do if You Suspect Botulism Contamination: Immediate Steps to Take

1. **Safety First**: If you even remotely suspect a jar might be contaminated, do not taste its contents. Dispose of it immediately, ensuring it's out of reach of children and pets.

2. **Medical Intervention**: If someone exhibits symptoms of botulism after consuming preserved foods, seek medical attention immediately. Time is of the essence, as the botulinum toxin acts rapidly, and early intervention can make a significant difference in outcomes.

3. **Inform Local Health Departments**: Report any suspected botulism cases to local health departments. They can provide guidance on testing the food and handling the situation, and it allows for broader monitoring of potential outbreaks.

4. **Safeguard the Surrounding Area**: Contaminated jars should be handled with gloves. Clean all surfaces that came into contact with the jar using a bleach solution to ensure no residual contamination.

The Role of Preservatives

Natural preservatives

Natural preservatives, as the term suggests, are compounds that nature generously offers, each with a unique mode of preserving food's integrity. In the age where artificial additives are under scrutiny, the shift towards natural preservatives aligns with a global movement prioritizing health and sustainability. By understanding their mechanisms and incorporating them wisely, we can preserve food's nutritional value, flavor, and safety.

• **Salt**: One of the oldest preservatives known to humankind, salt works by drawing out moisture from bacteria and fungi through osmosis, making the environment inhospitable for these spoilage agents.

• **Sugar**: While it's renowned for sweetening, sugar also acts as a preservative, especially in jams, jellies, and fruit preserves. Similar to salt, sugar extracts moisture, thus curbing microbial growth.

• **Vinegar**: A product of fermentation, vinegar's acidic nature is unfriendly to many pathogens. Historically, pickling in vinegar has been a favored method to extend the life of many perishables.

• **Citric Acid**: Found abundantly in citrus fruits, citric acid decreases the pH level of foods, making them less conducive to bacterial growth. It's a popular additive in jams, jellies, and some beverages.

• **Lemon Juice**: Another natural acidifier, lemon juice, can be used in various preserves, jams, and salsas. Apart from its preservation properties, it imparts a fresh and tangy flavor.

• **Rosemary Extract**: Not just a fragrant herb for culinary use, rosemary extract contains antioxidants that prevent the oxidation of fats, thus extending the shelf life of products, especially meats.

• **Honey**: Due to its high acidity and low water content, is naturally resistant to bacteria. Additionally, its enzyme glucose oxidase produces hydrogen peroxide, which imparts antibacterial properties.

The Mechanisms at Play

• **Dehydration**: Both salt and sugar, by virtue of their hygroscopic nature, bind to water molecules, depriving microorganisms of the moisture they need to thrive.

• **pH Alteration**: Acids like citric acid and vinegar create an acidic environment, reducing the pH of food. Most spoilage bacteria find it challenging to grow in these conditions.

• **Oxidation Prevention**: Some natural preservatives, including rosemary extract, act as antioxidants. They keep fats and oils from oxidizing and spoiling.

• **Antimicrobial Activity**: Compounds in certain natural preservatives directly counteract bacteria, molds, and yeasts. Honey, for example, has properties that inhibit the growth of these spoilage microorganisms.

Chemical preservatives

Chemical preservatives are synthetic or man-made substances introduced to food products to extend their shelf life by preventing or slowing spoilage caused by microorganisms. Their primary function is to inhibit the growth of bacteria, mold, yeast, and fungi, ensuring the food remains fresh and safe for consumption for an extended period.

Some common chemical preservatives include:

• **Benzoates** (e.g., Sodium benzoate): Frequently used in acidic foods like fruit juices, jams, and soft drinks.

• **Nitrites and Nitrates**: Common in cured meats, they help in preserving the pinkish hue of meats and preventing the growth of harmful bacteria.

• **Sulfites**: Often found in dried fruits and wines, they prevent browning and discoloration.

• **Propionates**: Used in baked goods to counteract molds.

Health Implications

• **Allergic Reactions**: Some individuals may exhibit allergic reactions to specific chemical preservatives. Sulfites, for instance, can cause asthma symptoms in persons with sulfite sensitivity.

• **Digestive Issues**: Certain preservatives, when consumed in significant amounts, might disrupt the natural balance of gut flora, leading to digestive discomfort.

• **Potential Carcinogenicity**: Some studies have linked chemical preservatives, such as nitrates and nitrites, to an increased risk of cancers when they transform into carcinogenic compounds within the body.

• **Neurological Effects**: There have been concerns and studies linking specific preservatives, like sodium benzoate, to hyperactivity in children, although conclusive evidence is still under review.

While chemical preservatives play an undeniable role in modern food production, addressing the growing demand for convenience and extended shelf life, it's essential to approach them with informed caution. By carefully scrutinizing food labels and being aware of the potential effects of these additives, consumers can make educated choices.

Moreover, as the world leans more towards organic and natural products, the food industry is gradually shifting. The rise of "clean labels" and preservative-free claims underscore the increasing demand for transparency and natural preservation methods.

The Importance of Temperature and Oxygen Control

Temperature is undeniably the conductor of microbial activity. It doesn't merely influence; it dictates bacterial activity.

1. *The Danger Zone*: Any seasoned chef or food preservationist will speak of the "danger zone" with warranted caution. This range, typically between 40°F (4.4°C) and 140°F (60°C), is the playground for bacteria. Within these limits, bacteria reproduce most rapidly, doubling sometimes in as little as 20 minutes.

2. *Cooler Temperatures*: Refrigeration and freezing, stalwarts of modern food preservation, slow down or halt bacterial growth. This state is not eternal, as freezing only puts most bacteria into a suspended state, and once thawed, they can become active again. In contrast, refrigeration slows down the bacterial lifecycle, prolonging the food's freshness.

3. *Higher Temperatures*: On the opposite end of the spectrum, heating food to temperatures above 140°F (60°C) can kill bacteria. This principle underpins methods such as canning, where food is heated to high temperatures to eliminate harmful microorganisms, then sealed in an airtight container.

Oxygen, the life-sustaining element that fuels our very breath, holds an intricate role in the food preservation. It is a character of both protagonist and antagonist; its presence can give rise to vibrant flavors, but also trigger decay and spoilage. For any serious preservationist or culinary enthusiast, understanding this duality is crucial. One must first recognize its two primary roles in food preservation:

1. *Promoter of Flavor Development*: Oxygen can enhance the maturation of certain food items, particularly in the domain of fermented goods and wines. Over time, wines evolve in the bottle due to subtle oxygen exposure, leading to deeper and more complex flavors. Cheeses like Camembert or Brie

also depend on oxygen to cultivate their signature mold rinds. So, in these controlled contexts, oxygen plays a revered role.

2. *Catalyst for Spoilage*: However, more often than not, oxygen is the agent of decay in food preservation. When fruits and vegetables are sliced, oxygen exposure catalyzes oxidation, leading to browning and degradation of vitamins and other essential nutrients. Fats and oils, when left exposed, can turn rancid in the presence of oxygen, impacting flavor negatively.

Oxygen is also crucial for the survival of aerobic bacteria. However, some foodborne pathogens thrive in its absence, which presents its own set of challenges.

1. *Aerobic Environment*: Foods exposed to air are at risk from aerobic bacteria. These bacteria, like their name suggests, need oxygen to grow. Proper sealing methods, such as vacuum sealing, can significantly reduce the available oxygen and thus the threat of these bacteria.

2. *Anaerobic Environment*: In the absence of oxygen, anaerobic bacteria, including the notorious Clostridium botulinum which causes botulism, can thrive. This is a concern in low-acid foods preserved in a vacuum-sealed environment. Ensuring the food's acidity is above a certain level, or using heat processing methods like pressure canning, becomes vital to neutralize these threats.

Moreover, food storage methods have evolved with a focus on minimizing oxygen's adverse effects.

1. **Vacuum Sealing**: By drawing out air and sealing foods in an airtight environment, vacuum sealing reduces the oxygen level, thus slowing microbial growth and oxidation. It's a preferred method for preserving the color, texture, and nutritional value of foods over extended periods.

2. **Modified Atmosphere Packaging** (MAP): This advanced technique modifies the internal atmosphere of packaging, often by replacing the oxygen with nitrogen or carbon dioxide. Used predominantly in commercial settings, MAP can extend the shelf life of meat and fresh produce significantly.

3. **Canning**: A tried-and-true method, canning exposes food to high temperatures to kill harmful microbes. The food is then packed in airtight jars, ensuring that the oxygen inside is minimal.

4. **Airtight Seals**: A well-sealed canning jar ensures that the minimal amount of oxygen present inside is not enough to support spoilage or the growth of aerobic bacteria. When canning, always check the integrity of the seal. A damaged seal can let air (and bacteria) in, spoiling the food.

5. **Oxygen Absorbers**: Often used in dried food preservation, these small sachets contain iron powder that rusts, or oxidizes, removing oxygen from the sealed package. They ensure an oxygen-free environment, keeping food fresh and extending shelf life.

But oxygen isn't always the foe. While efforts to thwart oxygen's adverse effects in preservation are abundant, it's vital to remember its beneficial roles. Fermentation, for instance, often requires oxygen, especially during the initial stages. Yeasts and certain bacteria need it to multiply and produce the flavors and textures cherished in foods like sourdough or kombucha.

The Interplay of Temperature and Oxygen

Together, temperature and oxygen can either be the guardians of food safety or its undoing. By maintaining foods at safe temperatures and managing oxygen exposure, one can substantially reduce the risk of spoilage and foodborne illnesses. Additionally, combining temperature and oxygen control with other preservation methods, like salting or acidifying, can further bolster the defense against unwelcome microbial guests.

Essential Tools for Safe Preservation

The gastronomic landscape of preservation is vast and varied. But like any accomplished artist or craftsman, a home preserver requires the right tools to craft their edible masterpieces safely. Each instrument has a role, ensuring that every jar sealed holds not just deliciousness but also the assurance of safety.

Thermometers

Thermometers provide immediate feedback on the processing temperature. Precision here is paramount. Ensuring your food reaches a particular temperature and maintains it for a designated period is a make-or-break factor in eliminating harmful bacteria.

1. **Candy/Jelly Thermometers**: Especially beneficial for those delving into jams, jellies, and syrups. These thermometers measure higher temperatures, ensuring the sugar concentration is just right to set your sweet preserves.

2. **Digital Instant-Read Thermometers**: Swift, precise, and easy-to-read, these thermometers are versatile and give an immediate temperature reading, crucial for steps that demand precision.

   • *Usage*: When employing a thermometer, it's essential to place it in the thickest part of the food but away from bones or the jar's sides. This ensures an accurate reading of the food's internal temperature. Always clean and sanitize thermometers before and after use.

   • *Calibration*: Over time, thermometers can lose their accuracy. To recalibrate, one common method involves the ice water test. Fill a glass with crushed ice and water, then immerse the thermometer. It should read 32°F (0°C). If not, adjust accordingly, usually with a small wrench or by following the manufacturer's instructions.

pH Meters

The acidity of preserved foods plays a pivotal role in determining their safety. A pH meter is an invaluable tool in this regard, providing a clear picture of where your food stands on the acidity scale.

1. **Digital pH Meters**: With clear digital displays, these meters offer accurate and easy-to-read measurements. They're particularly vital for foods where the safe pH threshold is critical, such as pickles and fermented foods.

2. **Litmus Paper**: Though not as precise as a digital meter, pH strips or litmus paper can provide a general idea of the acidity of your preparations. They're a quick and economical alternative.

- *Usage*: Before taking a reading, ensure that the pH meter's probe is clean and properly immersed in the food or liquid. Allow a few moments for the reading to stabilize.

- *Calibration*: Regular calibration is required to maintain accuracy. Use pH buffer solutions of known values, typically pH 4, 7, and 10. Immerse the probe in a buffer solution and adjust the meter to the corresponding pH value. Repeat for different pH levels.

Pressure Canners and Water Bath Canners

1. **Pressure Canners**: Essential for low-acid foods like meats, poultry, and vegetables. These devices use pressure to elevate the boiling point of water, ensuring the food inside the jars reaches temperatures high enough to kill dangerous pathogens.

- *Usage*: Always follow the manufacturer's instructions. Ensure the canner is clean, especially the vent ports and safety valves. Add the specified amount of water, place the filled jars inside, and secure the lid. Adjust the heat to achieve the desired pressure.

- *Calibration*: For dial gauge pressure canners, it's advised to have the gauge tested annually. If readings are off by more than 2 pounds, it's time to replace the gauge.

2. **Water Bath Canners**: Best for high-acid foods like tomatoes, fruits, jams, and jellies. They process jars in boiling water, ensuring a seal and safe preservation of the contents.

- *Usage*: Fill the canner with enough water to cover the jars by at least one inch. Once the water boils, place the jars inside using a jar lifter, ensuring they don't touch each other. Process for the recommended time, then carefully remove and let cool.

Jar Lifters, Funnels, and Bubble Freers

1. **Jar Lifters**: This tool ensures safe handling of hot jars, minimizing risks of burns and breakage.

2. **Funnels**: A wide-mouthed funnel simplifies the process of filling jars, ensuring minimal spillage and optimal headspace.

3. **Bubble Freers**: Air bubbles trapped in your preserves can affect the jar's internal pressure. A bubble freer, often a simple plastic tool, helps release these bubbles before sealing.

- *Usage*: Use jar lifters to move hot jars, ensuring a firm grip. Funnels can assist in pouring, ensuring minimal spillage. For bubble freers, slide them along the jar's interior to release trapped air, ensuring a safer seal.

Chapter 3
The Importance of Sterilization

What is Sterilization and Why is it Important?

Sterilization, in its most basic form, is the process of removing all kinds of microbial life, including fungi, bacteria, spores, and viruses. It goes beyond mere cleaning; it's about ensuring a sterile environment that it prevents the proliferation of organisms that could spoil food or, worse, harm those who consume it. These microorganisms, ever-present in our environment, are always in search of their next habitat. Fresh food, with its moisture and nutrients, provides an inviting space for these microscopic invaders. Left unchecked, they can rapidly multiply, leading to spoilage, off-flavors, and, in certain scenarios, foodborne illnesses.

Sterilization ensures the longevity of the preserved item. A jar of jelly, for instance, can sit on a shelf for years without fermenting or molding, thanks to the meticulous sterilization process it underwent.

More importantly, though, is the issue of safety. Certain pathogenic organisms, if allowed to thrive, can lead to severe health implications. Botulism can sometimes find its way into poorly preserved food. Sterilization effectively eliminates such threats, offering peace of mind with every bite.

The process itself involves subjecting the food, and the containers they're housed in, to high temperatures for a specified period. This heat treatment effectively denatures the proteins of the microorganisms, rendering them inactive. The result is a pristine environment inside the container, where the preserved food can remain untouched by microbial life until it's eventually opened.

The difference between cleaning, sanitizing, and sterilizing

Cleaning pertains to the removal of visible residues, dirt, and debris from surfaces. Using water, often combined with detergents, we can scrub away the daily accumulations: spilled sauces, scattered crumbs, or even the film of oil left from the evening's sautéing. The objective is straightforward - achieve a surface that looks clean to the naked eye.

However, looks can be deceiving. Enter **sanitizing**. While cleaning takes care of the apparent mess, sanitizing delves deeper. It targets the invisible realm, aiming to drastically reduce the number of pathogenic organisms on a surface to a safe level. This doesn't imply the elimination of all microbes; rather, it brings down their populations to a level where the risk of infection or contamination is minimal. The agents of sanitization are many – hot water, alcohol-based solutions, or even specific food-grade sanitizers. A surface that has been sanitized might not necessarily be free of all microbes, but it's deemed safe for contact with food.

And then, we have **sterilizing**. When a surface or tool is sterilized, it has undergone a process rigorous enough to annihilate all forms of microbial life, including bacteria, fungi, viruses, and even stubborn bacterial spores. High heat, often delivered through steam under pressure, is a common method. But chemical sterilants can also be deployed.

It's easy to misconstrue these as mere semantics. However, understanding and applying these differences becomes paramount. Cleaning ensures that our kitchen is devoid of visible contaminants, sanitizing ensures it is safe to work upon, and sterilizing ensures that it is an absolute blank slate, free from all microbial interferences.

Proper Methods for Sterilizing Jars and Lids for Canning

Sterilizing jars and lids isn't just a suggestion—it's a cardinal rule. This meticulous process ensures that your canned foods remain free from harmful microorganisms and spoilage, guaranteeing not only longevity but also the safety of consumption.

To start, it's essential to understand that while jars and lids must both undergo sterilization, they may have slightly different protocols due to their material and construction. Let's walk through the process.

Sterilizing the Jars:

1. **Preparation**: Before anything else, inspect your jars for any nicks, cracks, or abnormalities. These can compromise the jar's seal, rendering the entire process moot.

2. **Washing**: Even brand-new jars benefit from a good wash. Clean the jars thoroughly with warm, soapy water. If the jars have been used before, ensure they are free from any previous food residue.

3. **Boiling**: In a large pot or canner, fill it with water until it's about two-thirds full. Place the jars in the pot, ensuring they are fully submerged. Bring the water to a rolling boil. Once boiling, let the jars sit in this bubbling for 10 minutes. For altitudes above 1,000 feet, add an extra minute for every additional 1,000 feet in elevation.

4. **Drying and Cooling**: Using canning tongs, carefully take out the jars and place them upside down on a clean kitchen towel. This prevents any lingering water droplets from settling at the jar's base. Allow them to dry naturally.

Sterilizing the Lids:

1. **Washing**: Like jars, lids need a good preliminary wash. Using warm, soapy water, ensure they're squeaky clean.

2. **Simmering, Not Boiling**: Unlike jars, lids (especially those with rubber gaskets) should not be exposed to a rolling boil as it can compromise the sealing compound. Instead, place them in a pot of water and let it simmer – aiming for a temperature of about 180°F (82°C). Maintain this simmer for at least 10 minutes.

3. **Cooling**: Using tongs, remove the lids and place them on a clean towel, ensuring they don't touch each other.

How to Sterilize Utensils, Funnels, and Other Equipment

Some tools made of sensitive materials like rubber or silicone can lose their integrity or shape if boiled. For these:

1. Clean as usual with warm, soapy water.

2. Submerge in hot water — just off the boil — for about 10 minutes.

3. Place on a clean surface and allow to air dry.

Special Considerations for Measuring Devices

For tools like measuring cups or spoons, which might have engraved or embossed areas that can hide remnants of food, consider using a soft brush to ensure all residues are removed before sterilization.

Storage Post-Sterilization

Once the equipment is sterilized and dried, it's vital to store them in a place where they'll remain uncontaminated until use. Consider covering them with a clean cloth or storing them in a sealed container to keep out any potential contaminants.

Common Mistakes to Avoid When Sterilizing Jars and Equipment

Overlooking the Preliminaries

Before you even think about sterilization, every piece of equipment should be immaculately clean. Sometimes, individuals rush to the sterilization phase without adequately cleaning their tools, which can render the sterilization ineffective. The first step should always be a thorough wash with warm soapy water, ensuring all remnants of previous canning sessions or manufacturing residues are gone.

Skimping on Boil Time

One might assume that as soon as jars or equipment have seen some boiling water, they're good to go. However, cutting short the recommended boiling time can mean not all harmful bacteria are eradicated. Ensure that once the water is at a rolling boil, jars and tools remain submerged for a full 10 minutes. And remember, at higher altitudes, boiling times should be extended.

Overcrowding the Pot

In the bid to save time, there might be a temptation to cram as many jars or tools into the boiling pot as possible. Overcrowding can prevent the water from circulating freely around each item, leading to uneven sterilization. Always give each piece its own space in the pot.

Improper Drying

After boiling, some might opt to pat dry their jars and tools. This is a mistake. Introducing a cloth or paper towel can recontaminate the surface. Instead, items should be placed on a clean, dry towel and allowed to air dry naturally.

Ignoring the Lids

Metal lids and bands have their own set of sterilization rules. Boiling them for extended periods can compromise the seal. Lids should be placed in simmering water (not a full boil) for several minutes, but not for the duration of the jar sterilization process.

Using Damaged Jars

It's essential to inspect each jar for nicks, cracks, or other imperfections. A damaged jar might not seal correctly and can compromise the preservation process. Such jars should be recycled or repurposed for other uses.

Neglecting Storage Practices

After taking the time to properly sterilize, it's a mistake to then store jars and equipment in a dusty or open environment. Sterilized items should be kept in a clean, dry place, covered to prevent contamination from the surrounding environment.

Step-by-Step Guide to Using the Boiling-Water Bath Method for Sterilization

The boiling-water bath method is an age-old tradition in the realm of home preservation, long regarded for its effectiveness in sterilizing jars for canning.

Begin with quality jars specifically made for canning. These vessels, with their thick walls, can withstand the rigors of repeated heating. Lay a protective rack at the bottom of a large pot, ensuring the jars do not directly touch the base, preventing breakages and allowing water to circulate freely. Fill the pot with water, ensuring the jars are submerged by at least an inch. The water should be in a pre-boiled state as you introduce the jars, reducing the risk of thermal shock.

Once the jars, filled with their intended contents and properly sealed, are placed in the pot, bring the water to a vigorous boil. The magic number here is typically 10 minutes, but altitude and jar size can play a role, so it's paramount to consult trusted recipes or guidelines. Post boiling, turn off the heat and let the jars stand in the water for a few more minutes. Then, using jar lifters or tongs, remove the jars, placing them on a cloth-covered counter to cool, undisturbed, for up to 24 hours. However, it's recommended to fill the jars while they're still hot to prevent them from cracking when introduced back into the boiling water.

But what about verification? How can one be sure of complete sterilization? The proof lies in the 'pop' – that sound of the lid being sucked in, indicating a vacuum seal. This sound, complemented by visual inspection of a concave lid, assures that the jar is hermetically sealed.

When to use The Boiling-Water Bath Method for Sterilization and for which types of food

The boiling-water bath method is ideally suited for high-acid foods. Acidity is nature's own preservative, a deterrent to many of the harmful microorganisms that may lurk, waiting to spoil your culinary creations. Thus, when combined with the boiling-water bath technique, it creates an environment inhospitable to these unwelcome guests.

The tomatoes inherent acidity makes them perfect for this sterilization method. Whether you're crafting a chunky salsa, a silky tomato sauce, or a zesty chutney, the boiling-water bath method is your ally. Similarly, fruits like peaches, pears, and apples, whether in the form of jams, jellies, or even pie fillings, benefit immensely from this technique.

Pickles, too, find themselves in this league. Cucumbers, beets, and even certain peppers, once bathed in a vinegary brine, elevate their acid content. Here, the boiling-water bath method not only sterilizes but works to enhance flavor.

However, caution should prevail. Low-acid foods, such as meats, most vegetables, and poultry, are not suitable for this method. Their pH levels, being higher, can provide a breeding ground for the notorious Clostridium botulinum, the causative agent of botulism. For these foods, the pressure canning method is recommended.

The Pressure-Canning Method for Sterilization

Pressure canning, unlike its boiling-water bath counterpart, harnesses the power of heightened temperature achieved under pressure to sterilize and preserve. The method is particularly favored for low-acid foods, which includes most vegetables, meats, poultry, and fish. These low-acid foods are vulnerable to the dreaded Clostridium botulinum bacteria, which thrive in low-acid environments and are capable of producing the lethal botulinum toxin under specific conditions. The boiling-water bath method is insufficient for such foods, as water boils at 212°F (100°C) and cannot reach the higher temperatures needed to neutralize this threat. Enter pressure canning, which effortlessly attains temperatures above 240°F (115°C), effectively eliminating this perilous bacteria.

To understand the mechanics, it's crucial to delve a bit into the physics. In a sealed environment, as steam builds, it increases pressure, which in turn raises the boiling point of water. In a pressure canner, this sealed environment ensures that high temperatures are achieved rapidly and uniformly, ensuring each jar inside gets evenly processed.

The procedure typically commences with clean jars filled with food and the necessary liquid, leaving recommended headspace. Lids are placed, and jars are then positioned into the canner, which already contains some water. Once sealed, heat is applied. As the water inside the canner boils, steam is trapped, increasing the internal pressure. A gauge or weight is used to monitor and regulate this pressure.

However, pressure canning isn't a mere "set and forget" process. The altitude of your location plays a pivotal role. With increased elevation, atmospheric pressure drops, requiring adjustments in the pressure level or processing time. Always consult reliable guidelines or trusted recipes specific to your altitude.

After processing, the canner is turned off and left to depressurize naturally. Rushing this step can lead to underprocessing or the liquid being siphoned from jars. Once depressurized, jars are removed and left to cool, after which the sealing success is assessed.

The appeal of pressure canning isn't merely scientific; it offers an extended shelf life and locks in nutrition and flavor in a way few methods can rival. Moreover, it broadens the range of foods that can be safely preserved at home.

Proper procedures for sterilizing jars and food with pressure canning

Before the actual canning process begins, attention must first be directed towards the jars. These vessels, the primary containers for the preserved food, should be devoid of any chips or cracks. They must be washed in hot, soapy water, rinsed well, and then kept hot until they're filled. While older recommendations suggest sterilizing jars before filling, nowadays, if the processing time in the pressure canner is more than 10 minutes (which it typically is), pre-sterilization is deemed unnecessary as the extended processing will do the job.

As for the lids, modern two-piece lids are washed in warm soapy water, rinsed, and set aside to air dry. Remember, magnetic lifters can be invaluable tools, preventing direct hand contact with the inner side of the lid.

With jars prepped, we pivot our focus to the food. Prepare it according to a tested and trusted recipe. Whether you're dealing with vegetables, meats, or beans, ensure they're clean, peeled or trimmed if necessary, and cut to uniform sizes to ensure even cooking. If a hot pack method is suggested, heat the food in a boiling liquid before packing. For raw pack, uncooked food goes directly into the jars, then covered with boiling water or broth.

Once packed, release any trapped air bubbles using a non-metallic spatula, adjust headspace as recommended, wipe the jar rim to ensure no residues, place the lid, and then screw on the band until fingertip tight.

The magic then unfolds in the pressure canner. Add the required amount of water (generally 2-3 inches deep) to the canner and place filled jars on the rack. Seal the canner, turn on the heat, and let steam flow from the vent pipe. Once steam spurts consistently, allow it to vent for 10 minutes to drive out air. Then, place the weight or close the petcock, depending on the canner type, and wait for the pressure to rise.

Processing time starts once the required pressure is achieved. Maintain this pressure, adjusting the heat as necessary. Over-processing can compromise food texture, while under-processing can pose health risks.

When the designated time elapses, turn off the heat, and allow the canner to depressurize naturally. Rushing depressurization can compromise the seal and food quality. Once depressurized, open the lid, letting the steam escape away from you, and leave jars in the canner for another 10 minutes. Finally, using jar lifters, transfer jars to a cloth-covered space, free from drafts, and let them sit undisturbed for 12-24 hours.

The satisfaction of hearing the "pop" of jar lids sealing is a testament to a job well done. However, always check seals, label, date, and store in a cool, dark place. The result will be a pantry filled with wholesome, home-canned goods.

Safety precautions for using pressure canners

1. Begin by examining the pressure canner itself. It may show signs of wear, but one must ascertain that it's in working order. Inspect the gasket for flexibility; it should not be brittle or cracked. Equally important is the vent pipe; it should be clear of any debris. If using a dial-gauge canner, have the gauge tested annually to ensure its accuracy.

2. Familiarize yourself with the manufacturer's guidelines for your specific canner. Not every pressure canner is created equal, and subtle differences might exist in operation procedures.

3. One cannot overemphasize the importance of maintaining the correct pressure. A consistent, adequate pressure ensures that the temperature inside the canner remains high enough to kill harmful bacteria. Should the pressure drop below the recommended level during processing, one must restart the timer to ensure safety.

4. It's paramount to stay in the kitchen and monitor the process. This allows for prompt adjustments in the heat source to maintain the correct pressure and minimizes risks.

5. Once the processing time is complete, turn off the heat source. Allow the canner to depressurize naturally. Hastening this step can cause liquid to be drawn out of the jars, potentially compromising the seal. Moreover, opening a pressurized canner can be hazardous.

6. When the canner is fully depressurized, and it's time to open the lid, always ensure that you lift the side farthest from you first. This allows the steam to escape away from you, reducing the risk of steam burns.

7. Once jars are cooled, check the seal. Unsealed jars can be treated again within 24 hours, or the contents can be refrigerated. However, if spoilage is suspected — evident from off-odors, mold, or spurting liquid upon opening — the contents should be discarded.

8. Store jars in a cool, dark, and dry place. While the beauty of jars might tempt you to display them openly, direct light can degrade the food quality.

Altitude Adjustment

Altitude (Feet)	Water Bath Canning: Additional Processing Time	Pressure Canning: Weighted Gauge (PSI)	Pressure Canning: Dial Gauge (PSI)
0 to 1,000	None	10 PSI	11 PSI
1,001 to 3,000	Add 5 minutes	15 PSI	11 PSI
3,001 to 6,000	Add 10 minutes	15 PSI	13 PSI
6,001 to 8,000	Add 15 minutes	15 PSI	14 PSI
8,001 to 10,000	Add 20 minutes	15 PSI	15 PSI

Notes:

1. **Water Bath Canning:** For altitudes above 1,000 feet, increase the processing time as indicated. This is necessary because water boils at a lower temperature at higher altitudes, reducing the effectiveness of heat at killing harmful bacteria.

2. **Pressure Canning (Weighted Gauge):** This type of gauge jiggles several times per minute and regulates the pressure inside the canner. At higher altitudes, higher pressure is required to achieve the necessary temperature for safe canning.

3. **Pressure Canning (Dial Gauge):** Unlike weighted gauges, dial gauges show the exact pressure inside the canner. It's important to adjust the pressure according to your altitude for safe canning.

4. **Altitude Check:** Always check your exact altitude, as even small towns can have varying altitudes. Local government offices or online resources can provide this information.

5. **Regular Checks:** If using a pressure canner, regularly check your gauge for accuracy, as discrepancies can affect the safety of your canned goods.

Remember, these adjustments are essential for ensuring the safety of your canned food, as improper canning can lead to foodborne illnesses, including botulism.

The Dry-Heat Sterilization Method

Unlike methods employing steam or boiling water, dry-heat sterilization uses moisture-free hot air. The mechanism here is straightforward: the prolonged exposure to hot air eradicates microorganisms, rendering equipment or ingredients free of unwanted pathogens. The efficacy lies not just in the high temperatures, but in the duration of exposure.

This method proves especially adept for materials that might be compromised by moisture. Think of metal tools like knives, certain glassware, or even some spices and grains. These items can either rust, lose their efficacy, or become caked when exposed to steam or boiling water, making dry-heat sterilization the method of choice.

To effectively utilize this method, one would typically employ an oven. The items intended for sterilization are placed inside, ensuring they are spaced out to allow even heat distribution.

For effective dry-heat sterilization, preheat your oven to a temperature between 160°C to 170°C (320°F to 340°F). Once preheated, place your tray inside. Depending on what you're sterilizing, the duration can vary. Typically, a period of 90 minutes to 2 hours suffices for most items. It's crucial to remember that while higher temperatures can reduce the required time, they might also risk damaging the materials in question.

It's imperative to use an oven thermometer to ensure that the set temperature remains consistent. Fluctuating temperatures can compromise the efficacy of sterilization. Additionally, use oven mitts or tongs when placing or removing items, and allow them to cool gradually post-sterilization to avoid sudden temperature shocks that might damage glassware or other sensitive materials.

Once sterilized, carefully remove the items using oven mitts. Place them on a clean cloth or cooling rack, allowing them to cool slowly. If you're sterilizing jars for canning, this is the ideal time to fill them, while they're still warm, reducing the risk of contamination.

This process destroys bacteria, yeast, and mold spores that might contaminate your food or tools. The key is the combination of high heat and duration, ensuring complete elimination of unwanted microorganisms.

While dry-heat sterilization is effective, it's not universal in its application. Some materials, like rubber or certain plastics, might degrade or melt. Moreover, ensuring the consistent temperature throughout the process is paramount to its success. Uneven heating or fluctuating temperatures can compromise the sterilization.

Benefits of Dry-Heat Sterilization:

1. **Chemical-Free**: Unlike some sterilization processes which require chemical agents, dry-heat sterilization utilizes only heat, making it an all-natural option. This ensures that your food and tools remain free from any chemical residues, aligning with a more organic approach to preservation.

2. **Thoroughness**: When done correctly, dry-heat sterilization is exceptionally effective. The high temperatures involved ensure that a wide spectrum of microorganisms, including bacteria, molds, and yeasts, are obliterated.

3. **No Water-Related Complications**: With no moisture involved, there's no risk of water-borne contaminations or corrosion on metallic tools. This can be particularly beneficial for tools and equipment that may be vulnerable to rust.

4. **Suitable for Metal and Glass**: Dry-heat is ideal for sterilizing metallic instruments and glass containers, which can withstand high temperatures without damage.

Limitations of Dry-Heat Sterilization:

1. **Not Suitable for All Materials**: Plastics and certain rubber materials can melt or become deformed at the high temperatures involved in dry-heat sterilization. Thus, it's essential to ensure that whatever you're sterilizing can handle the heat.

2. **Longer Sterilization Time**: The process requires a prolonged exposure to heat to be effective, making it more time-consuming than methods like steam sterilization.

3. **Energy Intensive**: Keeping an oven heated for an extended period can consume a fair amount of energy, which might reflect on your electricity bill. This might also have environmental implications for those conscious about their carbon footprint.

4. **Requires Close Monitoring**: Unlike some methods, dry-heat sterilization necessitates regular monitoring to ensure consistent temperatures. This might not be convenient for everyone.

5. **Risk of Burns and Breakages**: The high temperatures mean there's a risk of burns if one isn't careful. Additionally, glassware can break if not cooled slowly post-sterilization.

Ensuring Proper Seals After Sterilization

A vacuum seal, in its essence, is the creation of an airtight environment within a jar or container. This is pivotal for several reasons:

1. **Oxygen Exclusion**: Oxygen is a friend to many spoilage microorganisms. By creating an oxygen-deprived environment, vacuum seals prevent the growth and multiplication of these unwanted guests, ensuring the food remains uncontaminated and fresh for a longer period.

2. **Retention of Quality**: With the absence of oxygen, the oxidation process is halted. This means that the food retains its color, texture, and flavor, ensuring that when the jar is eventually opened, it is as if time has stood still.

3. **Prevents Leakage**: A solid vacuum seal ensures that there is no leakage of the contents, especially liquids.

Achieving the perfect seal requires a touch of finesse and attention to detail. Here are some pointers:

1. **Cleanliness is Key**: Make sure the rims of the jars are clean before sealing. Even a minute particle can prevent a proper seal.

2. **Head Space**: While filling the jars, leave appropriate headspace. This space allows the contents to expand while boiling and ensures a tighter seal once cooled.

3. **Check the Lid**: Once the sterilization process is complete and the jars are cooled, press the center of the lid. If it doesn't pop back, you've achieved a vacuum seal. If it does, the jar hasn't sealed correctly and should be refrigerated and consumed soon.

4. **Visual Inspection**: A sealed jar will appear concave and should not move when gently poked. Additionally, when the jar is tapped, a sealed one produces a high-pitched sound, while an unsealed one has a duller thud.

5. **The Finger Lift**: Hold the jar at the edges of the lid, trying to lift it slightly. A well-sealed jar will hold firm, but if the seal is broken, the lid will come off easily.

6. **Check the Breaker**: The edge of the lid, often called the breaker, should be smooth to the touch. If there's a rough or sharp feel, it's possible the jar didn't seal correctly.

What to do with unsealed jars:

1. **Refrigerate and Consume**: Unsealed jars should be consumed within a week or so. Consider it an excuse to indulge in your handiwork sooner!

2. **Re-process**: First, ensure there's no residue on the jar's rim, as even a minuscule particle can thwart a perfect seal. Replace the lid, as its sealing compound might've been compromised during the first processing. Then, re-process the jar using the method initially employed, whether it's boiling-water bath or pressure canning.

3. **Freeze**: For those wary of re-processing, consider transferring the contents to a freezer-safe container and freezing it. While this does mean a shift from shelf-stable to freezer storage, the food's quality and safety remain intact.

4. **Examine for Errors**: Take a moment to ponder why the jar didn't seal. Was the jar's rim chipped? Was the lid old or damaged? Learning from these moments ensures future endeavors meet with success.

Proper Storage Conditions for Canned Goods

The essence of storing canned goods is not just about ensuring they have a spot on your shelf. It's about creating an environment where the contents remain as they were when the jar was sealed: fresh, flavorful, and free from harmful microorganisms.

1. The ideal storage place mimics a cave: cool, dark, and dry. These conditions decelerate the degradation of food quality and nutritional value. Aim for a consistent temperature between 50°F

and 70°F (10°C to 21°C). Excessive heat speeds up the degradation process, while extreme cold might cause jars to crack.

2. Light can degrade the color and nutritional quality of preserved foods. A pantry or a cupboard, away from direct sunlight, is optimal.

3. While your jars are airtight, the surrounding environment shouldn't be. Good air circulation prevents mold growth, a bane in storage areas.

4. Shelves are preferable over floors. This protects the jars from minor floods and also ensures a steady temperature as floors can get exceptionally cold in winters.

5. Resist the temptation to stack jars on top of each other. Not only does this put pressure on the lower jars, risking breakage, but a stacked jar's seal may be compromised. Instead, space jars apart, ensuring they don't touch each other, allowing for optimal air circulation.

6. Monthly check-ups are prudent. Look for signs of spoilage—cloudiness, mold, or an odd aroma. A bulging lid is a warning sign, indicating potential bacterial activity within.

7. A simple label with contents and date can save much guesswork in the future. When adding new jars, bring the older ones to the front to ensure they're consumed first.

How Long Canned Goods Can Be Stored Safely

Food Type	Canning Method	Approximate Shelf Life
Fruits	Water Bath Canning	12 to 18 months or beyond*
Jams and Jellies	Water Bath Canning	12 to 18 months**
Vegetables	Pressure Canning	12 to 18 months or beyond*
Red Meat	Pressure Canning	12 to 18 months or beyond***
Poultry	Pressure Canning	12 to 18 months or beyond***
Pork	Pressure Canning	12 to 18 months
Fish	Pressure Canning	12 to 18 months or beyond***
Pickles	Water Bath Canning	12 to 18 months or beyond*
Tomato Products	Water Bath/Pressure*	12 to 18 months or beyond*
Soups	Pressure Canning	12 to 18 months
Beans	Pressure Canning	12 to 18 months or beyond****
Stews	Pressure Canning	12 to 18 months
Dairy Products	Not Recommended	N/A

Notes:

* **High-Acid Foods**: Foods like fruits, tomatoes (with added acid), and pickles have a naturally high acid content which can contribute to a longer shelf life. When canned using the water bath method and stored in optimal conditions, they can often maintain quality for up to 2 years.

* **Low-Acid Vegetables**: Vegetables that are pressure canned and stored in optimal conditions may also last beyond the standard 18-month guideline. However, for safety and quality, it is still recommended to consume them within this period.

** **Jams and Jellies**: These high-sugar products can sometimes last longer due to sugar's preservative effect. However, they may lose their optimum flavor and texture beyond 18 months.

*** **Meats**: When pressure canned properly, meats like beef, poultry, and fish can sometimes last beyond 18 months. However, it's crucial to follow the recommended processing times and pressures for different types of meat to ensure safety.

**** **Dried Beans**: Pressure canned dried beans can sometimes last longer due to their low moisture content.

Sauces and Purees: Depending on their composition and acidity, some sauces and purees can have an extended shelf life. Acidification with lemon juice or vinegar is crucial for products like tomato sauce.

Important Considerations:

1. **Tomato Products:** They can be acidic enough for water bath canning, but due to varying acidity in different tomato varieties, acidification (adding lemon juice or vinegar) is recommended. Pressure canning can also be used, especially for low-acid recipes.

2. **Dairy Products:** Canning of dairy products is generally not recommended due to safety concerns.

3. **Always Follow Safe Canning Practices:** Use tested recipes and guidelines from reliable sources.

Chapter 4

Essential Equipment

Types of Canning Jars

Here's a list of the common types of jars used in canning and preserving:

1. **<u>Mason Jars</u>**: The quintessential choice for home canning. Mason Jars are equipped with a two-piece lid system that provides a vacuum seal, essential for long-term preservation.

2. **<u>Weck Jars</u>**: Originating from Germany, these jars have a distinctive clip and rubber seal closure. They're becoming increasingly popular for their aesthetic appeal and efficient seal.

3. **Fido** (or Bail and Seal) Jars: These European jars use a bail closure and rubber gasket. While they are often used for dry storage or fermentation, they aren't recommended for long-term canning due to potential seal issues.

4. **Straight-Sided Jars**: As the name implies, these jars have straight sides, making them perfect for freezing as well as canning.

5. **Quilted Crystal Jars**: These have a decorative, textured surface and are often used for jellies and jams that are given as gifts.

6. **Wide Mouth vs. Regular Mouth Jars**: Both are varieties of the Mason jar. Wide mouth jars have a wider opening, so they are ideal for large food items. Regular mouth jars have a narrower opening.

7. **Commercially Pre-packaged Jars**: These are jars that once held store-bought items. They aren't recommended for canning due to potential seal and breakage issues, but many still use them for refrigerated or dry storage.

8. **Half-Gallon Jars**: These large jars are used for preserving juice or fermenting larger batches.

9. **Pint & Quart Jars**: These are the most commonly used sizes for a variety of canning projects, from fruits and vegetables to pickles and relishes.

10. **Half-Pint & Quarter-Pint Jars**: Ideal for small-batch preserving like jams, jellies, and condiments.

Each type of jar is designed with a specific purpose in mind, ensuring the best possible preservation of the contents. Before embarking on any preservation project, it's essential to choose the right jar that matches the requirements of the produce and preservation method.

Lids and Bands

At the heart of a successful canning venture lies the principle of creating an airtight environment. And this is where the **lid** steps in. Often made of metal, the lid's primary function is to form an impeccable seal against the jar's mouth. This seal is typically backed by a rubber gasket or compound that softens with heat during the canning process, allowing it to snugly adhere to the jar.

When placing a lid, it's paramount to ensure that the jar's rim is clean and free of any food particles. Even a minuscule fragment can jeopardize the sealing process. A clean cloth or a damp paper towel works wonders to wipe down the rim before placing the lid. Once the lid is in position, it should sit flat, without any bubbles or warping, indicating a good initial placement.

Once the jar cools, the lid contracts, forming that precious vacuum seal that is the bedrock of preservation.

Bands, those screw-top metal rings, serve as loyal assistants to lids. While the lid ensures the seal, the band holds the lid in place during the canning process, allowing the necessary pressure to build and ensuring that the lid is perfectly positioned.

Over-tightening can be as detrimental as a loose fit. An overly tight band impedes the escape of air from the jar during processing, preventing the formation of the vacuum seal. On the other hand, a band that's too loose might allow the lid to float, making the sealing process inconsistent.

However, one must remember that once the jar has cooled and the seal is formed, the band's job is essentially done. It is advisable to remove bands during storage to prevent potential rusting or, worse, a false sense of security if a lid's seal has been compromised but is held tight by the band.

Here's a simple guide for the uninitiated: Place the lid on the jar, ensuring it sits centrally. Then, screw the band on until resistance is met, and then give it just a quarter turn more. The lid should have enough freedom to "pop" upwards during processing and then be pulled down as the jar cools, creating that sought-after vacuum seal.

Post-processing, once the jars have completely cooled, the bands have a diminished role. In fact, storing jars with bands can be counterproductive. If a seal fails during storage, a loosely fitted band can provide a false sense of security by keeping the lid in place. Without the band, a failed seal is quickly noticeable, as the lid will come off effortlessly.

It's essential to invest in high-quality lids and bands and to understand their proper usage. Reusing lids, for example, is a no-go; the sealing compound on the lid can degrade over time, and a reused lid may not provide the same level of protection.

Importance of using new lids for each canning session

At first glance, a lid's primary purpose appears deceptively simple: to seal. In practice, however, this seal is a complex interplay of materials designed to achieve the perfect vacuum, safeguarding the jar's contents from external contaminants. This is why, like the finest spices in a gourmet dish, a fresh lid's role is both subtle and indispensable.

New lids, straight out of the box, come equipped with a pristine sealing compound, a layer specifically designed to mold and adapt to the jar's rim, ensuring a near-perfect vacuum. Once used, this compound undergoes subtle changes, adapting to the specific contours of its paired jar. Reusing it presents the risk of a flawed seal due to the compound's prior adaptations.

While reusing lids may seem economical, the potential cost to health and the quality of the preserved goods far outweighs the savings. Imagine investing time and resources into preparing a batch of preserves, only to find them spoiled due to a compromised seal. Such disappointments are easily avoidable with the simple investment in new lids for each session.

We support the idea that today's culinary world is increasingly eco-conscious, and the idea of single-use items may seem counterintuitive. However, most canning lids are recyclable, ensuring that while they serve their primary purpose just once, they don't end up as environmental pollutants.

Jar Lifter

Ergonomically designed, a jar lifter typically features a curved, rubber-coated gripping end that contours around the jar's neck, providing a stable and secure grip. This ensures that the jar, even when slippery or wet, is held firmly, minimizing the risk of unfortunate accidents. After all, a dropped jar can lead not only to wasted produce but also to potential injury.

Beyond safety, the jar lifter offers an impeccable level of precision. When immersing jars into boiling water or lifting them out, ensuring they remain upright is paramount. Tilting can compromise the sealing process, allowing air bubbles to form or contents to spill. With a jar lifter's aid, one can deftly maneuver jars, maintaining their upright posture, thereby ensuring the integrity of the canning process.

Moreover, using a jar lifter aids in preserving the quality of your preserved items. Direct contact can lead to temperature fluctuations. These seemingly minor changes can have significant impacts, potentially leading to jar breakage or compromising the preservation environment.

Lastly, for those who find dedication in the details, using a jar lifter simply feels more professional. There's an undeniable charm in adorning one's canning sessions with tools that not only enhance safety but also elevate the entire process's elegance and efficiency.

Proper Technique for Lifting and Moving Jars with a Jar Lifter

To achieve a firm yet gentle grip, place the jar lifter's arms around the jar's neck, ensuring that both arms are equidistant from the jar's top. Squeeze the handles gently, and as the rubber grips embrace the glass, you'll feel a secure connection. It's this bond that allows the canner to lift jars with confidence, even amidst the turmoil of boiling water.

Lifting should be a smooth upward motion, avoiding any jerky movements that might compromise the jar or its contents. Remember, the goal is not just to extract the jar but to do so while maintaining its pristine internal environment. Once lifted, move the jar with steady hands to its next location, whether it's a countertop for cooling or back into the canning pot.

Setting the jar down is equally crucial. Gently lower it to ensure it lands softly on the surface, preventing any undue shock or stress on the glass. Releasing the jar is simply a matter of opening the jar lifter's handles, but it's advisable to do this slowly to ensure the jar remains stable once set down.

Maintenance of your jar lifter is also essential for effective technique. Ensure the rubber grips remain clean, as debris can compromise the grip. Similarly, periodically inspect for any signs of wear or tear, as a compromised jar lifter can pose risks.

Alternative tools for handling jars

While the jar lifter is the classic tool for handling hot jars, sometimes situations arise where one needs to think outside the box. In the expansive overview of canning, several other tools can double as jar handlers, each with its unique flair, ensuring both safety and efficiency.

The first in this lineup is the silicone oven mitt. With advancements in kitchenware technology, these mitts have proven to be heat resistant, offering adequate protection from scalding water or steam. Their flexible nature ensures a firm grip on the jars, providing stability during transport. When selecting a silicone mitt, opt for ones that run up the forearm, offering enhanced protection against splashes.

Tongs, especially those with rubberized or silicone grips, can also be adapted for this purpose. While they don't encircle the jar like a jar lifter, they offer a pincer-like grip that, when executed with care, can securely transfer jars. They're particularly handy for smaller jars or those with unique shapes. However, one must ensure that the tongs are held with both strength and delicacy to avoid any slippage.

Rubberized gardening gloves are another unconventional yet effective solution. Their textured grip ensures the jar won't slide, and the thick material acts as a barrier against heat. It's an ideal choice for those who wish for more tactile feedback during the handling process. However, they must be reserved strictly for canning purposes to prevent any contamination.

Another ingenious tool, often overlooked, is the canning rack. While its primary role is to keep jars off the bottom of the pot, it can also assist in raising and lowering jars into the water bath. By leveraging the handles of the canning rack, one can lift multiple jars simultaneously, ensuring uniform processing and reducing individual handling time.

Food-Grade Funnel

At first glance, the funnel may seem superfluous—a mere accessory. But as any seasoned preserver will attest, its value is incalculable.

Specifically designed for canning, these funnels typically come with a wide mouth, ensuring that even chunky preserves glide smoothly into the jar. The tapered design minimizes splashing, ensuring that the jar rims remain clean—a crucial aspect, as any residue can compromise the seal.

Beyond the cleanliness, the funnel embodies efficiency. When dealing with large batches, speed is of the essence, and every second counts. The funnel ensures a steady flow, eliminating the constant stop-start of cleaning up drips or spills. This precision not only accelerates the canning process but also ensures that the headspace—the gap between the preserve and the jar's lid—is consistent, which is paramount for proper sealing.

For those who champion perfection, funnels with headspace measurements are a blessing. These markers assist in filling the jar to the exact recommended level, ensuring the preserve's longevity and safety. It's a blend of art and science, made accessible even to the novice canner.

The term "food-grade" isn't mere nomenclature; it is a standard, a testament to the funnel's appropriateness for contact with food. Canning, as aficionados and beginners alike would know, is not just about preserving foods—it's about preserving them safely. Using materials that are not food-grade introduces the risk of unwanted and potentially harmful chemicals leaching into the foods we so lovingly prepare.

A food-grade funnel ensures that its composition is devoid of any toxicants that might adulterate your preserves. Especially when dealing with hot jams, sauces, or pickling liquids, non-food-grade materials can degrade, releasing undesirable and, at times, harmful substances. The food-grade funnel stands resilient against these temperatures, ensuring that the integrity of your canned goods remains unmarred.

Moreover, the very essence of preservation is to capture and extend the freshness of ingredients. A non-food-grade funnel, through its potential contamination, can ironically counteract this very goal, introducing agents that might spoil the food or alter its flavor profile.

Bubble Remover and Headspace Tool

As food is packed into jars, pockets of air often get trapped, resulting in these bubbles. If not addressed, they can compromise the vacuum seal, which is crucial for the long-term preservation of the jar's contents. Furthermore, trapped air bubbles can become a potential space for harmful bacteria to grow, especially if they are located near the food surface and away from the preserving liquid. This is where the simple yet effective bubble-removing tool, or even a plastic spatula, becomes indispensable. By sliding it around the jar's interior, one can release trapped air, ensuring a safer and aesthetically pleasing end product.

Equally compelling in the preservation is the concept of headspace. This refers to the space left between the top of the food or preserving liquid and the rim of the jar. The amount of headspace can influence the vacuum seal's effectiveness, which in turn affects the shelf life and safety of the preserved food. Different foods, due to their expansion rates when heated, require varied headspace. For instance, pickles might need a smaller headspace compared to fruit jams. A failure to adhere to recommended headspace measurements might result in the food expanding and breaking the seal, or, conversely, too much headspace might not allow the jar to seal properly at all.

The act of measuring this headspace, though it might seem like a detail, is essential. One must respect the guidelines provided in trusted canning recipes or by experienced canners. Using a ruler or specialized headspace tool ensures precision in this endeavor.

How to use a bubble remover and headspace tool

To start, the bubble remover is ingeniously designed to be both effective and gentle on the food. Usually crafted from plastic or another non-reactive material, it ensures that there's no metallic taste transferred to the food, while its curved or pointed end is perfect for reaching into the nooks of the jar. Once you've filled your jar with the desired contents and preserving liquid, you introduce the bubble remover, gently pushing it along the jar's inner walls. This motion allows trapped air bubbles, those covert threats to preservation, to rise to the surface and escape. It's a simple yet critical step in ensuring the longevity and safety of your preserves.

Then, we have the headspace tool, a dual-purpose gem. One end typically features a notched design, with each notch corresponding to a specific measurement, commonly 1/4-inch, 1/2-inch, and 1-inch intervals. After filling your jar, you'll align the appropriate notch with the jar's rim, allowing the tool to rest on the jar's edge. The other end of the tool should touch the top of the food or preserving liquid, granting an accurate reading of the headspace. Why is this crucial? The space you leave dictates the vacuum seal's strength - the very element that keeps contaminants at bay and ensures the jar's contents remain pristine.

But beyond its measuring prowess, the headspace tool doubles as a bubble remover in a pinch. Its slender design allows it to reach into the jar, ensuring no air pockets are left behind.

Recommended Headspace for Different Types of Foods

TYPE OF FOOD	RECOMMENDED HEADSPACE
Fruits	1/2 inch (1.27 cm)
Jams and Jellies	1/4 inch (0.64 cm)
Vegetables (Pressure Canned)	1 inch (2.54 cm)
Meats (Pressure Canned)	1 inch (2.54 cm)
Pickles	1/2 inch (1.27 cm)
Tomatoes (with added acid)	1/2 inch (1.27 cm)
Sauces and Purees	1/2 inch (1.27 cm)
Soups (Pressure Canned)	1 inch (2.54 cm)
Beans (Pressure Canned)	1 inch (2.54 cm)
Fish (Pressure Canned)	1 inch (2.54 cm)

Notes:

- The headspace may vary slightly based on specific recipes and canning guidelines. Always refer to the recipe and canning instructions for the best results.

- Ensuring the correct headspace is critical for ensuring that jars seal properly and to prevent overflow during processing.

- In general, liquids expand during processing, so more headspace is needed for liquid-heavy foods, especially when pressure canning.

- Always remove air bubbles from the jar before applying the lid to maintain the correct headspace.

Thermometer and Timer

Temperature is pivotal in annihilating potentially harmful microorganisms. Different bacteria and enzymes flourish at varying temperature ranges. By raising the heat beyond their survival threshold, we ensure the contents remain uncontaminated and safe for consumption. Yet, it's not merely about reaching a boiling crescendo; it's about sustaining that note. Each food type, be it fruit, vegetable, or meat, has its own optimal temperature, and straying even a few degrees can alter the balance between safety and the food's inherent qualities.

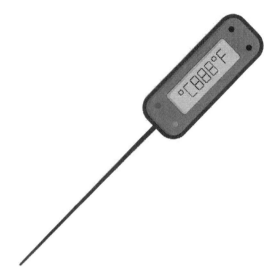

Then, there's time. Once the desired heat is achieved, maintaining it for a precise period ensures the thorough extermination of undesirables. Too brief an interval might leave harmful pathogens lurking, while overextending could compromise the food's nutritional value and palatability. Understanding the time signatures specific to each produce type and jar size is pivotal.

For a true reading, the thermometer probe should be immersed into the substance being measured, be it jam, sauce, or brine. Ensuring it doesn't touch the bottom or sides of the pot, which may be hotter than the food itself, guarantees a more accurate reading.

Using a dedicated timer does more than just measure seconds and minutes. It instills confidence in the process. Whether it's a tactile twist timer, a digital countdown device, or even a reliable app on one's smartphone, the critical thing is its accuracy and reliability.

It's worth noting that different altitudes can affect boiling points and, consequently, canning times. Therefore, alongside the thermometer's precision, a timer helps adjust and adhere to these varied requirements, ensuring uniformity in the preservation process regardless of one's location.

For those serious about their canning pursuits, timers with multiple simultaneous countdowns or alarms can be a godsend, especially when handling multiple batches or types of foods. This feature ensures that each jar gets its due time in the boiling bath or pressure canner without compromise.

Ideal Canning Times and Temperatures for Various Food Types

Remember, processing times can vary based on the canning method (water bath vs. pressure canning) and jar size.

Type of Food	Canning Method	Jar Size	Processing Time	Temperature (Pressure Canning)
Fruits	Water Bath	Pints/Quarts	20-25 min	-
Jams and Jellies	Water Bath	Half-Pints/Pints	10-15 min	-
Vegetables	Pressure Canning	Pints	20-25 min	11 psi (75.84 kPa)
		Quarts	25-30 min	11 psi (75.84 kPa)
Meats (Beef, Pork, Poultry)	Pressure Canning	Pints	75 min	11 psi (75.84 kPa)
		Quarts	90 min	11 psi (75.84 kPa)
Pickles	Water Bath	Pints/Quarts	10-15 min	-
Tomatoes (with acid)	Water Bath	Pints	35 min	-
		Quarts	45 min	-
Sauces and Purees	Water Bath	Pints	35 min	-
		Quarts	40-45 min	-
Soups	Pressure Canning	Pints	60-75 min	11 psi (75.84 kPa)
		Quarts	75-90 min	11 psi (75.84 kPa)
Beans	Pressure Canning	Pints	75 min	11 psi (75.84 kPa)
		Quarts	90 min	11 psi (75.84 kPa)
Fish	Pressure Canning	Half-Pints/Pints	100 min	11 psi (75.84 kPa)

Notes:

- The pressure levels (psi) are for a dial-gauge pressure canner at altitudes between 0 and 2,000 feet. Adjust pressure for higher altitudes.

- Times are approximate and may vary slightly based on specific recipes and canning guidelines.

- Always ensure that the jars are processed for the full recommended time and that the pressure is correctly maintained in pressure canning.

- For water bath canning, the water should be kept at a rolling boil throughout the processing time.

- Remember to adjust processing times for higher altitudes as required.

Water-Bath Canner

At its heart, a water-bath canner is simplicity personified—a large pot with a fitted lid and a rack at the bottom. This design, though elementary, is what lends the tool its efficacy. The process begins by filling the canner with water, placing filled jars on the rack, and boiling them for a specific duration. This boiling action does two essential things: it pushes out air from the jars, creating a vacuum seal, and it kills off spoilage organisms, ensuring that the preserved goods remain uncontaminated.

The primarily used of the water-bath canner is for high-acid foods like jams, jellies, fruits, and pickles. The inherent acidity of these foods, combined with the heat from the water bath, inhibits the growth of harmful bacteria, making the process relatively forgiving for those still refining their technique.

Ensuring the jars are covered by at least an inch of water is paramount. This ensures even and consistent heating. Remember, the water level will rise once jars are added, so it's wise to consider this when filling your canner. The rack plays a vital role in preventing the jars from direct contact with the pot's base, which could lead to breakage. And then there's the art of timing—each food type, based on its acidity and density, requires a specific boiling duration for optimal preservation.

Once the prescribed boiling time is reached, turn off the heat, remove the lid, and let the jars sit for a few minutes in the canner. Afterwards, place them on a towel in a draft-free spot. Giving them this resting period prevents the contents from boiling over when taken out of the hot water. Allow the jars to cool for at least 12 hours. You'll know the sealing has been successful when the jar lids are concave.

Once cooled, remove the bands, check the seals, and store in a cool, dark place. The bands can be reused, but remember, they're not what keeps the food fresh; it's the vacuum seal.

Alternative methods for water-bath canning without a specialized canner

Delving into the world of home preservation often brings forth the question: is specialized equipment a necessity or a luxury? Water-bath canning is traditionally done with a specialized canner. However, for those who are just beginning or perhaps find themselves in a situation without access to a water-bath canner, alternatives do exist.

1. Stockpot with a Rack: A large, deep stockpot can be a practical alternative to a specialized water-bath canner. The trick is ensuring that the jars do not come into direct contact with the pot's base. This can be achieved by placing a round cake cooling rack at the bottom. The main goal is to facilitate water circulation around the jars, ensuring even heat distribution.

2. Steam Canning: A more modern approach is using a steam canner, which utilizes steam to heat the jars instead of a water bath. The procedure is similar to water-bath canning but requires less water, heats up faster, and is considered suitable for many high-acid foods. However, always ensure that your recipe is compatible with steam canning before opting for this method.

3. Multi-Cookers: With the rise of multi-functional kitchen gadgets, devices like Instant Pots are sometimes erroneously believed to substitute for water-bath canners. It's crucial to note that while

some models might offer a "canning" setting, they aren't necessarily approved or tested for safe canning standards.

4. <u>Open Kettle Canning</u>: This method involves pouring hot, prepared food directly into jars and sealing them without processing. While it might sound straightforward and used to be quite popular, it's no longer recommended by food safety experts due to its inability to ensure a sterilized environment inside the jar.

Pressure Canner

The pressure canner is essential especially when preserving low-acid foods. This method is a blessing for both its versatility and its unmatched safety profile. Let us unfurl the distinct benefits that pressure canning brings to the table for low-acid food preservation.

1**. Unparalleled Safety**: Low-acid foods, such as green beans, corn, or meats, can be havens for the Clostridium botulinum bacteria, which thrives in low-oxygen environments. This bacteria is responsible for the botulism toxin. Pressure canning, with its ability to achieve temperatures above the boiling point of water (212°F or 100°C), ensures that these harmful bacteria are decimated, making it the only safe method for canning such foods.

2. **Retaining Nutritional Value**: The intense heat of pressure canning, while brief, effectively destroys enzymes and microorganisms without subjecting the food to prolonged heat. This means more of the food's original nutritional value, including essential vitamins and minerals, remains intact.

3. **Enhanced Flavor**: As with all canning methods, the goal is preservation without compromising taste. Pressure canning has a remarkable ability to intensify the flavor of the foods, especially broths and stews. The high pressure melds ingredients together, creating rich and deeply layered flavors.

4. **Economic and Sustainable**: With the ability to safely preserve seasonal bounty, pressure canning allows one to enjoy the flavors of particular seasons all year round. This not only contributes to savings in the household budget but also champions the cause of sustainability. By reducing dependency on commercially canned goods, we reduce the environmental impact of industrial processing and transportation.

5. **Flexibility in Meal Planning**: The sheer variety of low-acid foods that can be safely canned using a pressure canner—from meats to hearty soups—means that a well-stocked pantry can lead to spontaneous and diverse meal planning. A sudden craving for a mid-winter chili or a creamy potato soup can be readily satiated with a jar from the shelves.

6. **Longer Shelf Life**: Given the effectiveness of the pressure canning process in eliminating harmful bacteria and enzymes, foods canned using this method often have a longer shelf life compared to those preserved using other methods. This ensures longevity and reduces food wastage.

Difference between pressure canners and pressure cookers

The pressure canner and the pressure cooker, though seemingly analogous in their operations, serve distinct purposes. Let's demystify their differences to ensure clarity in their applications.

Foundational Mechanics: At the heart of both tools lies the principle of utilizing pressurized steam to achieve elevated temperatures. By trapping steam, they amplify the internal pressure, thus raising the boiling point of water and enabling the cooking or preservation of foods at temperatures beyond that of standard boiling water.

Purpose and Design:

- Pressure Canner: Specifically designed for the home preservation of foods, especially low-acid ones like meats, poultry, and most vegetables. Its construction caters to maintaining precise temperatures and pressures to ensure safe preservation and eliminate the risk of harmful pathogens, most notably botulism. Pressure canners typically come with a gauge to monitor the internal pressure, ensuring it stays within the required range.

- Pressure Cooker: Its primary role is to expedite the cooking process. Suitable for foods like beans, meats, or grains, pressure cookers slash cooking times significantly. Their design is often more compact, and while some modern pressure cookers have pressure indicators, they do not maintain the long, steady periods of exact pressures that canning requires.

Capacity and Size: Pressure canners are inherently larger, allowing numerous jars to be processed concurrently. Pressure cookers, conversely, are designed for meal preparation and tend to be smaller, accommodating the needs of day-to-day cooking.

Safety Considerations: Given that pressure canners aim to neutralize potential threats like Clostridium botulinum spores, they have robust safety features to sustain consistent high temperatures. Pressure cookers, while safe for cooking, may not always achieve the consistent temperatures necessary for safe canning.

Interchangeability: While pressure canners can be used as pressure cookers, the reverse is not always true. Utilizing a pressure cooker for canning, especially with low-acid foods, might not guarantee safety, posing a health risk.

In the next chapter, we will go into more detail about the differences between Water Bath and Pressure Canning, the basic steps for optimal food preservation with the various methods, common mistakes and troubleshooting.

Chapter 5

Water Bath vs. Pressure Canning: Understanding the Differences

In the wide world of home preservation, two techniques often come to the forefront, each boasting its distinctive mechanisms and advantages: water bath canning and pressure canning. These methods, though sharing the ultimate goal of preserving food, approach the task with differing science and technique. Here's a detailed exploration to help you discern which method best suits your preservation needs.

Core Mechanisms:

Water Bath Canning: This method involves immersing filled jars into a large pot of boiling water, ensuring they are fully covered. The heat from the boiling water processes the food, killing off potential spoilage organisms, and, as the jars cool, a vacuum seal forms, preventing any new bacteria from contaminating the contents.

Pressure Canning: This technique employs a specialized pot that can trap steam, raising the internal pressure and thus the boiling point of the water inside. As a result, foods inside the canner can reach higher temperatures than in a water bath, making it effective for neutralizing heat-resistant bacteria and spores.

Functional Differences:

Water Bath Canning: Ideally suited for high-acid foods, such as pickles, fruits, and jams, the boiling water effectively eliminates common spoilage organisms. However, the temperatures achieved are not high enough to eliminate botulism spores, making this method unsuitable for low-acid foods.

Pressure Canning: This method is indispensable for preserving low-acid foods like meats, fish, and most vegetables. The high temperatures achieved inside the canner (typically 240°F or 116°C) are sufficient to kill Clostridium botulinum spores, the primary concern in low-acid canning.

Operational Nuances:

Water Bath Canning: Typically more straightforward, it involves no pressure buildup, and the equipment is often simpler, making it more accessible for beginners.

Pressure Canning: Requires a bit more finesse. Users must monitor pressure levels, adjust heat sources, and ensure safety precautions are in place, given the high pressures involved.

Versatility and Results:

Water Bath Canning: While primarily for high-acid foods, its ease of use and lesser equipment cost make it a popular choice for many home preservers. The end results are jars of delicious preserves, perfect for desserts and breakfast spreads.

Pressure Canning: A versatile method, it preserves a broader range of foods safely. The end products are hearty jars of soups, stews, and vegetables, ready to grace dinner tables after months in the pantry.

Both water bath and pressure canning have unique attributes and roles in the preservation realm. While the water bath method revels in simplicity and is perfect for fruit-based delights and high-acid vegetables, pressure canning offers a comprehensive approach, ensuring a wider range of foods remain safe and delicious for prolonged periods.

In summary:

Water Bath Canning - High-Acid Foods: The innate beauty of water bath canning lies in its aptitude for high-acid foods. The method ensures a hostile environment for potential spoilage organisms, especially in foods with a pH of 4.6 or lower. This includes:

1. Fruits: Sweet jams, fruit sauces, marmalades.

2. Pickled Products: Be it cucumbers, beets, or even eggs, pickling not only adds flavor but also acid, making them suitable for this method.

3. Tomatoes: Although some varieties straddle the pH borderline, with the addition of lemon juice or citric acid, they become ideal for this method.

4. Fruit-based salsas, jellies, and chutneys.

Pressure Canning - Low-Acid Foods: Pressure canning shines when handling foods with a pH above 4.6. The intense heat, typically 240°F or higher, neutralizes resilient bacteria, especially the botulism-causing Clostridium botulinum spores. Foods in this category include:

1. Vegetables.

2. Meats and Poultry: This method ensures the preservation of these protein-rich foods, retaining their flavor and safety.

3. <u>Seafood</u>: From fish to shellfish, pressure canning offers the required heat treatment.

4. <u>Soups and Stews</u>: Mixed ingredient recipes, especially those with meat and veggies, necessitate the high temperatures of pressure canning.

Key Differences in Equipment

<u>Water Bath Canning</u>

Equipment: The water bath method employs a large pot, sometimes purpose-built with an accompanying wire rack. This rack helps suspend jars off the pot's base, ensuring even heat distribution.

1. **Water Bath Canner (or Large Stockpot)**: A dedicated water bath canner typically comes with a fitted rack, aiding in immersing and lifting jars. If one is using a large stockpot, ensure it's deep enough to cover the jars with at least an inch of water. The rack is essential, preventing jars from direct contact with the pot's bottom, which can lead to breakage.

2. **Rack**: To hold the jars in place, preventing them from touching each other or the pot's base.

3. **Canning Jars**: Tailored specifically for the purpose, these jars come in a variety of sizes. From diminutive jam jars to quart-sized jars, the choice often depends on the nature of the produce and personal preference.

4. **Lids and Bands**: Two-piece closures consist of a flat lid with a sealing compound and a threaded band that holds the lid during processing. It's paramount to use new lids each time to ensure a secure seal.

5. **Jar Lifter**: This tool, with its rubberized grip, is a canner's best ally, ensuring jars are safely immersed in and lifted out of boiling water, shielding hands from the scalding heat.

6. **Funnel**: Especially useful when dealing with liquids like brines or syrups, a funnel ensures a mess-free transfer of contents into jars.

7. **Bubble Remover & Headspace Tool**: This multipurpose tool assists in both the removal of air bubbles from filled jars and in measuring the correct headspace, which is crucial for proper sealing.

8. **Clean Cloths**: To wipe down jar rims after filling, ensuring no residue obstructs the sealing process.

9. **Thermometer**: While not always mandatory, it's useful to ascertain that the water bath achieves the desired temperature, especially crucial in higher altitude regions.

10. **Timer**: Timing is quintessential in canning. Over-processing can compromise the texture of the produce, while under-processing can risk preservation integrity.

11. **Magnetic Lid Lifter**: A small but valuable tool, especially when you need to retrieve sterilized lids from hot water.

Equipment:

1. **The Pressure Canner**: A pressure canner is designed to heat its contents to temperatures exceeding that of boiling water, a crucial factor for safely preserving low-acid foods. Opt for a model with a dial gauge or weighted gauge to monitor pressure accurately.

2. **Mason Jars**: These sturdy, thick-walled containers are designed to withstand the elevated temperatures and pressures of canning. Typically, they come in sizes ranging from half-pints to quarts, offering flexibility in portioning.

3. **Lids and Bands**: Two-piece lids consist of a flat, metal lid with a sealing compound and a separate metal band. The lid forms a vacuum-seal against the jar rim, while the band holds the lid in place during processing.

4. **Jar Lifter**: This tong-like tool is a boon when transferring hot jars in and out of the canner. Its rubberized grip ensures jars are securely held, minimizing accidents.

5. **Canning Rack**: Placed at the bottom of the pressure canner, this rack ensures jars don't sit directly on the heat source, preventing breakage. It also facilitates even heat distribution.

6. **Headspace Tool/Bubble Remover**: A dual-purpose tool, it helps in gauging the correct headspace (the gap between the food and the jar's rim) and aids in the removal of any trapped air bubbles inside the filled jars.

7. **Dial Gauge Tester (for dial-gauge canners)**: This device is pivotal for those using a dial-gauge canner, as it ensures the gauge is reading accurately, contributing to a safe canning process.

8. **Timer or Clock**: Precision is key in pressure canning. A reliable timer or clock ensures that foods are processed for the exact duration required, neither under-cooking nor over-cooking them.

9. **Canning Funnel**: This simple, yet invaluable, funnel ensures a mess-free transfer of food into jars. Its wide mouth is designed to fit jar openings perfectly.

10. **Clean Cloths**: Soft, lint-free cloths are essential for wiping jar rims before sealing, ensuring no food particles interfere with the sealing process.

11. **Thermometer**: While not always necessary, a thermometer can be useful, especially when troubleshooting or if suspecting that the canner is not reaching the correct temperature.

Water Bath Canning Basics

To begin, let's demystify acidity. At its core, acidity pertains to the pH level of a substance. On the pH scale, which ranges from 0 (highly acidic) to 14 (highly alkaline), foods registering below 4.6 are considered acidic. This natural acidity is a safeguard against many harmful bacteria, including the nefarious botulinum toxin.

Why acidity matters in Water Bath Canning

1. <u>Nature's Preservative</u>: High-acid environments, simply put, are inhospitable for many pathogenic microorganisms. By preserving foods with natural acidity, or by adding acidic agents like vinegar or lemon juice, the risks associated with spoilage and foodborne illnesses diminish considerably.

2. <u>Heat and Acidity</u>: The water bath canning process involves soaking the filled jars in boiling water. While this heat alone kills many bacteria, it's not always sufficient for those resilient ones lurking in low-acid foods. However, when combined with an acidic environment, the boiling process becomes doubly effective.

3. <u>Flavor Preservation</u>: Beyond safety, acidity plays a pivotal role in flavor retention. Many foods, like tomatoes or pickles, benefit from a tangy undertone, which is often intensified and refined during the canning process due to their acidic nature.

While many fruits are naturally acidic, there's a gamut of food items that reside in the gray area. Tomatoes, for instance, can vary in acidity depending on their variety and ripeness. For such foods, it's recommended to add an acidifying agent, ensuring safety without compromising on flavor.

Additionally, certain foods, like green beans or corn, are naturally low in acid. These aren't suitable for water bath canning unless they're pickled, which increases their acidity. If one wishes to can such items without pickling, they should opt for pressure canning.

Steps Involved in Water Bath Canning

1. **Preliminary Preparations**: Begin by selecting fresh, high-quality produce. Remember, the success of canning often lies in the initial choice of ingredients. Ensure your jars, lids, and bands are clean and free from any defects. Sterilize the jars by placing them in boiling water for 10 minutes and then placing them on a clean towel to air dry.

2. **Preparing the Food**: Wash your chosen produce thoroughly. Depending on the recipe, you may need to peel, chop, or core the ingredients. Once prepared, cook if necessary, and fill the sterilized jars, leaving an appropriate headspace.

3. **Adding Acidity (if required)**: For foods that might be on the borderline in terms of acidity, adding a touch of vinegar or lemon juice can tilt the balance, making the environment inhospitable for harmful microorganisms.

4. **Securing the Jars**: Once the jars are filled, run a spatula or bubble remover tool along the inside to remove any trapped air bubbles. Wipe the jar rims with a clean, damp cloth to remove any residue. Place the sterilized lid on the jar, ensuring it sits centered and flush against the jar rim. Secure it with a band, tightening just until fingertip-tight.

5. **Immersing in Boiling Water**: In your water bath canner or a large pot, fill it half with water and bring it to a simmer. Once the jars are prepared, place them in the canner using a jar lifter. Ensure the water level is at least an inch above the tops of the jars. Bring the water to a rolling boil.

6. **Processing Time**: Once the water reaches a rolling boil, start your timer. The processing time will vary based on the type of food you're canning and your altitude. Always refer to a trusted recipe or guideline to ensure the right duration.

7. **Cooling and Sealing**: After the designated processing time, turn off the heat and remove the jars using a jar lifter, placing them on a cloth or wooden surface away from drafts. Allow them to cool for 12-24 hours. As they cool, you may hear a "pop" sound – a sign of a successful vacuum seal.

8. **Verification**: Press the center of each lid, once the jar has cooled. If it doesn't pop back, it's sealed. Any jars that haven't sealed can be stored in the fridge for immediate consumption.

9. **Labeling and Storage**: Label each jar with its contents and the canning date. Store them in a cool, dark place, ideally between 50°F to 70°F.

Safety Precautions for Water Bath Canning

1. Inspect the Jars: Prior to canning, it's vital to examine jars for any nicks, cracks, or irregularities. Damaged jars can compromise the sealing process or shatter during the canning procedure, leading to wasted effort and potential injury.

2. Sterilization is Non-Negotiable: All jars, lids, and bands should be sterilized, especially if the processing time is less than 10 minutes. This ensures any lurking microorganisms are eradicated.

3. Mind the Fill Level: Overfilling or underfilling jars can result in improper sealing. Always leave the recommended headspace.

4. Eliminate Air Bubbles: After filling the jars, it's essential to remove air bubbles, which could affect the internal pressure and seal quality. Using a non-metallic spatula or bubble remover tool is ideal for this purpose.

5. Clean Rims Thoroughly: Any residue on the jar rim can prevent an airtight seal. After filling, wipe the rims with a clean, damp cloth.

6. Secure Bands, but Don't Over-tighten: Bands should be "fingertip tight" — secure, but not overly so. This allows for the expansion of air during processing and a proper vacuum seal as the jars cool.

7. Water Level is Key: Ensure the water in the canner covers the jar tops by at least an inch. Add more boiling water if necessary during the process to maintain this level.

8. Watch the Boil: Once the water in the canner reaches a rolling boil, that's when you start timing. The jars need to be processed for the full time recommended in the recipe, adjusted for altitude if necessary.

9. Safeguard Against Thermal Shock: When placing jars into the canner or removing them, it's advisable to use a jar lifter and ensure the environment isn't subject to sudden temperature changes, which could cause the glass to break.

10. Allow Jars to Cool Naturally: After processing, jars should be placed on a cloth or wooden surface away from drafts. They need to cool for 12-24 hours. Disturbing them or rushing the cooling process can prevent proper sealing.

11. Test the Seal: Once cooled, the seal should be checked. Lids should not flex up and down when pressing the center. Any jars that have not sealed properly should be refrigerated and consumed within a week.

Advantages of Water Bath Canning for Certain Foods

1. Natural Preservation of Acidic Foods: First and foremost, water bath canning is splendidly suited for high-acid foods, such as fruits, tomatoes with added acid, jams, jellies, and pickles. The inherent acidity of these foods creates an environment where harmful bacteria, including botulism-causing organisms, cannot thrive, ensuring a safe storage.

2. Retaining Delicate Flavors: Unlike pressure canning which subjects foods to higher temperatures, water bath canning often better preserves the delicate flavors, colors, and textures of certain foods. The resultant product, be it a jelly or a tangy compote, is close to its natural state in taste and appearance.

3. Simplified Process and Equipment: For the novice canner, the water bath method serves as a gentle introduction to the world of preservation. The equipment is straightforward - a large pot, a rack, and some jars. The process, devoid of the intricacies of pressure calibrations, is more accessible and less intimidating.

4. Reduced Energy Consumption: Water bath canning typically requires less energy than its pressure-based counterpart. The processing times, while varying depending on the specific food, are often shorter, making it an eco-friendlier option for those mindful of their carbon footprint.

5. Cost-Effective for Small Batches: For those engaging in small-batch canning, perhaps using fruits from a backyard tree or a local farmers' market haul, water bath canning is ideal. It doesn't demand the commitment of larger quantities necessary to justify the setup of a pressure canner.

6. Shelf Stability: When executed correctly, jars sealed via water bath canning have commendable shelf stability. This ensures that seasonal gluts can be enjoyed throughout the year.

Pressure Canning Basics

Pressure canning is fundamentally different from other preserving methods, primarily due to its use of heightened pressure to achieve higher temperatures than boiling water alone can provide. When water boils in a sealed pressure canner, it produces steam. As more steam builds, the pressure rises, which in turn raises the temperature inside. This higher temperature is the key to safely preserving low-acid foods.

1. Deciphering the Temperature Role: It's a well-established fact that the botulism bacteria, a serious threat in canned foods, can only be eradicated at temperatures beyond the boiling point of water (212°F or 100°C at sea level). Pressure canning consistently achieves temperatures of 240°F to 250°F (115°C to 121°C), ensuring that these bacteria and their spores are decisively eliminated.

2. <u>Pressure as a Control Mechanism</u>: Different altitudes affect the boiling point of water, which can, in turn, affect the canning process. With pressure canning, this variable is masterfully handled. By maintaining a consistent pressure—often 10 to 15 pounds per square inch (psi) for most recipes—the canning process ensures a uniform temperature, regardless of altitude.

3. <u>The Safety Implications</u>: The synergy between temperature and pressure in pressure canning is not just for the flavor or shelf life; it's fundamentally about safety. Low-acid foods, including many vegetables, meats, and poultry, are susceptible to Clostridium botulinum, the bacteria responsible for botulism. The elevated temperatures achieved through pressure canning are the only reliable method for home canners to ensure these foods are safe for long-term storage.

4. <u>Nutrient Retention</u>: While the primary aim is safety, the increased temperature from pressure canning, paradoxically, often results in better nutrient retention preservation. This is because, while the temperature is higher, the canning times can be shorter than other methods, leading to less overall nutrient loss.

Steps Involved in Pressure Canning

1. **Preparation of Ingredients**: Before anything else, select and prepare your ingredients. This includes washing, peeling, slicing, or dicing as necessary. Always choose fresh, high-quality produce to ensure the best flavor and safety.

2. **Sterilizing Equipment**: Jars, lids, and rings should be thoroughly cleaned and then sterilized. While some opt for a hot water bath for jars, others prefer the oven. Always follow manufacturers' instructions for sterilizing.

3. **Filling the Jars**: With your ingredients ready, fill the jars, leaving the headspace specified in your canning recipe. This space is vital for the expansion of food as it heats.

4. **Releasing Air Bubbles**: Using a non-metallic spatula or bubble remover, slide it down the side of the jar to release trapped air. This step is crucial to prevent jar breakage due to internal pressure.

5. **Wiping the Rim**: To achieve a good seal, wipe the jar's rim with a clean, dump cloth before placing the lid on it. Even a tiny food particle can prevent sealing.

6. **Placing Lids and Rings**: Position a sterilized lid on each jar and screw on the ring until it's finger-tight. It should be secure, but not overly tight.

7. **Loading the Pressure Canner**: Add the required amount of water to the pressure canner (typically 2-3 inches deep). Place the jars on the rack inside, ensuring they don't touch each other.

8. **Sealing and Heating**: Close the canner lid securely and turn up the heat. Allow the steam to vent for about 10 minutes before placing the weight or closing the vent.

9. **Processing Under Pressure**: Once the required pressure is achieved, maintain that level and start your timer. Adjust the heat as necessary to keep a consistent pressure. Always refer to specific recipes for accurate times and pressures.

10. **<u>Cooling Down</u>**: After the prescribed processing time, turn off the heat and let the canner cool naturally. Don't rush this step. Quick cooling might result in liquid loss from the jars or prevent them from sealing.

11. **<u>Removing and Cooling Jars</u>**: Once the canner has depressurized, open the lid, and remove the jars with the help of a jar lifter. Place them on a towel in a draft-free zone, spaced apart, to cool for 12-24 hours.

12. **<u>Checking the Seal</u>**: Once cooled, check for tightness by pressing the center part of the lid. If it doesn't pop back, it's sealed. Unopened jars should be stored in the refrigerator and consumed within a few days.

Safety Precautions for Pressure Canning

Before delving into the process, it's critical to thoroughly read the manufacturer's instructions for your pressure canner. Each model may have its unique operational nuances, and adhering to these guidelines ensures both safety and efficacy.

1. <u>Ensure Equipment Integrity</u>: Regularly inspect the canner for dents, warping, or other signs of wear. The sealing ring, over time, might become dry or cracked; it should be replaced if it's not pliable. Equally, ensure that the vent pipe isn't clogged.

2. <u>No Skimping on Processing Time</u>: The recommended processing times, based on scientific research, should be followed religiously. Under-processing could result in improperly preserved food, potentially leading to bacterial growth.

3. <u>Altitude Adjustments</u>: Remember, water boils at different temperatures with different altitude. Ensure that you adjust the processing pressure according to your altitude. Most canning recipes provide guidance on this.

4. <u>Venting is Vital</u>: Before reaching the desired pressure, allow the canner to vent for about 10 minutes. This step ensures the removal of air, allowing the canner to reach the necessary temperature for safe food preservation.

5. <u>Cooling Naturally</u>: Once the processing time is complete, turn off the heat and allow the canner cool on its own. Forcing it to cool, moving it, or immersing it in cold water might cause the jars to break or result in siphoning, where the contents leak from the jars.

6. <u>Monitor the Pressure</u>: Wait until the canner's pressure has completely dropped to zero before attempting to open it. Even then, open the lid away from you to avoid steam burns.

7. <u>Jar Handling</u>: Use jar lifters to remove hot jars and place them on a cloth or wooden surface away from drafts. A sudden temperature change could cause the glass to shatter.

8. <u>Store with Care</u>: Once the jars are cooled (usually after 12-24 hours), remove the bands and check the seals. Unopened jars should be stored in the refrigerator and consumed quickly or reprocessed. Store sealed jars in a cool, dark place.

Advantages of Pressure Canning for Certain Foods

1. Safety for Low-Acid Foods: Here lies the primary advantage. Foods like vegetables, meats, poultry, and seafood are low in acid, creating an ideal environment for the notorious Clostridium botulinum bacterium, which leads to botulism. Pressure canning reaches temperatures that effectively destroy these harmful organisms, making it the safest method for low-acid foods.

2. Nutrient Retention: Pressure canning's expedient nature - reaching higher temperatures in less time - often results in better retention of essential vitamins and minerals compared to other methods.

3. Versatility: From creamy soups to tender meats, pressure canning offers versatility. It's capable of preserving a broader range of textures and ingredients than other methods.

4. Economic and Environmental Benefits: Pressure canning allows for bulk preparation, saving both time and money in the long run. Plus, by reusing jars and reducing store-bought canned goods, one contributes to a more sustainable environment.

5. Storage Longevity: Foods preserved using the pressure canning method often have an extended shelf life compared to those preserved using other methods. The robust seal and absence of air within the jar create an environment where spoilage is greatly reduced.

6. Optimal Liquid Penetration: The heightened temperature and pressure ensure that the heat permeates even the densest of foods, guaranteeing an evenly processed product. This is particularly advantageous for thicker stews or densely packed jars.

Common Mistakes in Water Bath and Pressure Canning

1. Inaccurate Processing Time: Time is of the essence. Under-processing risks spoilage, while over-processing can turn your food to mush. Always refer to trusted recipes and adjust for altitude if necessary.

2. Overfilling Jars: The headspace, or the gap between the food and the lid, is critical. Too little space and the jar might not seal correctly, too much and food might discolor at the top. Aim for the recommended headspace for each recipe.

3. Using Damaged Jars: Cracks or chips, often imperceptible, can lead to breakage during canning or failed sealing. Thoroughly inspect each jar before use.

4. Skipping the Air Bubble Removal: This oversight in water bath canning can lead to inaccurate headspace. Use a non-metallic spatula or special tool to glide along the jar's interior before sealing.

5. Inconsistent Heat in Pressure Canning: Rapid fluctuations in temperature can lead to liquid loss. Ensure a steady heat, adjusting your burner as needed.

6. Ignoring Altitude Adjustments: Both water bath and pressure canning require adjustments for altitude. Water boils at lower temperatures at higher altitudes, meaning adjustments are essential for safety.

7. <u>Reusing Single-Use Lids</u>: Though tempting, reusing single-use lids compromises the seal's integrity. Always opt for fresh lids; consider it an investment in your food's safety and quality.

8. <u>Over-tightening Bands</u>: A common mistake. Bands should be "finger tight", allowing air to escape during processing, ensuring a vacuum seal upon cooling.

9. <u>Rapid Cooling of Pressure Canners</u>: A frequent error, often stemming from impatience. Allow the canner to cool naturally. Rapid cooling can cause jars to break or warp the canner's seal.

10. <u>Neglecting Equipment Check</u>: Gaskets, seals, and vents of pressure canners require periodic checks. Neglecting this can lead to inaccurate pressure levels and unsafe food.

Troubleshooting

1. **Jar Seals**:

Problem: The lid won't pop down or seal.

Solution: This could be due to a number of issues. Check the rim of the jar for any chips or cracks. Ensure that the headspace was correctly measured and that no residue remains on the rim. If the lid still refuses to seal, refrigerate and consume the contents within a week.

2. **Jar Breakage**:

Problem: Jars crack or break during the canning process.

Solution: Sudden temperature changes are usually the culprits. Always ensure jars are at room temperature, and never place them directly onto cold or metal surfaces. Using a rack at the bottom of your canner can also reduce the risk.

3. **Food Spoilage**:

Problem: Signs of mold, fermentation, or off-odors.

Solution: Sadly, there's no coming back from this. For your safety, discard the contents. Going forward, always adhere strictly to processing times and ensure you're working with sterilized equipment.

4. **Discolored Food**:

Problem: The food changes color after processing.

Solution: Over-processing or minerals in the water could be to blame. While it may not look as appetizing, it's generally safe to consume. Using distilled water can help avoid this in the future.

5. **Loss of Liquid**:

Problem: After processing, there's less liquid in the jar than you started with.

Solution: This can occur if jars are overfilled or if there's too much fluctuation in temperature during processing, especially in pressure canning. Always leave the recommended headspace and aim for consistent heat.

6. **Cloudy Brine**:

Problem: The liquid in pickled products appears cloudy.

Solution: This could result from the use of table salt instead of pickling salt. Always use the latter to ensure a crystal-clear brine.

Advanced Tips

1. Experiment with Raw Pack vs. Hot Pack: Raw packing involves placing fresh, raw ingredients in jars and then filling them with boiling water or syrup. Hot packing, conversely, requires simmering the food briefly before placing it in the jars. Both techniques have merits, but hot packing can result in a denser pack, fewer floaters, and often a better color retention in the finished product.

2. Seasonal Strategy: Canning at the peak of the season guarantees the best flavors. However, consider blending varieties of the same fruit or vegetable harvested at different times for a more complex flavor profile.

3. Test Acidity with a pH Meter: While many fruits are naturally high in acid, there are always exceptions. A pH meter can give precise readings, ensuring your food's acidity is conducive to safe preservation.

4. Evolve with Equipment: Investing in a steam canner, which uses steam in a confined space to heat jars, can be a game-changer for high-acid foods. It's quicker and uses less water than traditional water bath canning.

For Water Bath Canning:

1. Pre-Warm Your Jars: While it's not always essential, pre-warming jars can reduce the risk of thermal shock and breakage. It also ensures that your jars are sanitized before filling.

For Pressure Canning:

1. Venting is Essential: Always vent your pressure canner for 10 minutes before bringing it up to the desired pressure. This ensures all the air is expelled, creating a pure steam environment, which is crucial for accurate pressure building.

2. Two-Part Lid Technique: Some experts advise tightening the ring bands on lids and then backing off a quarter-inch. This can allow for necessary air escape during processing, ensuring a tighter vacuum seal upon cooling.

Chapter 6

Water Bath Recipes

CLASSIC TOMATO SALSA

PREPARATION TIME: 30 MINUTES
COOKING TIME: 20 MINUTES COOKING, 15 MINUTES PROCESSING
SERVINGS: 6 PINT-SIZED JARS (16 OUNCES EACH)

MAXIMUM STORAGE TIME: 1 YEAR (UNOPENED). ONCE OPENED, REFRIGERATE AND USE WITHIN 2 WEEKS
RECOMMENDED HEADSPACE: 1/2 INCH (12 MM)

INGREDIENTS

- 10 cups peeled and chopped ripe tomatoes (5 kg)
- 2 cups chopped onion (about 2 medium onions or 300 grams)
- 1 cup chopped green bell pepper (about 1 large pepper or 200 grams)
- 5 jalapeño peppers, seeds removed and finely chopped (adjust to taste)
- 4 cloves garlic, minced

- 1 cup apple cider vinegar (240 ml)
- 2 teaspoons salt (10 grams)
- 1/2 teaspoon ground black pepper (1 gram)
- 1/2 teaspoon ground cumin (1 gram)
- 1 teaspoon dried oregano (1 gram)
- 1/4 cup finely chopped fresh cilantro (15 grams)
- 6 clean pint-sized canning jars with lids and bands

INSTRUCTIONS

1. Blanch tomatoes in boiling water for 1 minute. Transfer to ice water, peel, and chop.
2. In a large pot, mix tomatoes, onion, green pepper, jalapeños, garlic, vinegar, salt, black pepper, cumin, and oregano.
3. Bring the mixture to a boil over medium heat, then reduce heat and simmer for 10 minutes.
4. Stir in fresh cilantro and cook for an additional 2 minutes.
5. Boil jars, lids, and bands for 10 minutes to sterilize them. Keep jars warm.
6. Ladle the hot salsa into jars, leaving 12 mm (1/2-inch) headspace. Remove any air bubbles.
7. Clean the rims, secure lids, and tighten rings finger-tight.
8. Soak the jars in boiling water for 15 minutes.
9. Take out the jars and leave to cool down for 12 to 24 hours. Check seals.

PREPARATION TIPS:
- Peeling the tomatoes ensures a smoother texture for the salsa.
- Dice the vegetables uniformly for consistent texture and flavor distribution.

NUTRITIONAL VALUE (PER SERVING - 1 TABLESPOON): Calories: 5, Carbohydrates: 1g, Fat: 0g, Protein: 0g, Sodium: 80mg, Sugar: 1g

CHARMING CHERRY TOMATO JAM

PREPARATION TIME: 20 MINUTES
COOKING TIME: 1 HOUR
SERVINGS: ABOUT 3-4 CUPS

MAXIMUM STORAGE TIME: 1 YEAR
RECOMMENDED HEADSPACE: LEAVE ABOUT 1/4-INCH (0.6 CM) HEADSPACE.

INGREDIENTS

- 6 cups (900g) of fresh cherry tomatoes, halved
- 1 cup (240 ml/200g) of sugar
- 2 tablespoons (30 ml) of fresh lemon juice
- 1 teaspoon (5 ml) of lemon zest
- 1/2 teaspoon (2.5 ml) of red chili flakes (optional)
- 1/4 teaspoon (1.25 ml) of sea salt
- 1/4 teaspoon (1.25 ml) of black pepper

INSTRUCTIONS

1. In a large, deep saucepan, combine the cherry tomatoes, sugar, lemon juice, lemon zest, red chili flakes (if using), sea salt, and black pepper.
2. Bring the mixture to a gentle boil over medium heat, stirring frequently to ensure that the sugar is completely dissolved.
3. Once boiling, reduce the heat to low and simmer for about 50-60 minutes, stirring regularly, until it has the consistency of a jam.
4. As the jam thickens, be sure to stir more frequently to avoid sticking.
5. Once the desired consistency is reached, remove from heat and allow to cool slightly.
6. Pour the jam to sterilized jars, leaving about 6 mm (1/4-inch) headspace. Clean the rims, secure lids, and tighten rings finger-tight.
7. Fill the water bath canner halfway with water and bring it to a simmer.
8. Carefully submerge the jars in the canner, making sure they are under water by at least 2.5 cm (1 inch).
9. Bring to a rolling boil, process for 10 minutes.
10. Turn off the heat, let the jars soak in the water for 5 minutes, then remove and let cool completely on a clean towel or cooling rack.

PREPARATION TIPS: To check the consistency, place a spoonful of the jam on a cold plate and let it sit for a minute. Run your finger over the jam - if it wrinkles, it's ready.

NUTRITIONAL VALUE PER SERVING: Calories: 85, Fat: 0.4g, Cholesterol: 0mg, Sodium: 60mg, Carbohydrates: 21g, Dietary Fiber: 1g, Sugar: 18g, Protein: 1g

HEARTY TOMATO BASIL SAUCE

PREPARATION TIME: 20 MINUTES
COOKING TIME: 60 MINUTES
SERVINGS: ABOUT 4-5 JARS (1 PINT EACH)

MAXIMUM STORAGE TIME: 1 YEAR
RECOMMENDED HEADSPACE: LEAVE ABOUT 1/2-INCH (1.25 CM) HEADSPACE

INGREDIENTS

- 2.2 kg of fresh tomatoes, peeled and chopped
- 1 cup (240 ml/160g) of fresh basil leaves, chopped
- 4 cloves of garlic, minced
- 2 tablespoons (30 ml) of olive oil
- 2 teaspoons (10 ml) of salt
- 1 teaspoon (5 ml) of black pepper
- 1 teaspoon (5 ml) of sugar
- 1/2 teaspoon (2.5 ml) of red pepper flakes (optional)

CONTINUED →

INSTRUCTIONS

1. Boil jars, lids, and bands for 10 minutes to sterilize them.
2. In a large saucepan, heat the olive oil over medium heat. Add the minced garlic and sauté for about 1-2 minutes.
3. Stir in the tomatoes, sugar, salt, black pepper, and red pepper flakes (if using). Bring to a simmer, and let it cook for about 45-50 minutes, stirring occasionally. About 10 minutes before the sauce is done, stir in the chopped basil.
4. Once the sauce has thickened, remove from heat. Puree the sauce using a hand blender for a smoother consistency or leave it chunky based on your preference.
5. Ladle the hot sauce into the prepared jars, leaving about 12 mm (1/2-inch) headspace.
6. Clean the rims, secure lids, and tighten rings finger-tight.
7. Soak the jars in a water bath canner, making sure they are under water by at least 2.5 cm (1 inch). Bring to a boil and process for 40 minutes.
8. Turn off the heat, let the jars soak in the water for 5 minutes, then carefully remove and allow to cool completely on a clean towel or cooling rack.

PREPARATION TIPS: To easily peel the tomatoes, score a small "x" on the bottom of each tomato and blanch them in boiling water for about 30-60 seconds, then transfer to a cold water bath.

NUTRITIONAL VALUE PER SERVING: Calories: 70, Fat: 3.5g, Cholesterol: 0mg, Sodium: 470mg, Carbohydrates: 9g, Dietary Fiber: 2g, Sugar: 6g, Protein: 2g

---

CLASSIC TOMATO BASIL SAUCE

PREPARATION TIME: 15 MINUTES
COOKING TIME: 1 HOUR
SERVINGS: ABOUT 3-4 JARS (16 OZ EACH)

MAXIMUM STORAGE TIME: 1 YEAR
RECOMMENDED HEADSPACE: LEAVE ABOUT 1/2-INCH (1.3 CM) HEADSPACE IN THE JARS.

INGREDIENTS

- 2.4 kg of fresh or canned tomatoes, chopped
- 1/2 cup (120 ml) of extra virgin olive oil
- 6 cloves garlic, finely chopped
- 1 cup (240 ml/20g) fresh basil leaves, chopped
- 1 teaspoon (5 ml/5g) sea salt
- 1/2 teaspoon (2.5 ml/2g) black pepper
- 1/2 teaspoon red pepper flakes (optional)
- 2 tablespoons (30 ml) balsamic vinegar

INSTRUCTIONS

1. In a large saucepan, heat the olive oil over medium heat. Add the garlic and sauté for about 1 minute.
2. Stir in the tomatoes, basil, salt, black pepper, and red pepper flakes if using. Bring the mixture to a boil.
3. Reduce heat to low and simmer uncovered for about 45-50 minutes, or until the sauce has thickened to your desired consistency, stirring occasionally. Stir in the balsamic vinegar and cook for an additional 2-3 minutes.
4. Carefully ladle the hot sauce into sterilized jars, leaving about 12 mm (1/2-inch) headspace. Clean the rims, secure lids, and tighten rings finger-tight.
5. Soak the jars in a water bath canner, making sure they are under water by at least 2.5 cm (1 inch). Bring to a boil and process for 40 minutes.
6. Turn off the heat, let the jars soak in the water for 5 minutes, then carefully remove and allow to cool completely on a clean towel or cooling rack.

NUTRITIONAL VALUE PER SERVING: Calories: 60, Fat: 5g, Cholesterol: 0mg, Sodium: 190mg, Carbohydrates: 4g, Dietary Fiber: 1g, Sugar: 2g, Protein: 1g

TANGY TOMATO BASIL SAUCE

PREPARATION TIME: 25 MINUTES
COOKING TIME: 2 HOURS
SERVINGS: ABOUT 4-5 JARS (16 OZ EACH)

MAXIMUM STORAGE TIME: 1 YEAR
RECOMMENDED HEADSPACE: LEAVE 1/2-INCH (1.3 CM) HEADSPACE IN THE JARS

INGREDIENTS

- 10 cups (2.4 L/2.2 kg) of fresh tomatoes, chopped
- 1 cup (240 ml/160g) of onion, finely chopped
- 5 cloves of garlic (25g), minced
- 1/4 cup (60 ml) of fresh basil, finely chopped
- 2 tablespoons (30 ml/30g) of olive oil
- 1/2 cup (120 ml/120g) of red wine vinegar
- 2 teaspoons (10 ml/10g) of sugar
- 1 teaspoon (5 ml/5g) of salt
- 1/2 teaspoon (2.5 ml/2g) of black pepper
- 1/2 teaspoon (2.5 ml/2g) of dried oregano

INSTRUCTIONS

1. In a large saucepan, heat the olive oil over medium heat. Add the onions and garlic, and sauté for about 5-7 minutes.
2. Stir in the tomatoes, red wine vinegar, sugar, salt, black pepper, and oregano. Bring the mixture to a boil.
3. Once boiling, reduce the heat to low and let simmer for about 1.5 hours, stirring occasionally. During this time, the sauce should reduce and thicken.
4. About 10 minutes before removing from heat, stir in the fresh basil.
5. Use an immersion blender to smooth the sauce to your desired consistency, if necessary.
6. Pour the hot sauce into sterilized jars, leaving about 12 mm (1/2-inch) headspace. Clean the rims, secure lids, and tighten rings finger-tight.
7. Soak the jars in a water bath canner, making sure they are under water by at least 2.5 cm (1 inch). Bring to a boil and process for 40 minutes.
8. Turn off the heat, let the jars soak in the water for 5 minutes, then remove and let cool completely on a clean towel or cooling rack.

NUTRITIONAL VALUE PER SERVING: Calories: 45, Fat: 2g, Cholesterol: 0mg, Sodium: 240mg, Carbohydrates: 6g, Dietary Fiber: 1g, Sugar: 4g, Protein: 1g

SMOKY TOMATO AND CHIPOTLE SALSA

PREPARATION TIME: 30 MINUTES
COOKING TIME: 20 MINUTES COOKING, 15 MINUTES PROCESSING
SERVINGS: 6 PINT-SIZED JARS (16 OUNCES EACH)

MAXIMUM STORAGE TIME: 1 YEAR (UNOPENED). ONCE OPENED, REFRIGERATE AND USE WITHIN 2 WEEKS
RECOMMENDED HEADSPACE: 1/2-INCH (12 MM)

INGREDIENTS

- 10 cups chopped tomatoes (5 kg of ripe tomatoes)
- 2 cups chopped onions (about 300 grams)
- 1 cup chopped green bell pepper (200 grams)
- 3 chipotle peppers in adobo sauce, finely chopped (adjust to taste)
- 4 cloves garlic, minced
- 1/2 cup apple cider vinegar (120 ml)
- 1/4 cup lime juice (about 2 limes)
- 2 teaspoons salt (10 grams)
- 1 teaspoon smoked paprika (2 grams)
- 1/2 teaspoon ground cumin (1 gram)
- 1/2 cup chopped fresh cilantro (30 grams)
- 6 clean pint-sized canning jars with lids and bands

71

CONTINUED →

INSTRUCTIONS

1. Blanch tomatoes in boiling water for 1 minute. Transfer to ice water, peel, and chop.
2. In a large pot, mix together chopped tomatoes, onions, green bell pepper, chipotle peppers, garlic, vinegar, lime juice, salt, smoked paprika, and cumin.
3. Bring the mixture to a simmer over medium heat, cooking for about 20 minutes or until desired consistency is reached.
4. Stir in fresh cilantro just before finishing the cooking.

5. Boil jars, lids, and bands for 10 minutes to sterilize them. Keep jars warm.
6. Ladle the hot salsa into jars, leaving 12 mm (1/2-inch) headspace. Remove any air bubbles.
7. Clean the rims, secure lids, and tighten rings finger-tight.
8. Soak the jars in boiling water for 15 minutes.
9. Take out the jars and leave to cool down for 12 to 24 hours. Check seals.

NUTRITIONAL VALUE (PER SERVING - 1 TABLESPOON): Calories: 10, Carbohydrates: 2g, Fat: 0g, Protein: 0g, Sodium: 80mg, Sugar: 1g

GARLIC BASIL TOMATO JAM

PREPARATION TIME: 20 MINUTES
COOKING TIME: 35 MINUTES COOKING, 10 MINUTES PROCESSING
SERVINGS: 5 HALF-PINT JARS (8 OUNCES EACH)

MAXIMUM STORAGE TIME: 1 YEAR (UNOPENED). ONCE OPENED, REFRIGERATE AND USE WITHIN 1 MONTH.
RECOMMENDED HEADSPACE: 1/4-INCH (6 MM)

INGREDIENTS

- 6 cups peeled and finely chopped tomatoes (3 kg)
- 3 cups granulated sugar (600 grams)
- 1/2 cup apple cider vinegar (120 ml)
- 1/4 cup lemon juice (about 2 lemons)
- 4 cloves garlic, minced

- 1/4 cup fresh basil leaves, finely chopped
- 1 teaspoon salt (5 grams)
- 1/2 teaspoon ground black pepper (1 gram)
- 5 clean half-pint canning jars with lids and bands

INSTRUCTIONS

1. Blanch tomatoes in boiling water for 1 minute. Transfer to ice water, peel, and finely chop.
2. In a large pot, combine tomatoes, lemon juice, apple cider vinegar, sugar, and garlic. Bring to a boil over medium heat, then reduce to a simmer. Cook, stirring frequently, until it has the consistency of a jam, about 35 minutes.
3. Stir in chopped basil, salt, and black pepper during the last 5 minutes of cooking.

4. Boil jars, lids, and bands for 10 minutes to sterilize them. Keep jars warm.
5. Ladle the hot tomato jam into jars, leaving 6 mm (1/4-inch) headspace. Remove any air bubbles.
6. Clean the rims, secure lids, and tighten rings finger-tight.
7. Soak the jars in boiling water for 10 minutes.
8. Take out the jars and leave to cool down for 12 to 24 hours. Check seals.

PREPARATION TIPS:
- Cooking the jam over medium heat and stirring frequently helps prevent burning.
- Finely chopping the basil leaves releases their flavor and aroma more effectively into the jam.

NUTRITIONAL VALUE (PER SERVING - 1 TABLESPOON): Calories: 25, Carbohydrates: 6g, Fat: 0g, Protein: 0g, Sodium: 20mg, Sugar: 6g

ZESTY TOMATO RELISH

PREPARATION TIME: 30 MINUTES
COOKING TIME: 20 MINUTES COOKING, 15 MINUTES PROCESSING
SERVINGS: 6 PINT-SIZED JARS (16 OUNCES EACH)

MAXIMUM STORAGE TIME: 1 YEAR (UNOPENED). ONCE OPENED, REFRIGERATE AND USE WITHIN 1 MONTH
RECOMMENDED HEADSPACE: LEAVE 1/2-INCH (12 MM) HEADSPACE IN THE JARS

INGREDIENTS

- 8 cups chopped tomatoes (4 kg of ripe tomatoes)
- 2 cups chopped green bell peppers (about 2 large peppers or 400 grams)
- 1 cup chopped red onion (about 1 large onion)
- 1 cup apple cider vinegar (240 ml)
- 3/4 cup granulated sugar (150 grams)

- 2 tablespoons mustard seeds (15 grams)
- 1 tablespoon celery seeds (8 grams)
- 2 teaspoons salt (10 grams)
- 1 teaspoon ground turmeric (2 grams)
- 1/2 teaspoon red pepper flakes (optional, to taste)
- 6 clean pint-sized canning jars with lids and bands

INSTRUCTIONS

1. In a large pot, mix together the tomatoes, green bell peppers, red onion, vinegar, sugar, mustard seeds, celery seeds, salt, turmeric, and red pepper flakes.
2. Bring the mixture to a boil over medium heat, then reduce heat and simmer for about 20 minutes, stirring occasionally.
3. Boil jars, lids, and bands for 10 minutes to sterilize them. Keep jars warm.
4. Fill the jars with the hot relish, leaving 12 mm (1/2-inch) headspace. Remove any air bubbles.
5. Clean the rims, secure lids, and tighten rings finger-tight.
6. Soak the jars in boiling water for 15 minutes.
7. Take out the jars and leave to cool down for 12 to 24 hours. Check seals.

PREPARATION TIPS:
- Chopping the vegetables uniformly ensures a consistent texture in the relish.
- The combination of spices provides a zesty flavor that complements the tomatoes.

NUTRITIONAL VALUE (PER SERVING - 1 TABLESPOON): Calories: 15, Carbohydrates: 3g, Fat: 0g, Protein: 0g, Sodium: 80mg, Sugar: 2g

---

SUN-DRIED TOMATO AND OLIVE TAPENADE

PREPARATION TIME: 20 MINUTES
COOKING TIME: NO COOKING REQUIRED, 10 MINUTES PROCESSING
SERVINGS: 6 HALF-PINT JARS (8 OUNCES EACH)

MAXIMUM STORAGE TIME: 6 MONTHS (UNOPENED). ONCE OPENED, REFRIGERATE AND USE WITHIN 1 MONTH
RECOMMENDED HEADSPACE: 1/2-INCH (12 MM)

INGREDIENTS

- 3 cups sun-dried tomatoes (not in oil, 300 grams)
- 1 cup pitted Kalamata olives (about 150 grams)

- 1/2 cup capers, drained
- 4 cloves garlic

CONTINUED →

- 1/4 cup olive oil (60 ml)
- 2 tablespoons balsamic vinegar (30 ml)
- 1 teaspoon dried basil (2 grams)
- 1 teaspoon dried oregano (2 grams)
- 1/2 teaspoon ground black pepper (1 gram)
- 6 clean half-pint canning jars with lids and bands

INSTRUCTIONS

1. In a food processor, combine sun-dried tomatoes, olives, capers, and garlic. Pulse until coarsely chopped.
2. Add olive oil, balsamic vinegar, basil, oregano, and black pepper to the mixture. Pulse until the ingredients are finely chopped and well combined, but not pureed.
3. Boil jars, lids, and bands for 10 minutes to sterilize them. Keep jars warm.
4. Spoon the tapenade into jars, leaving 12 mm (1/2-inch) headspace.
5. Clean the rims, secure lids, and tighten rings finger-tight.
6. Although tapenade is not typically processed due to its high acid content and oil, if you choose to can it, soak the jars in a boiling water canner for 10 minutes.
7. Take out the jars and leave to cool down for 12 to 24 hours. Check seals.

SHOPPING TIPS:
- Use high-quality sun-dried tomatoes for the best flavor.
- Opt for olives and capers that are not overly salty.

PREPARATION TIPS:
- Adjust the consistency of the tapenade according to your preference by pulsing more or less in the food processor.
- The tapenade should be rich and flavorful, perfect for spreading on crackers, bread, or as an accompaniment to cheese.

NUTRITIONAL VALUE (PER SERVING - 1 TABLESPOON): Calories: 35, Carbohydrates: 4g, Fat: 2g, Protein: 1g, Sodium: 150mg, Sugar: 2g

---

VEGETABLE CHUTNEYS AND RELISHES

SPICY CARROT AND GINGER CHUTNEY

PREPARATION TIME: 30 MINUTES
COOKING TIME: 50 MINUTES COOKING, 10 MINUTES PROCESSING
SERVINGS: 6 HALF-PINT JARS (8 OUNCES EACH)

MAXIMUM STORAGE TIME: 1 YEAR (UNOPENED). ONCE OPENED, REFRIGERATE AND USE WITHIN 2 MONTHS
RECOMMENDED HEADSPACE: LEAVE 1/4-INCH (6 MM) HEADSPACE IN THE JARS

INGREDIENTS

- 4 cups grated carrots (about 1 kg)
- 1 cup finely chopped onion (about 1 medium onion)
- 2 cups apple cider vinegar (480 ml)
- 1 cup brown sugar (packed) (200 grams)
- 1/4 cup finely chopped fresh ginger (50 grams)
- 1 teaspoon ground cinnamon (2 grams)
- 1/2 teaspoon ground cloves (1 gram)
- 1/2 teaspoon ground allspice (1 gram)
- 1/4 teaspoon cayenne pepper (adjust to taste)
- 1 teaspoon salt (5 grams)
- 6 clean half-pint canning jars with lids and bands

INSTRUCTIONS

1. In a large pot, mix together carrots, onion, vinegar, brown sugar, ginger, cinnamon, cloves, allspice, cayenne pepper, and salt.
2. Bring the mixture to a boil over medium heat, then reduce to a simmer. Cook, stirring regularly, until the it thickens and the carrots are tender, about 50 minutes.
3. Boil jars, lids, and bands for 10 minutes to sterilize them. Keep jars warm.
4. Fill the jars with the hot chutney, leaving 6 mm (1/4-inch) headspace. Remove any air bubbles.
5. Clean the rims, secure lids, and tighten rings finger-tight.
6. Soak the jars in boiling water for 10 minutes.
7. Take out the jars and leave to cool down for 12 to 24 hours. Check seals.

PREPARATION TIPS: The chutney should be thick but spreadable; adjust cooking time if necessary to achieve the desired consistency.

NUTRITIONAL VALUE (PER SERVING - 1 TABLESPOON): Calories: 15, Carbohydrates: 4g, Fat: 0g, Protein: 0g, Sodium: 40mg, Sugar: 3g

---

TANGY GREEN TOMATO AND APPLE CHUTNEY

PREPARATION TIME: 35 MINUTES
COOKING TIME: 40 MINUTES COOKING, 10 MINUTES PROCESSING
SERVINGS: 6 PINT-SIZED JARS (16 OUNCES EACH)

MAXIMUM STORAGE TIME: 1 YEAR (UNOPENED). ONCE OPENED, REFRIGERATE AND USE WITHIN 2 MONTHS
RECOMMENDED HEADSPACE: 1/2-INCH (12 MM)

INGREDIENTS

- 4 cups chopped green tomatoes (about 1 kg)
- 3 cups chopped apples (about 3-4 medium apples)
- 1 1/2 cups chopped onion (about 1 large onion)
- 1 cup raisins (150 grams)
- 1 cup brown sugar (packed) (200 grams)
- 3/4 cup apple cider vinegar (180 ml)
- 1/2 cup chopped candied ginger (100 grams)
- 1 tablespoon mustard seeds (10 grams)
- 2 teaspoons salt (10 grams)
- 1 teaspoon ground allspice (2 grams)
- 1/2 teaspoon ground cinnamon (1 gram)
- 1/4 teaspoon ground cloves (0.5 gram)
- 6 clean pint-sized canning jars with lids and bands

INSTRUCTIONS

1. In a large pot, mix together green tomatoes, apples, onions, raisins, brown sugar, vinegar, candied ginger, mustard seeds, salt, allspice, cinnamon, and cloves.
2. Bring the mixture to a boil over medium heat, then reduce heat and simmer, uncovered, for about 40 minutes or until the mixture thickens and the fruits and vegetables are tender.
3. Boil jars, lids, and bands for 10 minutes to sterilize them. Keep jars warm.
4. Fill the jars with the hot chutney, leaving 12 mm (1/2-inch) headspace. Remove any air bubbles.
5. Clean the rims, secure lids, and tighten rings finger-tight.
6. Soak the jars in boiling water for 10 minutes.
7. Take out the jars and leave to cool down for 12 to 24 hours. Check seals.

NUTRITIONAL VALUE (PER SERVING - 1 TABLESPOON): Calories: 20, Carbohydrates: 5g, Fat: 0g, Protein: 0g, Sodium: 80mg, Sugar: 4g

SWEET AND SPICY ZUCCHINI CHUTNEY

PREPARATION TIME: 30 MINUTES
COOKING TIME: 40 MINUTES COOKING, 10 MINUTES PROCESSING
SERVINGS: 6 PINT-SIZED JARS (16 OUNCES EACH)

MAXIMUM STORAGE TIME: 1 YEAR (UNOPENED). ONCE OPENED, REFRIGERATE AND USE WITHIN 2 MONTHS
RECOMMENDED HEADSPACE: LEAVE 1/2-INCH (12 MM) HEADSPACE IN THE JARS

INGREDIENTS

- 6 cups grated zucchini (about 3 medium zucchinis)
- 2 cups chopped onions (about 2 medium onions)
- 1 cup apple cider vinegar (240 ml)
- 1 cup brown sugar (packed) (200 grams)
- 1/2 cup raisins (75 grams)
- 2 cloves garlic, minced
- 2 tablespoons grated fresh ginger (30 grams)
- 1 tablespoon mustard seeds (10 grams)

- 1 teaspoon salt (5 grams)
- 1 teaspoon ground turmeric (2 grams)
- 1/2 teaspoon ground cinnamon (1 gram)
- 1/2 teaspoon ground nutmeg (1 gram)
- 1/4 teaspoon ground cloves (0.5 gram)
- 1/4 teaspoon cayenne pepper (adjust to taste)
- 6 clean pint-sized canning jars with lids and bands

INSTRUCTIONS

1. In a large pot, mix together grated zucchini, onions, vinegar, brown sugar, raisins, garlic, ginger, mustard seeds, salt, turmeric, cinnamon, nutmeg, cloves, and cayenne pepper.
2. Bring the mixture to a boil over medium heat, then reduce heat and simmer for about 40 minutes, or until the mixture thickens and the zucchini is tender.
3. Boil jars, lids, and bands for 10 minutes to sterilize them. Keep jars warm.
4. Fill the jars with the hot chutney, leaving 12 mm (1/2-inch) headspace. Remove any air bubbles.
5. Clean the rims, secure lids, and tighten rings finger-tight.
6. Soak the jars in boiling water for 10 minutes.
7. Take out the jars and leave to cool down for 12 to 24 hours. Check seals.

PREPARATION TIPS:
- Grating the zucchini provides a nice texture and allows it to absorb the flavors better.
- Ensure consistent stirring during cooking to prevent the chutney from sticking to the pot and to evenly distribute flavors.

NUTRITIONAL VALUE (PER SERVING - 1 TABLESPOON): Calories: 20, Carbohydrates: 5g, Fat: 0g, Protein: 0g, Sodium: 80mg, Sugar: 4g

ROASTED RED PEPPER AND EGGPLANT CHUTNEY

PREPARATION TIME: 45 MINUTES (INCLUDING ROASTING TIME)
COOKING TIME: 30 MINUTES COOKING, 10 MINUTES PROCESSING
SERVINGS: 6 PINT-SIZED JARS (16 OUNCES EACH)

MAXIMUM STORAGE TIME: 1 YEAR (UNOPENED). ONCE OPENED, REFRIGERATE AND USE WITHIN 2 MONTHS
RECOMMENDED HEADSPACE: LEAVE 1/2-INCH (12 MM) HEADSPACE IN THE JARS

INGREDIENTS

- 4 cups roasted red peppers, chopped (1 kg)
- 2 cups roasted eggplant, chopped (500 grams)
- 1 cup diced onions (about 1 medium onion)
- 3/4 cup apple cider vinegar (180 ml)
- 1/2 cup granulated sugar (100 grams)
- 1/4 cup golden raisins (50 grams)
- 3 cloves garlic, minced

- 1 tablespoon grated fresh ginger (15 grams)
- 1 teaspoon mustard seeds (5 grams)
- 1 teaspoon salt (5 grams)
- 1/2 teaspoon ground cumin (1 gram)
- 1/4 teaspoon cayenne pepper (optional, to taste)
- 6 clean pint-sized canning jars with lids and bands

INSTRUCTIONS

1. Roast red peppers and eggplant in the oven until tender. Peel and chop them.
2. In a large pot, mix together roasted red peppers, eggplant, onions, vinegar, sugar, raisins, garlic, ginger, mustard seeds, salt, cumin, and cayenne pepper.
3. Bring the mixture to a simmer over medium heat, cooking for about 30 minutes, or until thickened.
4. Boil jars, lids, and bands for 10 minutes to sterilize them. Keep jars warm.
5. Fill the jars with the hot chutney, leaving 12 mm (1/2-inch) headspace. Remove any air bubbles.
6. Clean the rims, secure lids, and tighten rings finger-tight.
7. Soak the jars in boiling water for 10 minutes.
8. Take out the jars and leave to cool down for 12 to 24 hours. Check seals.

SHOPPING TIPS: Roasting the vegetables beforehand adds depth and flavor to the chutney.

PREPARATION TIPS:
- Ensure thorough roasting of the vegetables for a smoky flavor.
- Chop the roasted vegetables into small, uniform pieces for even cooking and texture.
- Adjust the level of cayenne pepper to tailor the spice level to your preference.

NUTRITIONAL VALUE (PER SERVING - 1 TABLESPOON): Calories: 20, Carbohydrates: 4g, Fat: 0g, Protein: 0g, Sodium: 80mg, Sugar: 3g

CARAMELIZED ONION AND TOMATO CHUTNEY

PREPARATION TIME: 30 MINUTES
COOKING TIME: 40 MINUTES COOKING, 10 MINUTES PROCESSING
SERVINGS: 6 PINT-SIZED JARS (16 OUNCES EACH)

MAXIMUM STORAGE TIME: 1 YEAR (UNOPENED). ONCE OPENED, REFRIGERATE AND USE WITHIN 2 MONTHS
RECOMMENDED HEADSPACE: 1/2-INCH (12 MM)

CONTINUED →

INGREDIENTS

- 4 cups thinly sliced onions (about or 800 grams)
- 4 cups chopped ripe tomatoes (about 2 kg)
- 1 cup apple cider vinegar (240 ml)
- 3/4 cup brown sugar (packed) (150 grams)
- 1/2 cup raisins (75 grams)
- 3 cloves garlic, minced
- 2 tablespoons olive oil
- 1 teaspoon salt (5 grams)
- 1/2 teaspoon ground black pepper (1 gram)
- 1/2 teaspoon ground cinnamon (1 gram)
- 1/4 teaspoon ground cloves (0.5 gram)
- 1/4 teaspoon ground allspice (0.5 gram)
- 6 clean pint-sized canning jars with lids and bands

INSTRUCTIONS

1. In a large skillet, heat olive oil over medium heat. Add onions and cook for about 20 minutes, stirring often, until caramelized.
2. In a large pot, mix together caramelized onions, chopped tomatoes, vinegar, brown sugar, raisins, garlic, salt, black pepper, cinnamon, cloves, and allspice.
3. Bring the mixture to a simmer over medium heat, cooking for about 20 minutes, or until thickened.
4. Boil jars, lids, and bands for 10 minutes to sterilize them. Keep jars warm.
5. Fill the jars with the hot chutney, leaving 12 mm (1/2-inch) headspace. Remove any air bubbles.
6. Clean the rims, secure lids, and tighten rings finger-tight.
7. Soak the jars in boiling water for 10 minutes.
8. Take out the jars and leave to cool down for 12 to 24 hours. Check seals.

PREPARATION TIPS:
- Slowly caramelizing the onions brings out their natural sweetness and adds depth to the chutney.
- Stir the chutney regularly while cooking to ensure even thickening and to prevent burning.

NUTRITIONAL VALUE (PER SERVING - 1 TABLESPOON): Calories: 25, Carbohydrates: 6g, Fat: 0.5g, Sugar: 5g

---

CLASSIC CORN AND PEPPER RELISH

PREPARATION TIME: 30 MINUTES
COOKING TIME: 20 MINUTES COOKING, 10 MINUTES PROCESSING
SERVINGS: 6 PINT-SIZED JARS (16 OUNCES EACH)

MAXIMUM STORAGE TIME: 1 YEAR (UNOPENED). ONCE OPENED, REFRIGERATE AND USE WITHIN 1 MONTH
RECOMMENDED HEADSPACE: 1/2-INCH (12 MM)

INGREDIENTS

- 4 cups fresh corn kernels (about 6 ears of corn)
- 1 cup diced green bell pepper (200 grams)
- 2 cups diced red bell pepper (about 400 grams)
- 1 cup diced onion (about or 200 grams)
- 1 cup apple cider vinegar (240 ml)
- 3/4 cup sugar (150 grams)
- 2 teaspoons mustard seeds (10 grams)
- 1 teaspoon celery seeds (5 grams)
- 1 teaspoon salt (5 grams)
- 1/2 teaspoon turmeric (1 gram)
- 1/2 teaspoon ground black pepper (1 gram)
- 6 clean pint-sized canning jars with lids and bands

INSTRUCTIONS

1. In a large pot, mix together corn, red and green bell peppers, onion, vinegar, sugar, mustard seeds, celery seeds, salt, turmeric, and black pepper.
2. Bring the mixture to a boil over medium heat, then reduce heat and simmer for about 20 minutes, or

until the vegetables are tender and the flavors have melded.
3. Boil jars, lids, and bands for 10 minutes to sterilize them. Keep jars warm.
4. Fill the jars with the hot relish, leaving 12 mm (1/2-inch) headspace. Remove any air bubbles.

5. Clean the rims, secure lids, and tighten rings finger-tight.
6. Soak the jars in boiling water for 10 minutes.
7. Take out the jars and leave to cool down for 12 to 24 hours. Check seals.

NUTRITIONAL VALUE (PER SERVING - 1 TABLESPOON): Calories: 15, Carbohydrates: 3g, Fat: 0g, Protein: 0g, Sodium: 40mg, Sugar: 2g

---

SPICY CUCUMBER AND DILL RELISH

PREPARATION TIME: 40 MINUTES (INCLUDES RESTING TIME FOR CUCUMBERS)
COOKING TIME: 15 MINUTES COOKING, 10 MINUTES PROCESSING
SERVINGS: 6 PINT-SIZED JARS (16 OUNCES EACH)

MAXIMUM STORAGE TIME: 1 YEAR (UNOPENED). ONCE OPENED, REFRIGERATE AND USE WITHIN 1 MONTH
RECOMMENDED HEADSPACE: 1/2-INCH (12 MM)

INGREDIENTS

- 6 cups finely chopped cucumbers (about 1.5 kg)
- 2 cups finely chopped onions (about 300 grams)
- 1/4 cup salt (for draining cucumbers)
- 2 cups white vinegar (480 ml)
- 1 cup sugar (200 grams)
- 2 tablespoons dill seeds (10 grams)

- 1 tablespoon mustard seeds (5 grams)
- 1 teaspoon celery seeds (2 grams)
- 1/2 teaspoon turmeric (1 gram)
- 1-2 jalapeño peppers, finely chopped (to taste)
- 6 clean pint-sized canning jars with lids and bands

INSTRUCTIONS

1. In a large bowl, combine cucumbers and onions. Sprinkle with salt, mix well, and set aside for 2 hours to drain excess moisture. Rinse and drain thoroughly.
2. In a large pot, mix together the drained cucumber mixture, vinegar, sugar, dill seeds, mustard seeds, celery seeds, turmeric, and jalapeño peppers.
3. Bring the mixture to a boil over medium heat, then reduce heat and simmer for about 15 minutes, or until the cucumbers are tender but still crisp.

4. Boil jars, lids, and bands for 10 minutes to sterilize them. Keep jars warm.
5. Fill the jars with the hot relish, leaving 12 mm (1/2-inch) headspace. Remove any air bubbles.
6. Clean the rims, secure lids, and tighten rings finger-tight.
7. Soak the jars in boiling water for 10 minutes.
8. Take out the jars and leave to cool down for 12 to 24 hours. Check seals.

SHOPPING TIPS: For a milder relish, remove the seeds from the jalapeño peppers.

PREPARATION TIPS:
- Thoroughly rinsing and draining the cucumbers after salting is crucial to avoid an overly salty relish.
- Chop the cucumbers and onions finely for a uniform texture and quick pickling.
- Adjust the quantity of jalapeño peppers based on your preferred heat level.

NUTRITIONAL VALUE (PER SERVING - 1 TABLESPOON): Calories: 15, Carbohydrates: 3g, Fat: 0g, Protein: 0g, Sodium: 80mg, Sugar: 2g

BEET AND CARROT RELISH

PREPARATION TIME: 30 MINUTES
COOKING TIME: 25 MINUTES COOKING, 10 MINUTES PROCESSING
SERVINGS: 6 PINT-SIZED JARS (16 OUNCES EACH)

MAXIMUM STORAGE TIME: 1 YEAR (UNOPENED). ONCE OPENED, REFRIGERATE AND USE WITHIN 2 MONTHS
RECOMMENDED HEADSPACE: 1/2-INCH (12 MM)

INGREDIENTS

- 3 cups grated beets (about 4 medium beets)
- 2 cups grated carrots (about 4 medium carrots)
- 1 cup finely chopped onion (about 1 large)
- 1 cup apple cider vinegar (240 ml)
- 3/4 cup sugar (150 grams)
- 1/2 cup water (120 ml)
- 1 tablespoon mustard seeds (5 grams)
- 1 teaspoon salt (5 grams)
- 1/2 teaspoon ground black pepper (1 gram)
- 1/4 teaspoon ground cinnamon (0.5 gram)
- 6 clean pint-sized canning jars with lids and bands

INSTRUCTIONS

1. Peel and grate beets and carrots. Finely chop the onion.
2. In a large pot, mix together grated beets, carrots, onion, vinegar, sugar, water, mustard seeds, salt, black pepper, and cinnamon.
3. Bring the mixture to a simmer over medium heat, cooking for about 25 minutes, or until the flavors are well combined.
4. Boil jars, lids, and bands for 10 minutes to sterilize them. Keep jars warm.
5. Fill the jars with the hot relish, leaving 12 mm (1/2-inch) headspace. Remove any air bubbles.
6. Clean the rims, secure lids, and tighten rings finger-tight.
7. Soak the jars in boiling water for 10 minutes.
8. Take out the jars and leave to cool down for 12 to 24 hours. Check seals.

NUTRITIONAL VALUE (PER SERVING - 1 TABLESPOON): Calories: 20, Carbohydrates: 5g, Fat: 0g, Protein: 0g, Sodium: 80mg, Sugar: 4g

SWEET AND SOUR GREEN BEAN RELISH

PREPARATION TIME: 20 MINUTES
COOKING TIME: 30 MINUTES COOKING, 10 MINUTES PROCESSING
SERVINGS: 6 PINT-SIZED JARS (16 OUNCES EACH)

MAXIMUM STORAGE TIME: 1 YEAR (UNOPENED). ONCE OPENED, REFRIGERATE AND USE WITHIN 2 MONTHS
RECOMMENDED HEADSPACE: 1/2-INCH (12 MM)

INGREDIENTS

- 4 cups chopped fresh green beans (about 1 kg)
- 2 cups chopped red bell pepper (400 grams)
- 1 cup chopped onion (about 1 large onion)
- 1 cup chopped apple (about 1 large apple)
- 1 1/2 cups white vinegar (360 ml)
- 1 cup water (240 ml)
- 3/4 cup sugar (150 grams)
- 1 tablespoon mustard seeds (5 grams)
- 1 teaspoon celery seeds (2 grams)
- 1 teaspoon salt (5 grams)
- 1/2 teaspoon ground turmeric (1 gram)
- 6 clean pint-sized canning jars with lids and bands

INSTRUCTIONS

1. Chop green beans, red bell pepper, onion, and apple into uniform pieces.
2. In a large pot, mix together green beans, red bell pepper, onion, apple, vinegar, water, sugar, mustard seeds, celery seeds, salt, and turmeric.
3. Bring the mixture to a boil over medium heat, then reduce heat and simmer for about 30 minutes, or until the vegetables are tender and the flavors have melded.
4. Boil jars, lids, and bands for 10 minutes to sterilize them. Keep jars warm.
5. Fill the jars with the hot relish, leaving 12 mm (1/2-inch) headspace. Remove any air bubbles.
6. Clean the rims, secure lids, and tighten rings finger-tight.
7. Soak the jars in boiling water for 10 minutes.
8. Take out the jars and leave to cool down for 12 to 24 hours. Check seals.

PREPARATION TIPS: The sweet and sour combination in this relish is perfect as a condiment for grilled meats or as a flavorful addition to sandwiches and salads.

NUTRITIONAL VALUE (PER SERVING - 1 TABLESPOON): Calories: 15, Carbohydrates: 3g, Fat: 0g, Protein: 0g, Sodium: 80mg, Sugar: 2g

SPICED CAULIFLOWER AND CARROT RELISH

PREPARATION TIME: 25 MINUTES
COOKING TIME: 20 MINUTES COOKING, 10 MINUTES PROCESSING
SERVINGS: 6 PINT-SIZED JARS (16 OUNCES EACH)

MAXIMUM STORAGE TIME: 1 YEAR (UNOPENED). ONCE OPENED, REFRIGERATE AND USE WITHIN 2 MONTHS
RECOMMENDED HEADSPACE: 1/2-INCH (12 MM)

INGREDIENTS

- 3 cups chopped cauliflower (about 1 medium head)
- 2 cups grated carrots (about 4 medium carrots)
- 1 cup chopped sweet red pepper (200 grams)
- 1 cup chopped onion (about 1 large onion)
- 1 1/2 cups white vinegar (360 ml)
- 1 cup sugar (200 grams)

- 1/2 cup water (120 ml)
- 1 tablespoon yellow mustard seeds (5 grams)
- 1 teaspoon ground ginger (2 grams)
- 1 teaspoon turmeric (2 grams)
- 1/2 teaspoon cayenne pepper (adjust to taste)
- 1/2 teaspoon salt (2 grams)
- 6 clean pint-sized canning jars with lids and bands

INSTRUCTIONS

1. Chop cauliflower into small florets, grate carrots, and finely chop the red pepper and onion.
2. In a large pot, mix together cauliflower, carrots, red pepper, onion, vinegar, sugar, water, mustard seeds, ginger, turmeric, cayenne pepper, and salt.
3. Bring the mixture to a boil over medium heat, then reduce heat and simmer for about 20 minutes, or until the vegetables are tender and the flavors have melded.
4. Boil jars, lids, and bands for 10 minutes to sterilize them. Keep jars warm.
5. Fill the jars with the hot relish, leaving 12 mm (1/2-inch) headspace. Remove any air bubbles.
6. Clean the rims, secure lids, and tighten rings finger-tight.
7. Soak the jars in boiling water for 10 minutes.
8. Take out the jars and leave to cool down for 12 to 24 hours. Check seals.

NUTRITIONAL VALUE (PER SERVING - 1 TABLESPOON): Calories: 20, Carbohydrates: 4g, Fat: 0g, Protein: 0g, Sodium: 80mg, Sugar: 3g

VEGETABLE SAUCES AND SALSAS

ROASTED RED PEPPER AND BASIL SAUCE

PREPARATION TIME: 40 MINUTES (INCLUDING ROASTING TIME)
COOKING TIME: 20 MINUTES COOKING, 15 MINUTES PROCESSING
SERVINGS: 6 PINT-SIZED JARS (16 OUNCES EACH)

MAXIMUM STORAGE TIME: 1 YEAR (UNOPENED). ONCE OPENED, REFRIGERATE AND USE WITHIN 1 MONTH
RECOMMENDED HEADSPACE: 1/2-INCH (12 MM)

INGREDIENTS

- 6 large red bell peppers (about 1.5 kg)
- 2 tablespoons olive oil (30 ml)
- 1 large onion, chopped (about 200 grams)
- 4 cloves garlic, minced
- 1/2 cup chopped fresh basil (about 20 grams)

- 1/4 cup balsamic vinegar (60 ml)
- 1 teaspoon salt (5 grams)
- 1/2 teaspoon ground black pepper (1 gram)
- 1/2 teaspoon sugar (optional) (2 grams)
- 6 clean pint-sized canning jars with lids and bands

INSTRUCTIONS

1. Preheat the oven to 400°F (200°C). Arrange whole red peppers on a baking sheet and roast until the skins blister, about 30 minutes. Remove from the oven, cover with a bowl or foil for 10 minutes to steam, then peel and chop.
2. In a large saucepan, heat olive oil over medium heat. Sauté onion and garlic until translucent.
3. Add chopped roasted peppers, basil, salt, black pepper, balsamic vinegar, and sugar (if using) to the saucepan. Simmer for 10 minutes, allowing flavors to meld.
4. Use an immersion blender or stand blender to puree the sauce until smooth.
5. Boil jars, lids, and bands for 10 minutes to sterilize them. Keep jars warm.
6. Fill the jars with the hot sauce, leaving 12 mm (1/2-inch) headspace. Remove any air bubbles.
7. Clean the rims, secure lids, and tighten rings finger-tight.
8. Soak the jars in boiling water for 15 minutes.
9. Take out the jars and leave to cool down for 12 to 24 hours. Check seals.

PREPARATION TIPS:
- Roasting the peppers adds depth to the sauce with their natural sweetness.

NUTRITIONAL VALUE (PER SERVING - 1 TABLESPOON): Calories: 10, Carbohydrates: 2g, Fat: 0.5g, Protein: 0g, Sodium: 40mg, Sugar: 1g

SPICY TOMATO AND ZUCCHINI SAUCE

PREPARATION TIME: 30 MINUTES
COOKING TIME: 35 MINUTES COOKING, 15 MINUTES PROCESSING
SERVINGS: 6 PINT-SIZED JARS (16 OUNCES EACH)

MAXIMUM STORAGE TIME: 1 YEAR (UNOPENED). ONCE OPENED, REFRIGERATE AND USE WITHIN 1 MONTH
RECOMMENDED HEADSPACE: LEAVE 1/2-INCH (12 MM) HEADSPACE IN THE JARS

INGREDIENTS

- 8 cups chopped ripe tomatoes (about 4 kg)
- 4 cups grated zucchini (about 2 medium zucchinis)
- 2 cups chopped onions (about 2 medium onions)
- 1 cup chopped green bell pepper (about 1 large pepper or 200 grams)
- 4 cloves garlic, minced
- 2 tablespoons olive oil
- 1/4 cup chopped fresh basil (10 grams)
- 2 teaspoons salt (10 grams)
- 1 teaspoon ground black pepper (2 grams)
- 1 teaspoon dried oregano (2 grams)
- 1/2 teaspoon red pepper flakes (adjust to taste)
- 1/4 cup balsamic vinegar (60 ml)
- 6 clean pint-sized canning jars with lids and bands

INSTRUCTIONS

1. In a large pot, heat olive oil over medium heat. Sauté onions, garlic, and green bell pepper until soft.
2. Stir in the chopped tomatoes and grated zucchini. Bring to a simmer.
3. Add basil, salt, black pepper, oregano, red pepper flakes, and balsamic vinegar. Simmer for about 30 minutes, or until the sauce thickens and the vegetables are tender.
4. Boil jars, lids, and bands for 10 minutes to sterilize them. Keep jars warm.
5. Ladle the hot sauce into jars, leaving 12 mm (1/2-inch) headspace. Remove any air bubbles.
6. Clean the rims, secure lids, and tighten rings finger-tight.
7. Soak the jars in boiling water for 15 minutes.
8. Take out the jars and leave to cool down for 12 to 24 hours. Check seals.

PREPARATION TIPS:

- Grating the zucchini allows it to blend seamlessly into the sauce.
- Simmering the sauce for a sufficient time helps to develop the flavors and achieve the desired consistency.
- The addition of balsamic vinegar adds a slight tanginess and depth to the sauce.

NUTRITIONAL VALUE (PER SERVING - 1 TABLESPOON): Calories: 15, Carbohydrates: 3g, Fat: 0.5g, Protein: 0g, Sodium: 80mg, Sugar: 2g

CREAMY ROASTED GARLIC AND EGGPLANT SAUCE

PREPARATION TIME: 45 MINUTES (INCLUDING ROASTING TIME)
COOKING TIME: 20 MINUTES COOKING, 15 MINUTES PROCESSING
SERVINGS: 6 PINT-SIZED JARS (16 OUNCES EACH)

MAXIMUM STORAGE TIME: 1 YEAR (UNOPENED). ONCE OPENED, REFRIGERATE AND USE WITHIN 1 MONTH
RECOMMENDED HEADSPACE: 1/2-INCH (12 MM)

INGREDIENTS

- 4 cups roasted eggplant, peeled and chopped (about 2 medium eggplants or 1 kg)
- 2 heads of garlic, roasted and cloves squeezed out
- 1 cup chopped onion (about 1 medium onion)
- 2 cups chopped tomatoes (about 1 kg)
- 1/4 cup olive oil (60 ml)
- 1/4 cup chopped fresh basil (10 grams)
- 2 teaspoons salt (10 grams)
- 1 teaspoon ground black pepper (2 grams)
- 1/2 teaspoon dried thyme (1 gram)
- 1/4 cup balsamic vinegar (60 ml)
- 6 clean pint-sized canning jars with lids and bands

CONTINUED →

INSTRUCTIONS

1. Preheat the oven to 400°F (200°C). Roast whole eggplants and garlic heads until tender. Cool, peel, and chop the eggplant; squeeze out the garlic cloves.
2. In a large saucepan, heat olive oil over medium heat. Sauté onion until translucent.
3. Add roasted eggplant, roasted garlic, tomatoes, basil, salt, black pepper, thyme, and balsamic vinegar to the saucepan. Bring to a simmer.
4. Use an immersion blender or stand blender to puree the sauce until smooth.
5. Boil jars, lids, and bands for 10 minutes to sterilize them. Keep jars warm.
6. Ladle the hot sauce into jars, leaving 12 mm (1/2-inch) headspace. Remove any air bubbles.
7. Clean the rims, secure lids, and tighten rings finger-tight.
8. Soak the jars in boiling water for 15 minutes.
9. Take out the jars and leave to cool down for 12 to 24 hours. Check seals.

PREPARATION TIPS: Pureeing the sauce until smooth gives it a creamy texture, making it ideal for pasta, as a base for soups, or as a spread for bruschetta.

NUTRITIONAL VALUE (PER SERVING - 1 TABLESPOON): Calories: 20, Carbohydrates: 3g, Fat: 1g, Protein: 0g, Sodium: 80mg, Sugar: 2g

SWEET AND TANGY BELL PEPPER SAUCE

PREPARATION TIME: 30 MINUTES
COOKING TIME: 25 MINUTES COOKING, 15 MINUTES PROCESSING
SERVINGS: 6 PINT-SIZED JARS (16 OUNCES EACH)

MAXIMUM STORAGE TIME: 1 YEAR (UNOPENED). ONCE OPENED, REFRIGERATE AND USE WITHIN 1 MONTH
RECOMMENDED HEADSPACE: 1/2-INCH (12 MM)

INGREDIENTS

- 6 cups chopped bell peppers (mix of red, yellow, and orange, about 1.5 kg)
- 2 cups chopped tomatoes (about 500 grams)
- 1 cup apple cider vinegar (240 ml)
- 1 cup sugar (200 grams)
- 1/2 cup finely chopped onion (about 1 small onion)
- 2 cloves garlic, minced
- 1 tablespoon mustard seeds (5 grams)
- 1 teaspoon salt (5 grams)
- 1/2 teaspoon ground black pepper (1 gram)
- 1/4 teaspoon cayenne pepper (adjust to taste)
- 6 clean pint-sized canning jars with lids and bands

INSTRUCTIONS

1. Chop bell peppers and tomatoes into small pieces. Finely chop the onion and mince the garlic.
2. In a large pot, mix together bell peppers, tomatoes, vinegar, sugar, onion, garlic, mustard seeds, salt, black pepper, and cayenne pepper.
3. Bring the mixture to a boil over medium heat, then reduce heat and simmer for about 25 minutes, or until the sauce thickens and the vegetables are tender.
4. Boil jars, lids, and bands for 10 minutes to sterilize them. Keep jars warm.
5. Ladle the hot sauce into jars, leaving 12 mm (1/2-inch) headspace. Remove any air bubbles.
6. Clean the rims, secure lids, and tighten rings finger-tight.
7. Soak the jars in boiling water for 15 minutes.
8. Take out the jars and leave to cool down for 12 to 24 hours. Check seals.

GRILLED CORN AND BLACK BEAN SALSA

PREPARATION TIME: 30 MINUTES (INCLUDING GRILLING TIME)
COOKING TIME: 10 MINUTES COOKING, 15 MINUTES PROCESSING
SERVINGS: 6 PINT-SIZED JARS (16 OUNCES EACH)

MAXIMUM STORAGE TIME: 1 YEAR (UNOPENED). ONCE OPENED, REFRIGERATE AND USE WITHIN 2 WEEKS
RECOMMENDED HEADSPACE: 1/2-INCH (12 MM)

INGREDIENTS

- 4 cups grilled corn kernels (about 6 ears of corn)
- 2 cups cooked black beans (about 400 grams, can be from canned black beans, rinsed and drained)
- 1 cup diced red bell pepper (about 1 large pepper)
- 1 cup diced green bell pepper (about 1 large pepper or 200 grams)
- 1 cup diced red onion (about 1 medium onion)
- 1/2 cup chopped fresh cilantro (about a bunch)

- 2 jalapeño peppers, seeds removed and finely chopped (adjust to taste)
- 1/2 cup apple cider vinegar (120 ml)
- 1/4 cup lime juice (about 2 limes)
- 2 teaspoons salt (10 grams)
- 1 teaspoon ground cumin (2 grams)
- 6 clean pint-sized canning jars with lids and bands

INSTRUCTIONS

1. Grill corn ears until slightly charred. Let cool, then cut kernels off the cob.
2. In a large bowl, mix together grilled corn, black beans, red and green bell peppers, red onion, cilantro, jalapeños, vinegar, lime juice, salt, and cumin.
3. Transfer the mixture to a large pot and bring to a simmer over medium heat, cooking for about 10 minutes.

4. Boil jars, lids, and bands for 10 minutes to sterilize them. Keep jars warm.
5. Fill the jars with the hot salsa, leaving 12 mm (1/2-inch) headspace. Remove any air bubbles.
6. Clean the rims, secure lids, and tighten rings finger-tight.
7. Soak the jars in boiling water for 15 minutes.
8. Take out the jars and leave to cool down for 12 to 24 hours. Check seals.

PREPARATION TIPS:
- Grilling the corn adds a smoky flavor to the salsa.
- Finely chopping the vegetables ensures a consistent texture and easy scooping with chips.
- Adjust the amount of jalapeño peppers to control the heat level of the salsa.

NUTRITIONAL VALUE (PER SERVING - 1 TABLESPOON): Calories: 15, Carbohydrates: 3g, Fat: 0g, Protein: 1g, Sodium: 80mg, Sugar: 1g

---

ROASTED VEGETABLE SALSA

PREPARATION TIME: 40 MINUTES (INCLUDING ROASTING TIME)
COOKING TIME: 20 MINUTES COOKING, 15 MINUTES PROCESSING
SERVINGS: 6 PINT-SIZED JARS (16 OUNCES EACH)

MAXIMUM STORAGE TIME: 1 YEAR (UNOPENED). ONCE OPENED, REFRIGERATE AND USE WITHIN 2 WEEKS
RECOMMENDED HEADSPACE: LEAVE 1/2-INCH (12 MM) HEADSPACE IN THE JARS

CONTINUED →

INGREDIENTS

- 3 cups chopped tomatoes (about 1.5 kg)
- 2 cups chopped zucchini (about 2 medium zucchinis)
- 1 cup chopped red onion (about 1 large onion)
- 1 cup chopped bell peppers (mix of colors, about 2 medium peppers or 400 grams)
- 2 cloves garlic, minced
- 1/4 cup olive oil
- 1/2 cup chopped fresh cilantro (about a bunch)
- 1/4 cup lime juice (about 2 limes)
- 2 teaspoons salt (10 grams)
- 1 teaspoon ground black pepper (2 grams)
- 1/2 teaspoon ground cumin (1 gram)
- 1-2 jalapeño peppers, finely chopped (to taste)
- 6 clean pint-sized canning jars with lids and bands

INSTRUCTIONS

1. Preheat the oven to 400°F (200°C). Toss tomatoes, zucchini, onion, and bell peppers with olive oil and spread on a baking sheet. Roast until slightly charred, about 30 minutes. Cool and chop roughly.
2. In a large pot, mix together the roasted vegetables, minced garlic, cilantro, lime juice, salt, black pepper, cumin, and jalapeño peppers.
3. Bring the mixture to a simmer over medium heat, cooking for about 20 minutes.
4. Boil jars, lids, and bands for 10 minutes to sterilize them. Keep jars warm.
5. Fill the jars with the hot salsa, leaving 12 mm (1/2-inch) headspace. Remove any air bubbles.
6. Clean the rims, secure lids, and tighten rings finger-tight.
7. Soak the jars in boiling water for 15 minutes.
8. Take out the jars and leave to cool down for 12 to 24 hours. Check seals.

PREPARATION TIPS:

- Roasting the vegetables before combining them adds depth to the salsa with their natural sweetness.
- Chopping the roasted vegetables into small, uniform pieces ensures a consistent texture.
- Adjust the amount of jalapeño pepper according to your preference for heat.

NUTRITIONAL VALUE (PER SERVING - 1 TABLESPOON): Calories: 15, Carbohydrates: 2g, Fat: 1g, Protein: 0g, Sodium: 80mg, Sugar: 1g

SPICY TOMATO AND ROASTED EGGPLANT SALSA

PREPARATION TIME: 45 MINUTES (INCLUDING ROASTING TIME)
COOKING TIME: 20 MINUTES COOKING, 15 MINUTES PROCESSING
SERVINGS: 6 PINT-SIZED JARS (16 OUNCES EACH)

MAXIMUM STORAGE TIME: 1 YEAR (UNOPENED). ONCE OPENED, REFRIGERATE AND USE WITHIN 2 WEEKS
RECOMMENDED HEADSPACE: LEAVE 1/2-INCH (12 MM) HEADSPACE IN THE JARS

INGREDIENTS

- 4 cups chopped ripe tomatoes (about 2 kg)
- 2 cups roasted eggplant, peeled and chopped (about 1 large eggplant or 500 grams)
- 1 cup chopped red onion (about 1 large onion)
- 1 cup chopped green bell pepper (200 grams)
- 3 cloves garlic, minced
- 1/4 cup olive oil (for roasting eggplant)
- 1/2 cup apple cider vinegar (120 ml)
- 1/4 cup chopped fresh basil (10 grams)
- 2 tablespoons chopped fresh parsley (6 grams)
- 2 teaspoons salt (10 grams)
- 1 teaspoon ground black pepper (2 grams)
- 1 teaspoon dried oregano (2 grams)
- 1-2 jalapeño peppers, finely chopped (to taste)
- 6 clean pint-sized canning jars with lids and bands

INSTRUCTIONS

1. Preheat the oven to 400°F (200°C). Slice the eggplant, brush with olive oil, and roast until tender, about 30 minutes. Cool, peel, and chop.
2. In a large pot, mix together the chopped tomatoes, roasted eggplant, red onion, green bell pepper, garlic, vinegar, basil, parsley, salt, black pepper, oregano, and jalapeño peppers.
3. Bring the mixture to a simmer over medium heat, cooking for about 20 minutes.
4. Boil jars, lids, and bands for 10 minutes to sterilize them. Keep jars warm.
5. Fill the jars with the hot salsa, leaving 12 mm (1/2-inch) headspace. Remove any air bubbles.
6. Clean the rims, secure lids, and tighten rings finger-tight.
7. Soak the jars in boiling water for 15 minutes.
8. Take out the jars and leave to cool down for 12 to 24 hours. Check seals.

PREPARATION TIPS:

- Roasting the eggplant beforehand adds a smoky depth to the salsa.
- Finely chopping the vegetables ensures a well-blended texture and flavor in every scoop.

NUTRITIONAL VALUE (PER SERVING - 1 TABLESPOON): Calories: 15, Carbohydrates: 2g, Fat: 1g, Protein: 0g, Sodium: 80mg, Sugar: 1g

---

JAMS, JELLIES, AND MARMALADES

GINGER-PEACH JAM

PREPARATION TIME: 20 MINUTES
COOKING TIME: 40 MINUTES
SERVINGS: ABOUT 3-4 JARS (8 OZ EACH)

MAXIMUM STORAGE TIME: 1 YEAR
RECOMMENDED HEADSPACE: LEAVE ABOUT 1/4-INCH (0.6 CM) HEADSPACE IN THE JARS

INGREDIENTS

- *8 cups (1.9 L/1.5 kg) of fresh peaches, peeled, pitted, and chopped*
- *1/4 cup (60 ml/25g) of fresh ginger, finely grated*

- *1/4 cup (60 ml) of lemon juice*
- *3 cups (720 ml/600g) of granulated sugar*
- *1 packet (49g) of fruit pectin (optional)*

INSTRUCTIONS

1. In a large pot, combine the chopped peaches, ginger, and lemon juice. Bring the mixture to a boil over medium-high heat, stirring occasionally.
2. Once boiling, stir in the sugar until it is fully dissolved. Continue to boil for about 10-15 minutes, stirring often to avoid sticking.
3. If using, stir in the pectin and continue to boil for another 10-15 minutes. You can test the set by placing a small spoonful on a cold plate and freezing for 1-2 minutes; it should wrinkle slightly when pushed.
4. Fill the sterilized jars with the hot jam, leaving about 0.6 cm (1/4-inch) headspace. Clean the rims, secure lids, and tighten rings finger-tight.
5. Soak the jars in a water bath canner, making sure they are under water by at least 2.5 cm (1 inch). Bring to a boil and process for 10 minutes.
6. Turn off the heat, let the jars soak in the water for 5 minutes, then remove and let cool completely on a clean towel or cooling rack.

NUTRITIONAL VALUE PER SERVING: Calories: 45, Fat: 0g, Cholesterol: 0mg, Sodium: 1mg, Carbohydrates: 11g, Dietary Fiber: 0g, Sugars: 10g, Protein: 0g

SPICED PEACH JAM RECIPE

PREPARATION TIME: 30 MINUTES
COOKING TIME: 20 MINUTES
SERVINGS: 6 PINT-SIZED JARS (16 OUNCES EACH)

MAXIMUM STORAGE TIME: 1 YEAR (UNOPENED). ONCE OPENED, REFRIGERATE AND USE WITHIN 3 WEEKS.
RECOMMENDED HEADSPACE: 1/4-INCH (0.6 CM)

INGREDIENTS

- 8 cups of peeled and chopped peaches (about 12 medium peaches)
- 4 cups of granulated sugar (800 grams)
- 1/4 cup lemon juice (60 ml)
- 2 teaspoons ground cinnamon (5 grams)
- 1 teaspoon ground nutmeg (2 grams)
- 1/2 teaspoon ground cloves (1 gram)
- 6 clean pint-sized canning jars with lids and bands

INSTRUCTIONS

1. Boil jars, lids, and bands for 10 minutes to sterilize them. Keep the jars warm.
2. In a large saucepan, combine the chopped peaches, lemon juice, and sugar. Stir well.
3. Bring the mixture to a boil over medium-high heat, stirring frequently. Reduce heat and simmer until the it thickens, about 20 minutes.
4. Stir in cinnamon, nutmeg, and cloves.
5. Fill the warm jars with the hot jam, leaving 6 mm (1/4-inch) headspace. Remove any air bubbles.
6. Wipe the rims clean and place the lids on the jars. Apply the bands and tighten until fingertip tight.
7. Soak the jars in boiling water for 10 minutes.
8. Take out the jars and leave to cool down for 12 to 24 hours. Check the seals; the lid should not flex when pressed.

PREPARATION TIPS: Fill and close the jars while they are still warm to ensure proper sealing.

NUTRITIONAL VALUE (PER SERVING - 1 TABLESPOON): Calories: 50, Carbohydrates: 13g, Fat: 0g, Protein: 0g, Sodium: 0mg, Sugar: 13g

---

CLASSIC APPLE CINNAMON JAM

PREPARATION TIME: 20 MINUTES
COOKING TIME: 15 MINUTES
SERVINGS: MAKES ABOUT 6 HALF-PINT JARS

MAXIMUM STORAGE TIME: UP TO 1 YEAR IN A COOL, DARK PLACE
RECOMMENDED HEADSPACE: 1/4 INCH (6 MM)

INGREDIENTS

- 4 lbs apples, peeled, cored, and finely chopped
- 3 cups (600 g) sugar
- 1/2 cup (120 ml) water
- 1/4 cup (60 ml) lemon juice
- 2 tsp ground cinnamon

INSTRUCTIONS

1. Combine all ingredients in a large saucepan.
2. Cook over medium heat until the mixture thickens.
3. Fill the sterilized jars with the hot jam, leaving 6 mm (1/4-inch) headspace.
4. Soak in a water bath canner for 10 minutes.

SPICED BLUEBERRY PRESERVES

PREPARATION TIME: 15 MINUTES
COOKING TIME: 20 MINUTES
SERVINGS: MAKES ABOUT 5 HALF-PINT JARS

MAXIMUM STORAGE TIME: UP TO 18 MONTHS
RECOMMENDED HEADSPACE: LEAVE 1/4 INCH (6 MM) HEADSPACE

INGREDIENTS

- 5 cups (700 g) blueberries
- 2 1/2 cups (500 g) sugar
- 1 tsp ground nutmeg
- 1 tsp ground allspice
- 1/4 cup (60 ml) lemon juice

INSTRUCTIONS

1. Crush blueberries slightly in a large saucepan.
2. Add sugar, spices, and lemon juice, stirring until sugar dissolves.
3. Boil until it reaches jam consistency.
4. Ladle into jars, leaving 6 mm (1/4-inch) headspace.
5. Soak in a water bath for 15 minutes.

NUTRITIONAL VALUE (PER SERVING): Calories: 90, Fat: 0g, Carbohydrates: 23g, Protein: 0g

STRAWBERRY VANILLA JAM

PREPARATION TIME: 20 MINUTES
COOKING TIME: 20 MINUTES
SERVINGS: MAKES ABOUT 4 HALF-PINT JARS

MAXIMUM STORAGE TIME: UP TO 1 YEAR
RECOMMENDED HEADSPACE: LEAVE 1/4 INCH (6 MM) HEADSPACE

INGREDIENTS

- 4 cups (560 g) strawberries, hulled and halved
- 3 cups (600 g) sugar
- 1 vanilla bean, split and scraped
- 1/4 cup (60 ml) lemon juice

INSTRUCTIONS

1. Mash strawberries in a pot, add sugar and vanilla.
2. Bring to a boil, stirring, until it thickens.
3. Stir in lemon juice, boil for 5 more minutes.
4. Ladle into jars, leaving 6 mm (1/4-inch) headspace.
5. Soak in a water bath for 10 minutes.

PREPARATION TIPS:
- Cut larger strawberries into smaller pieces for uniform texture.

NUTRITIONAL VALUE (PER SERVING): Calories: 100, Fat: 0g, Carbohydrates: 25g, Protein: 0g

BLACKBERRY SAGE JAM

PREPARATION TIME: 15 MINUTES
COOKING TIME: 20 MINUTES
SERVINGS: MAKES ABOUT 5 HALF-PINT JARS

MAXIMUN STORAGE TIME: UP TO 18 MONTHS
RECOMMENDED HEADSPACE: LEAVE 1/4 INCH (6 MM) HEADSPACE

INGREDIENTS

- 4 cups (560 g) blackberries
- 2 1/2 cups (500 g) sugar
- 1/4 cup (60 ml) finely chopped fresh sage
- 1/4 cup (60 ml) lemon juice

INSTRUCTIONS

1. Mash blackberries and sugar in a pot. Add sage, boil until thick.
2. Stir in lemon juice, continue boiling for 5 minutes.
3. Ladle into jars, leaving 1/4 inch (6 mm) headspace. Process in a water bath for 15 minutes.

NUTRITIONAL VALUE (PER SERVING): Calories: 70, Fat: 0g, Carbohydrates: 17g, Protein: 1g

BERRY BLISS JAM RECIPE

PREPARATION TIME: 25 MINUTES
COOKING TIME: 15 MINUTES
SERVINGS: 6 PINT-SIZED JARS (16 OUNCES EACH)

MAXIMUM STORAGE TIME: 1 YEAR (UNOPENED). ONCE OPENED, REFRIGERATE AND USE WITHIN 3 WEEKS.
RECOMMENDED HEADSPACE: 1/4 INCH (6 MM)

INGREDIENTS

- 4 cups strawberries, hulled and crushed (1 kg)
- 2 cups blueberries, crushed (about 300 grams)
- 4 cups granulated sugar (800 grams)
- 1/4 cup lemon juice (60 ml)
- 1 packet of fruit pectin (powdered, 49 grams)
- 6 clean pint-sized canning jars with lids and bands

INSTRUCTIONS

1. Boil jars, lids, and bands for 10 minutes to sterilize them. Keep jars warm.
2. In a large saucepan, combine crushed blueberries, strawberries, and lemon juice. Gradually stir in pectin.
3. Bring the mixture to a full boil over high heat, stirring continuously. Add sugar and return to a boil. Boil for 1 minute, stirring.
4. Fill the warm jars with the hot jam, leaving 6 mm (1/4-inch) headspace. Remove air bubbles.
5. Clean the rims, secure lids, and tighten rings finger-tight.
6. Soak the jars in boiling water for 10 minutes.
7. Take out the jars and leave to cool down for 12 to 24 hours. Check seals.

PREPARATION TIPS:
- Crush berries with a potato masher or in a food processor for a smoother texture.
- Ensure a full rolling boil to properly activate the pectin for setting the jam.
- Fill and close jars while still warm to ensure proper sealing.

RASPBERRY RHUBARB JAM RECIPE

PREPARATION TIME: 20 MINUTES
COOKING TIME: 15 MINUTES (JAM COOKING) + 10 MINUTES (WATER BATH CANNING)
SERVINGS: 5 PINT-SIZED JARS (16 OUNCES EACH)

MAXIMUM STORAGE TIME: 1 YEAR (UNOPENED). ONCE OPENED, REFRIGERATE AND USE WITHIN 1 MONTH
RECOMMENDED HEADSPACE: 1/4 INCH (6 MM)

INGREDIENTS

- *3 cups chopped rhubarb (about 300 grams)*
- *3 cups fresh raspberries (about 360 grams)*
- *4 cups granulated sugar (800 grams)*

- *1/4 cup lemon juice (60 ml)*
- *5 clean pint-sized canning jars with lids and bands*

INSTRUCTIONS

1. In a large saucepan, combine rhubarb, raspberries, sugar, and lemon juice.
2. Bring to a boil over medium heat, stirring constantly. Once boiling, reduce heat to a simmer and cook until the mixture thickens (about 15 minutes).
3. Boil jars, lids, and bands for 10 minutes to sterilize them. Keep the jars warm.
4. Fill the jars with the hot jam, leaving 6 mm (1/4-inch) headspace. Remove any air bubbles.
5. Clean the rims, secure lids, and tighten rings finger-tight.
6. Soak the jars in boiling water for 10 minutes.
7. Take out the jars and leave to cool down for 12 to 24 hours. Check seals.

PREPARATION TIPS:
- Cut rhubarb into small, even pieces for uniform cooking.
- Constant stirring is essential to prevent burning and ensure even cooking.
- Fill and seal jars while they're still warm to maintain proper sealing.

NUTRITIONAL VALUE (PER SERVING - 1 TABLESPOON): Calories: 45, Carbohydrates: 11g, Fat: 0g, Protein: 0g, Sodium: 0mg, Sugar: 11g

TROPICAL MANGO JAM RECIPE

PREPARATION TIME: 25 MINUTES
COOKING TIME: 15 MINUTES (JAM COOKING) + 10 MINUTES (WATER BATH CANNING)
SERVINGS: 4 PINT-SIZED JARS (16 OUNCES EACH)

MAXIMUM STORAGE TIME: 1 YEAR (UNOPENED). ONCE OPENED, REFRIGERATE AND USE WITHIN 1 MONTH
RECOMMENDED HEADSPACE: 1/4 INCH (6 MM)

INGREDIENTS

- 6 cups of peeled and diced ripe mangoes (1.5 kg)
- 3 cups granulated sugar (600 grams)
- 1/4 cup lime juice (60 ml)

- 1 teaspoon grated fresh ginger (2 grams)
- 1/2 teaspoon ground cinnamon (1 gram)
- 4 clean pint-sized canning jars with lids and bands

INSTRUCTIONS

1. In a large saucepan, combine mangoes, sugar, lime juice, ginger, and cinnamon.
2. Bring the mixture to a boil over medium-high heat, stirring frequently. Reduce heat and simmer until the mixture thickens (about 15 minutes).
3. While the mixture is cooking, boil jars, lids, and bands for 10 minutes to sterilize them. Keep jars warm.
4. Fill the warm jars with the hot jam, leaving 6 mm (1/4-inch) headspace. Remove any air bubbles.
5. Clean the rims, secure lids, and tighten rings finger-tight.
6. Soak the jars in boiling water for 10 minutes.
7. Take out the jars and leave to cool down for 12 to 24 hours. Check seals.

PREPARATION TIPS:
- Stirring the jam frequently prevents burning and ensures even thickening.
- Fill and close jars while still warm to ensure proper sealing.

BLACKBERRY MINT JELLY

PREPARATION TIME: 20 MINUTES
COOKING TIME: 10 MINUTES COOKING, 10 MINUTES PROCESSING
SERVINGS: 6 HALF-PINT JARS (8 OUNCES EACH)

MAXIMUM STORAGE TIME: 1 YEAR (UNOPENED). ONCE OPENED, REFRIGERATE AND USE WITHIN 3 WEEKS.
RECOMMENDED HEADSPACE: 1/4 INCH (6 MM)

INGREDIENTS

- 4 cups blackberry juice (2 kg of fresh blackberries)
- 3 cups granulated sugar (600 grams)
- 1/4 cup fresh mint leaves, finely chopped

- 2 tablespoons lemon juice (30 ml)
- 1 pouch liquid pectin (3 ounces or 85 grams)
- 6 clean half-pint canning jars with lids and bands

INSTRUCTIONS

1. Crush the blackberries in a large pot and heat over low heat for 10 minutes. Strain through a cheesecloth or jelly bag to extract the juice.

2. Boil jars, lids, and bands for 10 minutes to sterilize them. Keep jars warm.

3. In a large pot, combine blackberry juice, sugar, mint leaves, and lemon juice. Bring to a rolling boil over high heat, stirring constantly. Stir in the liquid pectin and return to a full rolling boil. Boil for 1 minute.
4. Remove from heat. Fill the jars with the hot jelly, leaving 6 mm (1/4-inch) headspace. Remove any air bubbles.
5. Clean the rims, secure lids, and tighten rings finger-tight.
6. Soak the jars in boiling water for 10 minutes.
7. Take out the jars and leave to cool down for 12 to 24 hours. Check seals.

PREPARATION TIPS:

- When extracting juice, gently mash the blackberries to release more juice but avoid over-pulping which can make the jelly cloudy.
- Use a large pot for boiling the mixture as it tends to foam up.

NUTRITIONAL VALUE (PER SERVING – 1 TABLESPOON): Calories: 50, Carbohydrates: 13g, Fat: 0g, Protein: 0g, Sodium: 0mg, Sugar: 13g

APPLE CINNAMON JELLY

PREPARATION TIME: 30 MINUTES (FOR JUICE EXTRACTION AND PREPARATION)
COOKING TIME: 10 MINUTES COOKING, 10 MINUTES PROCESSING

SERVINGS: 6 HALF-PINT JARS (8 OUNCES EACH)
MAXIMUM STORAGE TIME: 1 YEAR (UNOPENED). ONCE OPENED, REFRIGERATE AND USE WITHIN 3 WEEKS
RECOMMENDED HEADSPACE: 1/4 INCH (6 MM)

INGREDIENTS

- *4 cups apple juice (preferably fresh, about 2 kg)*
- *3 1/2 cups granulated sugar (700 grams)*
- *2 cinnamon sticks*
- *2 tablespoons lemon juice (30 ml)*
- *1 pouch liquid pectin (3 ounces or 85 grams)*
- *6 clean half-pint canning jars with lids and bands*

INSTRUCTIONS

1. Crush the apples and simmer over low heat for about 20 minutes. Strain through a jelly bag or cheesecloth to obtain clear apple juice.
2. Boil jars, lids, and bands for 10 minutes to sterilize them. Keep jars warm.
3. In a large pot, combine apple juice, cinnamon sticks, sugar, and lemon juice. Bring to a rolling boil over high heat, stirring. Remove cinnamon sticks.
4. Stir in liquid pectin and return to a full boil. Boil for 1 minute, stirring constantly.
5. Fill the jars with the hot jelly, leaving 1 6 mm (1/4-inch) headspace. Remove any air bubbles.
6. Clean the rims, secure lids, and tighten rings finger-tight.
7. Soak the jars in boiling water for 10 minutes, starting the timer when water returns to a boil.
8. Take out the jars and leave to cool down for 12 to 24 hours. Check seals.

PREPARATION TIPS:
- Ensure a thorough extraction of juice for a clear jelly.
- The addition of cinnamon sticks during boiling infuses a warm, spicy flavor.

NUTRITIONAL VALUE (PER SERVING - 1 TABLESPOON): Calories: 55, Carbohydrates: 14g, Fat: 0g, Protein: 0g, Sodium: 0mg, Sugar: 14g

RASPBERRY LEMONADE JELLY

PREPARATION TIME: 25 MINUTES (FOR JUICE EXTRACTION AND PREPARATION)
COOKING TIME: 10 MINUTES COOKING, 10 MINUTES PROCESSING
SERVINGS: 6 HALF-PINT JARS (8 OUNCES EACH)

MAXIMUM STORAGE TIME: 1 YEAR (UNOPENED). ONCE OPENED, REFRIGERATE AND USE WITHIN 3 WEEKS
RECOMMENDED HEADSPACE: LEAVE 1/4 INCH (6 MM) HEADSPACE

INGREDIENTS

- 3 cups raspberry juice (about 1.5 kg of fresh raspberries)
- 1 cup fresh lemon juice (about 5-6 large lemons)
- 4 1/2 cups granulated sugar (900 grams)
- 1 pouch liquid pectin (3 ounces or 85 grams)
- 6 clean half-pint canning jars with lids and bands

INSTRUCTIONS

1. Crush raspberries and simmer over low heat for 10 minutes. Strain through a jelly bag or cheesecloth to obtain clear raspberry juice. Combine with lemon juice.
2. Boil jars, lids, and bands for 10 minutes to sterilize them. Keep jars warm.
3. In a large pot, combine raspberry-lemon juice and sugar. Bring to a rolling boil over high heat, stirring.
4. Stir in liquid pectin and return to a full boil. Boil for 1 minute, stirring constantly.
5. Fill the jars with the hot jelly, leaving 6 mm (1/4-inch) headspace. Remove any air bubbles.
6. Clean the rims, secure lids, and tighten rings finger-tight.
7. Soak the jars in boiling water for 10 minutes, starting the timer when water returns to a boil.
8. Take out the jars and leave to cool down for 12 to 24 hours. Check seals.

PREPARATION TIPS: Ensure thorough straining of raspberry juice to avoid seeds in your jelly.

NUTRITIONAL VALUE (PER SERVING - 1 TABLESPOON): Calories: 50, Carbohydrates: 13g, Fat: 0g, Protein: 0g, Sodium: 0mg, Sugar: 13g

SPICED GRAPE JELLY

PREPARATION TIME: 30 MINUTES (FOR JUICE EXTRACTION AND PREPARATION)
COOKING TIME: 10 MINUTES COOKING, 10 MINUTES PROCESSING
SERVINGS: 6 HALF-PINT JARS (8 OUNCES EACH)

MAXIMUM STORAGE TIME: 1 YEAR (UNOPENED). ONCE OPENED, REFRIGERATE AND USE WITHIN 3 WEEKS
RECOMMENDED HEADSPACE: LEAVE 1/4 INCH (6 MM) HEADSPACE

INGREDIENTS

- 4 cups grape juice (fresh, 2 kg of grapes)
- 3 1/2 cups granulated sugar (700 grams)
- 1 cinnamon stick
- 2 cloves
- 1 star anise
- 2 tablespoons lemon juice (30 ml)
- 1 pouch liquid pectin (3 ounces or 85 grams)
- 6 clean half-pint canning jars with lids and bands

INSTRUCTIONS

1. Crush grapes in a large pot and simmer over low heat for 20 minutes. Strain through a jelly bag to get a clear grape juice.
2. Boil jars, lids, and bands for 10 minutes to sterilize them. Keep jars warm.
3. In a large pot, combine grape juice, sugar, cinnamon stick, cloves, star anise, and lemon juice. Bring to a rolling boil over high heat, stirring. Remove the spices.
4. Stir in liquid pectin and return to a full rolling boil. Boil for 1 minute, stirring constantly.
5. Fill the jars with the hot jelly, leaving 6 mm (1/4-inch) headspace. Remove any air bubbles.
6. Clean the rims, secure lids, and tighten rings finger-tight.
7. Soak the jars in boiling water for 10 minutes, starting the timer when water returns to a boil.
8. Take out the jars and leave to cool down for 12 to 24 hours. Check seals.

PREPARATION TIPS: Ensure thorough straining of the grape juice to avoid cloudiness in the jelly.

NUTRITIONAL VALUE (PER SERVING - 1 TABLESPOON): Calories: 55, Carbohydrates: 14g, Fat: 0g, Protein: 0g, Sodium: 0mg, Sugar: 14g

STRAWBERRY VANILLA JELLY

PREPARATION TIME: 20 MINUTES (FOR JUICE EXTRACTION AND PREPARATION)
COOKING TIME: 10 MINUTES COOKING, 10 MINUTES PROCESSING
SERVINGS: 6 HALF-PINT JARS (8 OUNCES EACH)

MAXIMUM STORAGE TIME: 1 YEAR (UNOPENED). ONCE OPENED, REFRIGERATE AND USE WITHIN 3 WEEKS
RECOMMENDED HEADSPACE: LEAVE 1/4 INCH (6 MM) HEADSPACE

INGREDIENTS

- 4 cups strawberry juice (about 2 kg of fresh strawberries)
- 3 cups granulated sugar (600 grams)
- 1 vanilla bean, split and scraped (or 1 teaspoon vanilla extract)
- 2 tablespoons lemon juice (30 ml)

- 1 pouch liquid pectin (3 ounces or 85 grams)

INSTRUCTIONS

1. Crush strawberries in a large pot and simmer over low heat for 10 minutes. Strain through a jelly bag or cheesecloth to obtain clear strawberry juice.
2. Boil jars, lids, and bands for 10 minutes to sterilize them. Keep jars warm.
3. In a large pot, combine strawberry juice, sugar, vanilla bean seeds (or extract), and lemon juice. Bring to a rolling boil over high heat, stirring.
4. Stir in liquid pectin and return to a full rolling boil. Boil for 1 minute, stirring constantly.
5. Remove vanilla bean pod (if used). Fill the jars with the hot jelly, leaving 6 mm (1/4-inch) headspace. Remove any air bubbles.
6. Clean the rims, secure lids, and tighten rings finger-tight.
7. Soak the jars in boiling water for 10 minutes, starting the timer when water returns to a boil.
8. Take out the jars and leave to cool down for 12 to 24 hours. Check seals.

NUTRITIONAL VALUE (PER SERVING - 1 TABLESPOON): Calories: 50, Carbohydrates: 13g, Fat: 0g, Protein: 0g, Sodium: 0mg, Sugar: 13g

SWEET & TANGY APPLE CIDER JELLY

PREPARATION TIME: 15 MINUTES
COOKING TIME: 50 MINUTES
SERVINGS: ABOUT 3-4 CUPS

MAXIMUM STORAGE TIME: 1 YEAR
RECOMMENDED HEADSPACE: LEAVE ABOUT 1/4-INCH (0.6 CM) HEADSPACE

INGREDIENTS

- 4 cups (960 ml) of fresh apple cider
- 3 cups (600g) of sugar
- 1 packet (49g) of fruit pectin
- 1 tablespoon (15 ml) of lemon juice

INSTRUCTIONS

1. In a large pot, combine the apple cider, lemon juice, and fruit pectin. Stir the mixture well to thoroughly blend the pectin.
2. Place the pot on medium-high heat and bring the mixture to a rolling boil, stirring constantly.
3. Once boiling, add the sugar all at once, continuing to stir as you bring the mixture back to a rolling boil.
4. Once it reaches a boil again, cook for another 1-2 minutes, ensuring the sugar has completely dissolved.
5. Remove from heat and skim off any foam that may have formed on the surface with a metal spoon.
6. Allow the mixture to cool slightly before carefully ladling into sterilized jars, leaving about 1/4-inch (0.6 cm) headspace.
7. Clean the rims, secure lids, and tighten rings finger-tight.
8. Fill the water bath canner halfway with water and bring it to a simmer. Carefully submerge the jars in the canner, making sure they are under water by at least 2.5 cm (1 inch). Bring to a boil and process for 10 minutes.
9. Turn off the heat, let the jars soak in the water for 5 minutes, then remove and let cool completely on a clean towel or cooling rack.

NUTRITIONAL VALUE PER SERVING: Calories: 60, Fat: 0g, Cholesterol: 0mg, Sodium: 0mg, Carbohydrates: 16g, Dietary Fiber: 0g, Sugars: 16g, Protein: 0g

ZESTY APPLE CIDER JELLY

PREPARATION TIME: 20 MINUTES
COOKING TIME: 40 MINUTES
SERVINGS: ABOUT 4-5 JARS (8 OZ EACH)

MAXIMUM STORAGE TIME: 1 YEAR
RECOMMENDED HEADSPACE: LEAVE ABOUT 1/4-INCH (0.6 CM) HEADSPACE

INGREDIENTS

- 4 cups (960 ml/950g) of fresh apple cider
- 1/4 cup (60 ml) of lemon juice
- 1 package (1.75 oz/49g) fruit pectin
- 5 cups (1200 ml/1 kg) of sugar

INSTRUCTIONS

1. Sterilize your jars and lids by washing them in warm, soapy water, and set them aside to air dry.
2. In a large pot, combine the apple cider, fruit pectin, and lemon juice. Bring the mixture to a rolling boil over medium-high heat, stirring constantly.
3. Once boiling, stir in the sugar all at once, returning the mixture to a rolling boil. Continue to boil for 1 to 2 minutes, stirring constantly.
4. Remove the pot from the heat and skim off any foam with a metal spoon.

5. Fill the prepared jars with the hot jelly, leaving about 6 mm (1/4-inch) headspace. Clean the rims, secure lids, and tighten rings finger-tight.
6. Soak the jars in a water bath canner, making sure they are under water by at least 2.5 cm (1 inch). Bring to a boil and process for 10 minutes.
7. Turn off the heat, let the jars soak in the water for 5 minutes, then carefully remove and allow to cool completely on a clean towel or cooling rack.

NUTRITIONAL VALUE PER SERVING: Calories: 45, Fat: 0g, Cholesterol: 0mg, Sodium: 0mg, Carbohydrates: 12g, Dietary Fiber: 0g, Sugars: 12g, Protein: 0g

RASPBERRY LEMON MARMALADE

PREPARATION TIME: 15 MINUTES
COOKING TIME: 25 MINUTES
SERVINGS: MAKES ABOUT 5 HALF-PINT JARS

MAXIMUM STORAGE TIME: UP TO 18 MONTHS
RECOMMENDED HEADSPACE: LEAVE 1/4 INCH (6 MM) HEADSPACE

INGREDIENTS

- 4 cups (560 g) raspberries
- 3 cups (600 g) sugar
- 1/2 cup (120 ml) lemon juice
- 2 tbsp lemon zest

INSTRUCTIONS

1. Combine raspberries, sugar, and lemon juice in a pot. Boil until it thickens, stir in zest.
2. Ladle into jars, leaving 6 mm (1/4-inch) headspace.
3. Soak in a water bath for 15 minutes.

NUTRITIONAL VALUE (PER SERVING): Calories: 80, Fat: 0g, Carbohydrates: 20g, Protein: 0g

TANGY ORANGE AND GINGER MARMALADE

PREPARATION TIME: 45 MINUTES (INCLUDING PREPARING THE FRUIT)
COOKING TIME: 30 MINUTES COOKING, 10 MINUTES PROCESSING
SERVINGS: 6 HALF-PINT JARS (8 OUNCES EACH)

MAXIMUM STORAGE TIME: 1 YEAR (UNOPENED). ONCE OPENED, REFRIGERATE AND USE WITHIN 3 WEEKS.
RECOMMENDED HEADSPACE: LEAVE 1/4 INCH (6 MM) HEADSPACE

INGREDIENTS

- 6 medium-sized oranges (total weight 1.2 kg)
- 2 lemons (total weight approx 300 grams)
- 4 cups water (approx 950 ml)
- 1/4 cup finely grated fresh ginger (about 50 grams)
- 5 cups granulated sugar (1 kg)
- 6 clean half-pint canning jars with lids and bands

CONTINUED →

INSTRUCTIONS

1. Wash oranges and lemons thoroughly. Peel the skin thinly, avoiding the white pith, and cut it into thin strips. Remove and discard the white pith of the fruit and chop the flesh, removing any seeds.
2. In a large pot, combine the peel, chopped fruit, and water. Bring to a boil, then reduce the heat and simmer for about 20 minutes or until the peel is tender.
3. Stir in the sugar and grated ginger. Bring the mixture to a rolling boil, stirring frequently to ensure that the sugar is completely dissolved. Continue boiling until it reaches the setting point (about 10 minutes). Perform a gel test by dropping a small amount on a cold plate; it should wrinkle when pushed with a finger.
4. While the marmalade is cooking, boil jars, lids, and bands for 10 minutes to sterilize them. Keep jars warm.
5. Fill the jars with the hot marmalade, leaving 6 mm (1/4-inch) headspace. Remove any air bubbles.
6. Clean the rims, secure lids, and tighten rings finger-tight.
7. Soak the jars in boiling water for 10 minutes, starting the timer when water returns to a boil.
8. Take out the jars and leave to cool down for 12 to 24 hours. Check seals.

PREPARATION TIPS:

- Removing the white pith thoroughly helps avoid bitterness in the marmalade.
- Thinly slicing the peel will result in a more delicate texture and even distribution in the marmalade.
- The gel test is crucial for ensuring the right consistency. If it doesn't wrinkle, continue boiling and check every few minutes.

NUTRITIONAL VALUE (PER SERVING - 1 TABLESPOON): Calories: 40, Carbohydrates: 10g, Fat: 0g, Protein: 0g, Sodium: 0mg, Sugar: 10g

CHERRY-LIME MARMALADE

PREPARATION TIME: 35 MINUTES (INCLUDING PREPARING THE FRUIT)
COOKING TIME: 25 MINUTES COOKING, 10 MINUTES PROCESSING
SERVINGS: 6 HALF-PINT JARS (8 OUNCES EACH)

MAXIMUM STORAGE TIME: 1 YEAR (UNOPENED). ONCE OPENED, REFRIGERATE AND USE WITHIN 3 WEEKS
RECOMMENDED HEADSPACE: LEAVE 1/4 INCH (6 MM) HEADSPACE

INGREDIENTS

- *4 cups pitted and finely chopped cherries*
- *2 limes, zest and juice (zest finely grated)*
- *4 cups granulated sugar (800 grams)*
- *3 cups water (approx 700 ml)*
- *1 pouch liquid pectin (3 ounces or 85 grams)*
- *6 clean half-pint canning jars with lids and bands*

INSTRUCTIONS

1. Wash the cherries and limes thoroughly. Pit the cherries and finely chop them. Zest the limes and squeeze their juice.
2. In a large pot, combine the cherries, lime juice, lime zest, and water. Bring to a boil, then reduce heat and simmer for 15 minutes.
3. Stir in the sugar until dissolved. Bring the mixture back to a rolling boil.
4. Stir in the liquid pectin and return to a full boil. Boil for 1 minute, stirring constantly.
5. While the marmalade cooks, boil jars, lids, and bands for 10 minutes to sterilize them. Keep jars warm.
6. Ladle the hot marmalade into jars, leaving 6 mm (1/4-inch) headspace. Remove any air bubbles.

7. Clean the rims, secure lids, and tighten rings finger-tight.
8. Soak the jars in boiling water for 10 minutes.
9. Take out the jars and leave to cool down for 12 to 24 hours. Check seals.

PREPARATION TIPS:
- Finely chopping the cherries allows for a smoother marmalade texture.
- Ensure all equipment is sterilized to maintain the marmalade's longevity and prevent contamination.

NUTRITIONAL VALUE (PER SERVING - 1 TABLESPOON): Calories: 45, Carbohydrates: 11g, Fat: 0g, Protein: 0g, Sodium: 0mg, Sugar: 11g

PEACH AND THYME MARMALADE

PREPARATION TIME: 30 MINUTES (INCLUDING PREPARING THE FRUIT)
COOKING TIME: 20 MINUTES COOKING, 10 MINUTES PROCESSING
SERVINGS: 6 HALF-PINT JARS (8 OUNCES EACH)

MAXIMUM STORAGE TIME: 1 YEAR (UNOPENED). ONCE OPENED, REFRIGERATE AND USE WITHIN 3 WEEKS
RECOMMENDED HEADSPACE: LEAVE 1/4 INCH (6 MM) HEADSPACE

INGREDIENTS

- *5 cups peeled and chopped peaches (about 5-6 medium peaches or 1 kg)*
- *3 cups granulated sugar (600 grams)*
- *1/4 cup lemon juice (about 60 ml)*
- *2 tablespoons fresh thyme leaves*
- *1/2 cup water (about 120 ml)*
- *1 pouch liquid pectin (3 ounces or 85 grams)*
- *6 clean half-pint canning jars with lids and bands*

INSTRUCTIONS

1. Wash and peel the peaches. Remove pits and chop the flesh finely.
2. In a large pot, combine peaches, thyme, lemon juice, sugar, and water. Bring to a boil over medium heat, stirring to ensure that the sugar is completely dissolved.
3. Add the liquid pectin, bring the mixture back to a rolling boil, and boil for 1 minute, stirring constantly.
4. While the marmalade is cooking, boil jars, lids, and bands for 10 minutes to sterilize them. Keep jars warm.
5. Ladle the hot marmalade into jars, leaving 6 mm (1/4-inch) headspace. Remove any air bubbles.
6. Clean the rims, secure lids, and tighten rings finger-tight.
7. Soak the jars in boiling water for 10 minutes.
8. Take out the jars and leave to cool down for 12 to 24 hours. Check seals.

PREPARATION TIPS:
- Finely chopping the peaches will help them break down and blend into a smooth texture more easily.
- The addition of fresh thyme gives a savory twist to the sweet peach flavor, creating a unique and complex taste profile.

NUTRITIONAL VALUE (PER SERVING - 1 TABLESPOON): Calories: 40, Carbohydrates: 10g, Fat: 0g, Protein: 0g, Sodium: 0mg, Sugar: 10g

MIXED BERRY AND LAVENDER MARMALADE

PREPARATION TIME: 25 MINUTES (INCLUDING PREPARING THE FRUIT)
COOKING TIME: 20 MINUTES COOKING, 10 MINUTES PROCESSING
SERVINGS: 6 HALF-PINT JARS (8 OUNCES EACH)

MAXIMUM STORAGE TIME: 1 YEAR (UNOPENED). ONCE OPENED, REFRIGERATE AND USE WITHIN 3 WEEKS
RECOMMENDED HEADSPACE: LEAVE 1/4 INCH (6 MM) HEADSPACE

INGREDIENTS

- *3 cups mixed berry juice (combination of strawberries, blueberries, raspberries – about 1.5 kg of fresh berries)*
- *1 cup water (240 ml)*
- *4 cups granulated sugar (800 grams)*
- *2 tablespoons dried lavender flowers*
- *2 tablespoons lemon juice (30 ml)*
- *1 pouch liquid pectin (3 ounces or 85 grams)*

INSTRUCTIONS

1. Crush the berries in a large pot and simmer over low heat for 10 minutes. Strain through a jelly bag or cheesecloth to obtain clear mixed berry juice.
2. Boil jars, lids, and bands for 10 minutes to sterilize them. Keep jars warm.
3. In a large pot, combine water, berry juice, sugar, lemon juice, and lavender. Bring to a rolling boil over high heat, stirring to ensure that the sugar is dissolved.
4. Stir in liquid pectin and return to a full boil. Boil for 1 minute, stirring constantly.
5. Ladle the hot marmalade into jars, leaving 6 mm (1/4-inch) headspace. Remove any air bubbles.
6. Clean the rims, secure lids, and tighten rings finger-tight.
7. Soak the jars in boiling water for 10 minutes.
8. Take out the jars and leave to cool down for 12 to 24 hours. Check seals.

PREPARATION TIPS:
- Ensure thorough straining of the berry juice to avoid seeds in your marmalade.
- The addition of lavender offers a delicate floral note that pairs beautifully with the mixed berries.

NUTRITIONAL VALUE (PER SERVING - 1 TABLESPOON): Calories: 45, Carbohydrates: 11g, Fat: 0g, Protein: 0g, Sodium: 0mg, Sugar: 11g

PINEAPPLE KIWI MARMALADE

PREPARATION TIME: 30 MINUTES (INCLUDING PREPARING THE FRUIT)
COOKING TIME: 20 MINUTES COOKING, 10 MINUTES PROCESSING
SERVINGS: 6 HALF-PINT JARS (8 OUNCES EACH)

MAXIMUM STORAGE TIME: 1 YEAR (UNOPENED). ONCE OPENED, REFRIGERATE AND USE WITHIN 3 WEEKS
RECOMMENDED HEADSPACE: LEAVE 1/4 INCH (6 MM) HEADSPACE

INGREDIENTS

- *3 cups finely chopped pineapple (750 grams)*
- *2 cups finely chopped kiwi (about 500 grams)*
- *1/2 cup water (120 ml)*
- *4 cups granulated sugar (800 grams)*
- *2 tablespoons lemon juice (30 ml)*
- *1 pouch liquid pectin (3 ounces or 85 grams)*

INSTRUCTIONS

1. Peel and finely chop the pineapple and kiwi.
2. In a large pot, combine chopped pineapple, kiwi, water, and lemon juice. Bring to a simmer over medium heat, cooking for about 10 minutes.
3. Stir in the sugar and continue to cook, stirring frequently to ensure that the sugar is dissolved.
4. Bring the mixture to a full rolling boil. Stir in liquid pectin and continue to boil for 1 minute, stirring constantly.
5. Boil jars, lids, and bands for 10 minutes to sterilize them. Keep jars warm.
6. Ladle the hot marmalade into jars, leaving 6 mm (1/4-inch) headspace. Remove any air bubbles.
7. Clean the rims, secure lids, and tighten rings finger-tight.
8. Soak the jars in boiling water for 10 minutes.
9. Take out the jars and leave to cool down for 12 to 24 hours. Check seals.

PREPARATION TIPS:

- Finely chopping the fruit ensures a more even texture and better distribution of flavors.
- The addition of lemon juice not only adds a slight tartness to balance the sweetness but also aids in setting the marmalade.
- Make sure to constantly stir the marmalade during the cooking process to avoid sticking and to ensure even cooking.

NUTRITIONAL VALUE (PER SERVING - 1 TABLESPOON): Calories: 40, Carbohydrates: 10g, Fat: 0g, Protein: 0g, Sodium: 0mg, Sugar: 10g

FRUIT SAUCES AND SALSAS

SUNNY PEACH PRESERVE

PREPARATION TIME: 30 MINUTES
COOKING TIME: 20 MINUTES
SERVINGS: 6 HALF-PINT JARS

MAXIMUM STORAGE TIME: 1 YEAR
RECOMMENDED HEADSPACE: LEAVE ABOUT 1/4 INCH (0.6 CM) HEADSPACE

INGREDIENTS

- *4 cups (900g) peeled, pitted, and chopped peaches*
- *2 cups (480 ml/400g) granulated sugar*
- *1 tablespoon (15 ml) lemon juice*
- *1 teaspoon (5 ml) vanilla extract*

INSTRUCTIONS

1. In a large saucepan, mix peaches and sugar; let stand for 15 minutes.
2. Stir in lemon juice, bring to a boil over medium heat, stirring regularly.
3. Reduce heat, simmer until thickened, about 15-20 minutes.
4. Remove from heat, stir in vanilla extract.
5. Ladle into sterilized jars, leaving 1/4 inch (0.6 cm) headspace. Wipe the rims clean, then place the lids and rings on the jars.
6. Soak in a water bath canner for 10 minutes.

PREPARATION TIPS: Peel peaches by blanching in boiling water for 30 seconds, then soaking in ice water.

NUTRITIONAL VALUE (PER SERVING): Calories: 115, Fat: 0g, Sodium: 1mg, Carbohydrates: 29g, Sugars: 28g, Protein: 1g

WHOLESOME BERRY MEDLEY COMPOTE

PREPARATION TIME: 15 MINUTES
COOKING TIME: 30 MINUTES
SERVINGS: ABOUT 3-4 CUPS

MAXIMUM STORAGE TIME: 1 YEAR
RECOMMENDED HEADSPACE: LEAVE ABOUT 1/4-INCH (0.6 CM) HEADSPACE IN THE JARS.

INGREDIENTS

- 2 cups (300g) of fresh strawberries, hulled and halved
- 1 cup (240 ml/150g) of fresh blueberries
- 1 cup (240 ml/120g) of fresh raspberries
- 1/2 cup (120 ml/100g) of sugar
- 2 tablespoons (30 ml) of lemon juice
- 1 teaspoon (5 ml) of lemon zest
- 1/2 teaspoon (2.5 ml) of vanilla extract (optional)

INSTRUCTIONS

1. In a large saucepan, combine the strawberries, blueberries, raspberries, sugar, lemon juice, and lemon zest.
2. Bring the mixture to a simmer over medium heat, stirring regularly.
3. Reduce the heat to low and continue to simmer for about 20-25 minutes, or until the fruit has broken down and the mixture has thickened slightly.
4. Add vanilla extract if using, and remove from heat.
5. Allow the compote to cool slightly before transferring it to sterilized jars, leaving about 1/4-inch (0.6 cm) headspace.
6. Wipe the rims of the jars, clean, then place the lids on the jars. Apply bands and tighten until fingertip tight.
7. Fill the water bath canner halfway with water and bring it to a simmer.
8. Carefully submerge the jars in the canner, making sure they are under water by at least 2.5 cm (1 inch).
9. Bring to a rolling boil, process for 10 minutes.
10. Turn off heat, let jars soak in the water for 5 minutes, then remove and let cool completely on a clean towel or cooling rack.

PREPARATION TIPS: You can adjust the sugar level based on your personal preference.

NUTRITIONAL VALUE PER SERVING: Calories: 60, Fat: 0g, Cholesterol: 0mg, Sodium: 0mg, Carbohydrates: 15g, Dietary Fiber: 2g, Sugars: 12g, Protein: 0g

SPICED PEAR BUTTER

PREPARATION TIME: 20 MINUTES
COOKING TIME: 2 HOURS
SERVINGS: ABOUT 3-4 JARS (8 OZ EACH)

MAXIMUM STORAGE TIME: 1 YEAR
RECOMMENDED HEADSPACE: LEAVE ABOUT 1/4-INCH (0.6 CM) HEADSPACE IN THE JARS

INGREDIENTS

- 10 cups (2.4 L/1.8 kg) of fresh pears, peeled, cored, and chopped
- 1/2 cup (120 ml/100g) of brown sugar
- 1/4 cup (60 ml/60g) of apple cider
- 1 teaspoon (5 ml/5g) of cinnamon
- 1/2 teaspoon (2.5 ml/2g) of nutmeg
- 1/4 teaspoon (1.25 ml/1g) of ground cloves
- 1 tablespoon (15 ml) of lemon juice

INSTRUCTIONS

1. In a large pot, combine pears, brown sugar, apple cider, cinnamon, nutmeg, and cloves. Bring to a boil over medium-high heat.
2. Once boiling, reduce the heat to low and simmer for about 1.5 to 2 hours or until the mixture thickens and becomes a butter-like consistency, stirring occasionally to prevent sticking.
3. Stir in lemon juice and continue to cook for an additional 5 minutes.
4. Use an immersion blender to smooth the pear butter to your desired consistency, if necessary.
5. While the pear butter is still hot, ladle it into sterilized jars, leaving about 1/4-inch (0.6 cm) headspace. Clean the rims, secure lids, and tighten rings finger-tight.
6. Submerge the jars in a water bath canner, making sure they are under water by at least 2.5 cm (1 inch). Bring to a rolling boil and process for 10 minutes.
7. Turn off heat, let jars soak in the water for 5 minutes, then remove and let cool completely on a clean towel or cooling rack.

NUTRITIONAL VALUE PER SERVING: Calories: 40, Fat: 0g, Cholesterol: 0mg, Sodium: 2mg, Carbohydrates: 11g, Dietary Fiber: 2g, Sugars: 8g, Protein: 0g

---

CHERRY ALMOND PRESERVE

PREPARATION TIME: 25 MINUTES
COOKING TIME: 35 MINUTES
SERVINGS: MAKES ABOUT 6 HALF-PINT JARS

MAXIMUM STORAGE TIME: UP TO 1 YEAR
RECOMMENDED HEADSPACE: LEAVE 1/4 INCH (6 MM) HEADSPACE

INGREDIENTS

- 5 cups (700 g) pitted cherries
- 3 cups (600 g) sugar
- 1/4 cup (60 ml) almond extract
- 1/4 cup (60 ml) lemon juice

INSTRUCTIONS

1. Crush cherries slightly, add sugar, and heat.
2. Boil until thickened, stir in lemon juice and almond extract.
3. Ladle into jars, leaving 1/4 inch (6 mm) headspace.
4. Soak in a water bath for 20 minutes.

NUTRITIONAL VALUE (PER SERVING): Calories: 85, Fat: 0g, Carbohydrates: 21g, Protein: 1g

CINNAMON APPLE BUTTER RECIPE

PREPARATION TIME: 30 MINUTES (PLUS ADDITIONAL TIME FOR COOLING COOKED APPLES)
COOKING TIME: 1 HOUR (STOVETOP COOKING) + 10 MINUTES (WATER BATH CANNING)
SERVINGS: 5 PINT-SIZED JARS (16 OUNCES EACH)

MAXIMUM STORAGE TIME: 1 YEAR (UNOPENED). ONCE OPENED, REFRIGERATE AND USE WITHIN 1 MONTH
RECOMMENDED HEADSPACE: LEAVE 1/4 INCH (6 MM) HEADSPACE

INGREDIENTS

- 10 cups of peeled, cored, and sliced apples (about 3 kg of apples)
- 2 cups granulated sugar (400 grams)
- 1/2 cup brown sugar (100 grams)
- 1/4 cup apple cider vinegar (60 ml)

- 2 teaspoons ground cinnamon (5 grams)
- 1/2 teaspoon ground nutmeg (1 gram)
- 1/4 teaspoon ground cloves (0.5 gram)
- 5 clean pint-sized canning jars with lids and bands

INSTRUCTIONS

1. In a large pot, combine apples, sugars, and apple cider vinegar. Cook over medium heat until apples are soft, about 20 minutes. Once softened, blend the mixture until smooth.
2. Return the puree to the pot. Stir in cinnamon, nutmeg, and cloves. Simmer the mixture, stirring frequently, until it thickens and reduces (about 40 minutes).
3. While the apple mixture is cooking, boil jars, lids, and bands for 10 minutes to sterilize them. Keep jars warm.
4. Ladle the hot apple butter into warm jars, leaving 6 mm (1/4-inch) headspace. Remove air bubbles.
5. Clean the rims, secure lids, and tighten rings finger-tight.
6. Soak the jars in boiling water for 10 minutes.
7. Take out the jars and leave to cool down for 12 to 24 hours. Check seals.

PREPARATION TIPS:
- Cooking apples until soft before pureeing ensures a smooth texture.
- Constant stirring during the reduction phase prevents sticking and burning.
- Fill and close jars while still warm to ensure proper sealing.

NUTRITIONAL VALUE (PER SERVING - 1 TABLESPOON): Calories: 30, Carbohydrates: 8g, Fat: 0g, Protein: 0g, Sodium: 1mg, Sugar: 7g

---

MANGO PINEAPPLE SALSA

PREPARATION TIME: 30 MINUTES
COOKING TIME: 15 MINUTES COOKING, 10 MINUTES PROCESSING
SERVINGS: 5 PINT-SIZED JARS (16 OUNCES EACH)

MAXIMUM STORAGE TIME: 1 YEAR (UNOPENED). ONCE OPENED, REFRIGERATE AND USE WITHIN 1 WEEK.
RECOMMENDED HEADSPACE: LEAVE 1/2 INCH (12 MM) HEADSPACE

INGREDIENTS

- 2 cups diced fresh mango (about 2 large mangoes)

- 2 cups diced fresh pineapple (about 1/2 pineapple)

- *1 cup diced red bell pepper (or 200 grams)*
- *1 cup diced red onion (about 1 large onion)*
- *1/2 cup finely chopped cilantro (about a bunch)*
- *2 jalapeño peppers, seeds removed and finely chopped (adjust to taste)*
- *1/2 cup apple cider vinegar (120 ml)*
- *1/4 cup lime juice (about 2 limes)*
- *1 teaspoon salt (5 grams)*
- *1/2 teaspoon ground cumin (1 gram)*
- *5 clean pint-sized canning jars with lids and bands*

INSTRUCTIONS

1. In a large pot, mix together mango, pineapple, red bell pepper, red onion, cilantro, jalapeños, vinegar, lime juice, salt, and cumin.
2. Cooking: Bring the mixture to a simmer over medium heat, cooking for about 10 minutes.
3. Boil jars, lids, and bands for 10 minutes to sterilize them. Keep jars warm.
4. Fill the jars with the hot salsa, leaving 12 mm (1/2-inch) headspace. Remove air bubbles.
5. Wipe rims, then place the lids on the jars. Apply bands and tighten until fingertip tight.
6. Soak the jars in boiling water for 10 minutes.
7. Take out the jars and leave to cool down for 12 to 24 hours. Check seals.

PREPARATION TIPS:

- Dice the fruits and vegetables uniformly for a consistent texture in the salsa.
- Adjust the amount of jalapeños based on your preferred spice level.

NUTRITIONAL VALUE (PER SERVING - 1 TABLESPOON): Calories: 15, Carbohydrates: 4g, Fat: 0g, Protein: 0g, Sodium: 40mg, Sugar: 3g

---

SPICY PEACH AND TOMATO SALSA

PREPARATION TIME: 25 MINUTES
COOKING TIME: 15 MINUTES COOKING, 10 MINUTES PROCESSING
SERVINGS: 5 PINT-SIZED JARS (16 OUNCES EACH)

MAXIMUM STORAGE TIME: 1 YEAR (UNOPENED). ONCE OPENED, REFRIGERATE AND USE WITHIN 1 WEEK.
RECOMMENDED HEADSPACE: LEAVE 1/2 INCH (12 MM) HEADSPACE

INGREDIENTS

- *3 cups diced fresh peaches (600 grams)*
- *2 cups diced tomatoes (400 grams)*
- *1 cup diced red onion (200 grams)*
- *1/2 cup finely chopped green bell pepper*
- *2 jalapeño peppers, seeds removed and chopped*
- *1/2 cup chopped fresh cilantro*
- *1/2 cup apple cider vinegar (120 ml)*
- *1/4 cup lime juice (about 2 limes)*
- *2 cloves garlic, minced*
- *1 teaspoon salt (5 grams)*
- *1/2 teaspoon ground black pepper (1 gram)*
- *5 clean pint-sized canning jars with lids and bands*

INSTRUCTIONS

1. In a large pot, mix together peaches, tomatoes, red onion, green bell pepper, jalapeños, cilantro, vinegar, lime juice, garlic, salt, and black pepper.
2. Bring the mixture to a simmer over medium heat, cooking for about 15 minutes.
3. Boil jars, lids, and bands for 10 minutes to sterilize them. Keep jars warm.
4. Fill the jars with the hot salsa, leaving 12 mm (1/2 inch) headspace. Remove air bubbles.
5. Wipe rims, clean, then place the lids on the jars. Apply bands and tighten until fingertip tight.
6. Soak the jars in boiling water for 10 minutes.
7. Take out the jars and leave to cool down for 12 to 24 hours. Check seals.

KIWI AND PINEAPPLE SALSA

PREPARATION TIME: 30 MINUTES
COOKING TIME: 15 MINUTES COOKING, 10 MINUTES PROCESSING
SERVINGS: 5 PINT-SIZED JARS (16 OUNCES EACH)

MAXIMUM STORAGE TIME: 1 YEAR (UNOPENED). ONCE OPENED, REFRIGERATE AND USE WITHIN 1 WEEK.
RECOMMENDED HEADSPACE: 1/2 INCH (12 MM)

INGREDIENTS

- *2 cups diced kiwi (about 5-6 kiwis or 500 grams)*
- *2 cups diced pineapple (about 500 grams)*
- *1 cup diced red bell pepper (about 200 grams)*
- *1 cup diced red onion (about 200 grams)*
- *1/2 cup finely chopped cilantro*
- *2 jalapeño peppers, seeds removed and finely chopped (adjust to taste)*

- *1/2 cup white vinegar (120 ml)*
- *1/4 cup lime juice (about 2 limes)*
- *2 teaspoons honey (optional for a hint of sweetness)*
- *1 teaspoon salt (5 grams)*
- *1/2 teaspoon ground cumin (1 gram)*
- *5 clean pint-sized canning jars with lids and bands*

INSTRUCTIONS

1. In a large pot, mix together kiwi, pineapple, red bell pepper, red onion, cilantro, jalapeños, vinegar, lime juice, honey (if using), salt, and cumin.
2. Bring the mixture to a simmer over medium heat, cooking for about 15 minutes.
3. Boil jars, lids, and bands for 10 minutes to sterilize them. Keep jars warm.
4. Fill the jars with the hot salsa, leaving 12 mm (1/2 inch) headspace. Remove air bubbles.
5. Wipe rims, clean, then place the lids on the jars. Apply bands and tighten until fingertip tight.
6. Soak the jars in boiling water for 10 minutes.
7. Take out the jars and leave to cool down for 12 to 24 hours. Check seals.

PREPARATION TIPS:
- Dice the kiwi and pineapple into small, even pieces for a consistent texture.
- Adjust the amount of jalapeños based on your preference for spice.

NUTRITIONAL VALUE (PER SERVING - 1 TABLESPOON): Calories: 10, Carbohydrates: 2g, Fat: 0g, Protein: 0g, Sodium: 40mg, Sugar: 2g

---

SPICY BLUEBERRY-CUCUMBER SALSA

PREPARATION TIME: 20 MINUTES
COOKING TIME: 10 MINUTES COOKING, 10 MINUTES PROCESSING
SERVINGS: 5 PINT-SIZED JARS (16 OUNCES EACH)

MAXIMUM STORAGE TIME: 1 YEAR (UNOPENED). ONCE OPENED, REFRIGERATE AND USE WITHIN 1 WEEK.
RECOMMENDED HEADSPACE: LEAVE 1/2 INCH (12 MM) HEADSPACE

INGREDIENTS

- *3 cups fresh blueberries (about 450 grams)*
- *2 cups finely diced cucumber (about 300 grams)*
- *1 cup finely diced red onion (about 200 grams)*

- *1/2 cup finely chopped red bell pepper (100 grams)*
- *1/4 cup finely chopped fresh mint leaves*
- *2 jalapeño peppers, seeds removed and finely chopped*

- 1/2 cup apple cider vinegar (120 ml)
- 1/4 cup lime juice (about 2 limes)
- 2 tablespoons honey (30 ml)
- 1 teaspoon salt (5 grams)
- 1/2 teaspoon ground black pepper (1 gram)
- 5 clean pint-sized canning jars with lids and bands

INSTRUCTIONS

1. In a large bowl, gently mix together blueberries, cucumber, red onion, red bell pepper, mint, jalapeños, vinegar, lime juice, honey, salt, and black pepper. Transfer to a large pot.
2. Bring the mixture to a gentle simmer over medium heat, cooking for about 10 minutes.
3. Boil jars, lids, and bands for 10 minutes to sterilize them. Keep jars warm.
4. Fill the jars with the hot salsa, leaving 12 mm (1/2 inch) headspace. Remove air bubbles.
5. Wipe the rims, clean, then place the lids on the jars. Apply bands and tighten until fingertip tight.
6. Soak the jars in boiling water for 10 minutes.
7. Take out the jars and leave to cool down for 12 to 24 hours. Check seals.

NUTRITIONAL VALUE (PER SERVING - 1 TABLESPOON): Calories: 15, Carbohydrates: 3g, Fat: 0g, Protein: 0g, Sodium: 40mg, Sugar: 2g

APPLE AND CRANBERRY SALSA

PREPARATION TIME: 25 MINUTES
COOKING TIME: 15 MINUTES COOKING, 10 MINUTES PROCESSING
SERVINGS: 5 PINT-SIZED JARS (16 OUNCES EACH)

MAXIMUM STORAGE TIME: 1 YEAR (UNOPENED). ONCE OPENED, REFRIGERATE AND USE WITHIN 1 WEEK.
RECOMMENDED HEADSPACE: 1/2 INCH (12 MM)

INGREDIENTS

- 3 cups finely diced apples (600 grams)
- 2 cups fresh cranberries (about 200 grams)
- 1 cup finely diced green bell pepper (200 grams)
- 1 cup finely diced red onion (200 grams)
- 1/2 cup finely chopped cilantro
- 2 jalapeño peppers, seeds removed and finely chopped (adjust to taste)
- 1/2 cup white vinegar (120 ml)
- 1/4 cup orange juice (about 1 orange)
- 2 tablespoons brown sugar (30 grams)
- 1 teaspoon salt (5 grams)
- 1/2 teaspoon ground cinnamon (1 gram)

INSTRUCTIONS

1. In a large pot, mix together apples, cranberries, green bell pepper, red onion, cilantro, jalapeños, vinegar, orange juice, brown sugar, salt, and cinnamon.
2. Bring the mixture to a simmer over medium heat, cooking for about 15 minutes or until cranberries burst and apples are tender.
3. Boil jars, lids, and bands for 10 minutes to sterilize them. Keep jars warm.
4. Fill the jars with the hot salsa, leaving 12 mm (1/2-inch) headspace. Remove air bubbles.
5. Wipe the rims, clean, then place the lids on the jars. Apply bands and tighten until fingertip tight.
6. Soak the jars in boiling water for 10 minutes.
7. Take out the jars and leave to cool down for 12 to 24 hours. Check seals.

NUTRITIONAL VALUE (PER SERVING - 1 TABLESPOON): Calories: 15, Carbohydrates: 4g, Fat: 0g, Protein: 0g, Sodium: 40mg, Sugar: 3g

FRUIT CHUTNEYS AND RELISHES

SWEET APPLE CHUTNEY

PREPARATION TIME: 20 MINUTES
COOKING TIME: 1 HOUR
SERVINGS: ABOUT 3-4 JARS (16 OZ EACH)

MAXIMUM STORAGE TIME: 1 YEAR
RECOMMENDED HEADSPACE: LEAVE ABOUT 1/2-INCH (1.3 CM) HEADSPACE

INGREDIENTS

- 8 cups (900g) of apples, peeled, cored, and diced
- 1/2 cup (120 ml/100g) of onion, finely chopped
- 1/2 cup (120 ml/75g) of raisins
- 1/4 cup (60 ml/60g) of ginger, finely chopped
- 1/2 cup (120 ml/120g) of brown sugar

- 1/2 teaspoon (2.5 ml/2g) of cinnamon
- 1/4 teaspoon (1.25 ml/1g) of cloves
- 1/4 teaspoon (1.25 ml/1g) of nutmeg
- 1 cup (240 ml/240g) of apple cider vinegar
- 1 teaspoon (5 ml/6g) of sea salt

INSTRUCTIONS

1. In a large saucepan, combine apples, onion, raisins, ginger, brown sugar, cinnamon, cloves, nutmeg, apple cider vinegar, and sea salt.
2. Bring the mixture to a boil over medium-high heat, stirring frequently to ensure the sugar dissolves completely.
3. Reduce heat to low and let simmer for about 45-50 minutes, or until the mixture thickens and obtains a chutney-like consistency, stirring occasionally.
4. Remove from heat once the desired consistency is reached.
5. Carefully spoon the hot chutney into sterilized jars, leaving about 1/2-inch (1.3 cm) headspace. Clean the rims, secure lids, and tighten rings finger-tight.
6. Soak the jars in a water bath canner, making sure they are under water by at least 2.5 cm (1 inch). Bring to a boil and process for 15 minutes.
7. Turn off heat, let the jars soak in the water for 5 minutes, then carefully remove and let cool completely on a clean towel or cooling rack.

NUTRITIONAL VALUE PER SERVING: Calories: 70, Fat: 0g, Cholesterol: 0mg, Sodium: 75mg, Carbohydrates: 18g, Dietary Fiber: 1g, Sugars: 16g, Protein: 0g

SPICY PINEAPPLE AND MANGO CHUTNEY

PREPARATION TIME: 20 MINUTES
COOKING TIME: 30 MINUTES
SERVINGS: 6 PINT-SIZED JARS (16 OUNCES EACH)

MAXIMUM STORAGE TIME: 1 YEAR (UNOPENED). ONCE OPENED, REFRIGERATE AND USE WITHIN 1 MONTH.
RECOMMENDED HEADSPACE: 1/2 INCH (12 MM)

INGREDIENTS

- 4 cups diced fresh pineapple (about 1 medium pineapple or 800 grams)
- 4 cups diced ripe mango (about 3 large mangoes)
- 1 medium red onion, finely chopped (150 grams)

- 1 cup apple cider vinegar (240 ml)
- 1 cup brown sugar (packed) (200 grams)
- 1/2 cup raisins (100 grams)

- 2 garlic cloves, minced
- 1 tablespoon freshly grated ginger (15 grams)
- 1 teaspoon ground cinnamon (2 grams)
- 1/2 teaspoon ground allspice (1 gram)
- 1/2 teaspoon ground cloves (1 gram)
- 1/2 teaspoon red pepper flakes (1 gram)
- 1/4 teaspoon salt (1 gram)
- 6 clean pint-sized canning jars with lids and bands

INSTRUCTIONS

1. In a large saucepan, mix together pineapple, mango, onion, vinegar, brown sugar, raisins, garlic, ginger, cinnamon, allspice, cloves, red pepper flakes, and salt.
2. Bring the mixture to a boil over medium heat. Reduce heat and simmer, stirring occasionally, until the mixture thickens and becomes syrupy, about 30 minutes.
3. While the chutney cooks, boil jars, lids, and bands for 10 minutes to sterilize them. Keep jars warm.
4. Fill the jars with the hot chutney, leaving 12 mm (1/2 inch) headspace. Remove any air bubbles.
5. Clean the rims, secure lids, and tighten rings finger-tight.
6. Soak the jars in boiling water for 15 minutes.
7. Take out the jars and leave to cool down for 12 to 24 hours. Check seals.

SHOPPING TIPS:
- Choose ripe but firm mangoes and a fresh pineapple for the best flavor.
- Organic fruits and spices can enhance the taste and quality of the chutney.

PREPARATION TIPS:
- Dice the fruits uniformly for even cooking.
- Regular stirring during cooking helps avoid the chutney sticking to the pan.
- Fill and seal jars while they are still warm to ensure proper sealing.

NUTRITIONAL VALUE (PER SERVING - 1 TABLESPOON): Calories: 35, Carbohydrates: 9g, Fat: 0g, Protein: 0g, Sodium: 5mg, Sugar: 8g

PEACH AND GINGER CHUTNEY

PREPARATION TIME: 30 MINUTES
COOKING TIME: 45 MINUTES
SERVINGS: MAKES ABOUT 6 HALF-PINT JARS

MAXIMUM STORAGE TIME: UP TO 12 MONTHS
RECOMMENDED HEADSPACE: LEAVE 1/2 INCH (12 MM) HEADSPACE

INGREDIENTS

- 6 cups (900 g) peaches, peeled and diced
- 1 cup (200 g) brown sugar
- 1/2 cup (120 ml) apple cider vinegar
- 1/4 cup (60 ml) finely chopped ginger
- 1 tsp ground cinnamon
- 1/2 tsp ground cloves

INSTRUCTIONS

1. Combine all ingredients in a large pot.
2. Bring to a boil, then simmer until thickened.
3. Ladle into jars, leaving 1/2 inch (12 mm) headspace.
4. Process for 20 minutes in a water bath.

NUTRITIONAL VALUE (PER SERVING): Calories: 70, Fat: 0g fat, Carbohydrates: 18g, Protein: 1g

APPLE CRANBERRY CHUTNEY

PREPARATION TIME: 25 MINUTES
COOKING TIME: 35 MINUTES
SERVINGS: 5 PINT-SIZED JARS (16 OUNCES EACH)

MAXIMUM STORAGE TIME: 1 YEAR (UNOPENED). OPENED JARS SHOULD BE REFRIGERATED AND USED WITHIN 1 MONTH
RECOMMENDED HEADSPACE: 1/2 INCH (12 MM)

INGREDIENTS

- *4 cups diced apples (about 4 medium apples)*
- *2 cups fresh or frozen cranberries (200 grams)*
- *1 cup finely chopped red onion (about 100 grams)*
- *1 cup apple cider vinegar (240 ml)*
- *3/4 cup brown sugar (packed) (150 grams)*
- *1/2 cup golden raisins (100 grams)*

- *2 teaspoons grated orange zest (5 grams)*
- *1 teaspoon ground cinnamon (2 grams)*
- *1/2 teaspoon ground ginger (1 gram)*
- *1/4 teaspoon ground cloves (0.5 gram)*
- *1/4 teaspoon salt (1 gram)*
- *5 clean pint-sized canning jars with lids and bands*

INSTRUCTIONS

1. In a large saucepan, combine apples, cranberries, onion, vinegar, brown sugar, raisins, orange zest, cinnamon, ginger, cloves, and salt.
2. Bring the mixture to a boil over medium heat, then reduce heat to low. Simmer, stirring occasionally, until the mixture thickens and cranberries burst, about 35 minutes.
3. Boil jars, lids, and bands for 10 minutes to sterilize them. Keep jars warm.
4. Fill the jars with the hot chutney, leaving 12 mm (1/2 inch) headspace. Remove any air bubbles.
5. Clean the rims, secure lids, and tighten rings finger-tight.
6. Soak in a water bath canner for 15 minutes.
7. Take out the jars and leave to cool down for 12 to 24 hours.
Check seals.

PREPARATION TIPS:
- Chop apples uniformly for consistent texture.
- Stir the chutney regularly to avoid sticking and ensure even cooking.
- Warm jars prior to filling to prevent thermal shock.

NUTRITIONAL VALUE (PER SERVING - 1 TABLESPOON): Calories: 30, Carbohydrates: 8g, Fat: 0g, Protein: 0g, Sodium: 5mg, Sugar: 7g

PEAR AND GOLDEN RAISIN CHUTNEY

PREPARATION TIME: 25 MINUTES
COOKING TIME: 30 MINUTES
SERVINGS: 5 PINT-SIZED JARS (16 OUNCES EACH)

MAXIMUM STORAGE TIME: 1 YEAR (UNOPENED). OPENED JARS SHOULD BE REFRIGERATED AND USED WITHIN 1 MONTH
RECOMMENDED HEADSPACE: 1/2 INCH (12 MM)

INGREDIENTS

- *5 cups peeled and chopped pears (about 1 kg)*
- *1 cup golden raisins (200 grams)*

- *1 large sweet onion, finely chopped (200 grams)*
- *1 cup white wine vinegar (240 ml)*

- 3/4 cup granulated sugar (150 grams)
- 1/2 cup water (120 ml)
- 2 tablespoons grated fresh ginger (30 grams)
- 1 teaspoon mustard seeds (2 grams)
- 1/2 teaspoon ground cinnamon (1 gram)
- 1/4 teaspoon ground nutmeg (0.5 gram)
- 1/4 teaspoon salt (1 gram)
- 1/4 teaspoon crushed red pepper flakes (optional)
- 5 clean pint-sized canning jars with lids and bands

INSTRUCTIONS

1. In a large saucepan, mix pears, golden raisins, onion, vinegar, sugar, water, ginger, mustard seeds, cinnamon, nutmeg, salt, and red pepper flakes.
2. Bring the mixture to a boil over medium heat, then reduce to a simmer. Cook, stirring regularly, until thickened, about 30 minutes.
3. Boil jars, lids, and bands for 10 minutes to sterilize them. Keep jars warm.
4. Fill the jars with the hot chutney, leaving 12 mm (1/2 inch) headspace. Remove air bubbles.
5. Clean the rims, secure lids, and tighten rings finger-tight.
6. Soak the jars in boiling water for 15 minutes, starting the timer once the water boils.
7. Take out the jars and leave to cool down for 12 to 24 hours. Check seals.

PREPARATION TIPS:

- Chop the pears evenly for consistent cooking and texture.
- Stir the chutney regularly to prevent burning.
- Warm the jars prior to filling to avoid thermal shock.

NUTRITIONAL VALUE (PER SERVING - 1 TABLESPOON): Calories: 30, Carbohydrates: 8g, Fat: 0g, Protein: 0g, Sodium: 5mg, Sugar: 7g

---

CHERRY AND APPLE CHUTNEY

PREPARATION TIME: 30 MINUTES
COOKING TIME: 40 MINUTES
SERVINGS: 6 PINT-SIZED JARS (16 OUNCES EACH)

MAXIMUM STORAGE TIME: 1 YEAR (UNOPENED). ONCE OPENED, REFRIGERATE AND USE WITHIN 1 MONTH
RECOMMENDED HEADSPACE: 1/2 INCH (12 MM)

INGREDIENTS

- 3 cups pitted and chopped fresh cherries (about 600 grams)
- 3 cups peeled and chopped apples (about 3 medium apples or 600 grams)
- 1 1/2 cups finely chopped red onion (150 grams)
- 1 cup apple cider vinegar (240 ml)
- 1 cup granulated sugar (200 grams)
- 1/2 cup dried cranberries (100 grams)
- 1/4 cup chopped crystallized ginger (40 grams)
- 2 teaspoons yellow mustard seeds (5 grams)
- 1 teaspoon ground cinnamon (2 grams)
- 1/2 teaspoon ground allspice (1 gram)
- 1/2 teaspoon salt (1 gram)
- 1/4 teaspoon ground cloves (0.5 gram)
- 6 clean pint-sized canning jars with lids and bands

INSTRUCTIONS

1. In a large saucepan, combine cherries, apples, onion, vinegar, sugar, cranberries, ginger, mustard seeds, cinnamon, allspice, salt, and cloves.
2. Bring to a boil over medium heat, then reduce heat to low. Simmer, stirring regularly, until the fruits soften, about 40 minutes.
3. Boil jars, lids, and bands for 10 minutes to sterilize them. Keep jars warm.

CONTINUED →

4. Fill the jars with the hot chutney, leaving 12 mm (1/2 inch) headspace. Remove air bubbles.
5. Clean the rims, secure lids, and tighten rings finger-tight.
6. Soak the jars in boiling water for 15 minutes.
7. Take out the jars and leave to cool down for 12 to 24 hours. Check seals.

PREPARATION TIPS:
- Ensure the cherries are pitted thoroughly to avoid any hard bits in the chutney.
- Chop the apples and cherries evenly for consistent cooking.

NUTRITIONAL VALUE (PER SERVING - 1 TABLESPOON): Calories: 35, Carbohydrates: 9g, Fat: 0g, Protein: 0g, Sodium: 5mg, Sugar: 8g

SPICY APPLE AND PEPPER RELISH

PREPARATION TIME: 30 MINUTES
COOKING TIME: 20 MINUTES
SERVINGS: 6 PINT-SIZED JARS (16 OUNCES EACH)

MAXIMUM STORAGE TIME: 1 YEAR (UNOPENED). ONCE OPENED, REFRIGERATE AND USE WITHIN 1 MONTH
RECOMMENDED HEADSPACE: 1/2 INCH (12 MM)

INGREDIENTS

- 4 cups finely chopped apples (about 800 grams)
- 2 cups finely chopped red bell pepper (about 2 large peppers or 300 grams)
- 1 cup finely chopped onion (about 1 large)
- 1 cup apple cider vinegar (240 ml)
- 3/4 cup granulated sugar (150 grams)
- 1/2 cup water (120 ml)
- 1/4 cup finely chopped jalapeño peppers (seeds removed) (about 2 jalapeños or 50 grams)
- 2 teaspoons mustard seeds (5 grams)
- 1 teaspoon salt (5 grams)
- 1/2 teaspoon ground turmeric (1 gram)
- 6 clean pint-sized canning jars with lids and bands

INSTRUCTIONS

1. In a large saucepan, mix apples, red bell pepper, onion, vinegar, sugar, water, jalapeño peppers, mustard seeds, salt, and turmeric.
2. Bring the mixture to a boil over medium heat, then reduce to a simmer. Cook, stirring regularly, until the mixture thickens, about 20 minutes.
3. Boil jars, lids, and bands for 10 minutes to sterilize them. Keep jars warm.
4. Fill the jars with the hot relish, leaving 12 mm (1/2 inch) headspace. Remove air bubbles.
5. Clean the rims, secure lids, and tighten rings finger-tight.
6. Soak the jars in boiling water for 15 minutes, starting the timer once the water boils.
7. Take out the jars and leave to cool down for 12 to 24 hours. Check seals.

PREPARATION TIPS:
- Finely chopping the ingredients ensures a uniform texture.
- Removing seeds from jalapeños adjusts the heat level to a mild but noticeable warmth.
- Stir the relish frequently during cooking to prevent sticking.

NUTRITIONAL VALUE (PER SERVING - 1 TABLESPOON): Calories: 20, Carbohydrates: 5g, Fat: 0g, Protein: 0g, Sodium: 40mg, Sugar: 4g

SPICED PEAR AND CRANBERRY RELISH

PREPARATION TIME: 25 MINUTES
COOKING TIME: 35 MINUTES
SERVINGS: 6 PINT-SIZED JARS (16 OUNCES EACH)

MAXIMUM STORAGE TIME: 1 YEAR (UNOPENED). ONCE OPENED, REFRIGERATE AND USE WITHIN 1 MONTH
RECOMMENDED HEADSPACE: 1/2 INCH (12 MM)

INGREDIENTS

- 4 cups diced ripe pears (about 4 large pears)
- 2 cups fresh cranberries (about 200 grams)
- 1 cup finely chopped sweet onion (200 grams)
- 1 cup brown sugar (packed) (200 grams)
- 3/4 cup apple cider vinegar (180 ml)
- 1/2 cup water (120 ml)
- 1/4 cup raisins (50 grams)

- 2 teaspoons grated orange zest (5 grams)
- 1 teaspoon ground cinnamon (2 grams)
- 1/2 teaspoon ground ginger (1 gram)
- 1/4 teaspoon ground allspice (0.5 gram)
- 1/4 teaspoon ground cloves (0.5 gram)
- 1/4 teaspoon salt (1 gram)
- 6 clean pint-sized canning jars with lids and bands

INSTRUCTIONS

1. In a large saucepan, mix pears, cranberries, onion, brown sugar, vinegar, water, raisins, orange zest, cinnamon, ginger, allspice, cloves, and salt.
2. Bring to a boil over medium heat, then reduce to a simmer. Cook, stirring occasionally, until the cranberries pop, about 35 minutes.
3. Fill the sterilized jars with the hot relish, leaving 12 mm (1/2 inch) headspace. Remove air bubbles.
4. Clean the rims, secure lids, and tighten rings finger-tight.
5. Soak the jars in boiling water for 15 minutes, starting the timer once the water boils.
6. Take out the jars and leave to cool down for 12 to 24 hours. Check seals.

PREPARATION TIPS: Dice the pears evenly to ensure a consistent texture throughout the relish.

NUTRITIONAL VALUE (PER SERVING - 1 TABLESPOON): Calories: 20, Carbohydrates: 5g, Fat: 0g, Protein: 0g, Sodium: 10mg, Sugar: 4g

CRANBERRY ORANGE RELISH

PREPARATION TIME: 25 MINUTES
COOKING TIME: 20 MINUTES
SERVINGS: 5 PINT-SIZED JARS (16 OUNCES EACH)

MAXIMUM STORAGE TIME: 1 YEAR (UNOPENED). ONCE OPENED, REFRIGERATE AND USE WITHIN 1 MONTH
RECOMMENDED HEADSPACE: 1/2 INCH (12 MM)

INGREDIENTS

- 4 cups fresh cranberries (about 400 grams)
- 2 large oranges, peeled, seeded, and finely chopped (about 2 cups or 300 grams)
- 1 1/2 cups granulated sugar (300 grams)
- 1 cup water (240 ml)
- 1/2 cup finely chopped red onion (about 50 grams)

- 1/2 cup apple cider vinegar (120 ml)
- 1/4 cup raisins (50 grams)
- 1 teaspoon ground cinnamon (2 grams)
- 1/2 teaspoon ground ginger (1 gram)
- 1/4 teaspoon ground allspice (0.5 gram)
- 5 clean pint-sized canning jars with lids and bands

CONTINUED →

INSTRUCTIONS

1. In a large saucepan, combine cranberries, oranges, sugar, water, onion, vinegar, raisins, cinnamon, ginger, and allspice. Bring to a boil over medium heat, then reduce to a simmer. Cook for about 20 minutes, stirring regularly, until cranberries burst and mixture thickens.
2. Boil jars, lids, and bands for 10 minutes to sterilize them. Keep jars warm.
3. Fill the jars with the hot relish, leaving 12 mm (1/2 inch) headspace. Remove air bubbles.
4. Clean the rims, secure lids, and tighten rings finger-tight.
5. Soak the jars in boiling water for 15 minutes.
6. Take out the jars and leave to cool down for 12 to 24 hours. Check seals.

NUTRITIONAL VALUE (PER SERVING - 1 TABLESPOON): Calories: 25, Carbohydrates: 6g, Fat: 0g, Protein: 0g, Sodium: 1mg, Sugar: 5g

---

PEACH AND RED PEPPER RELISH

PREPARATION TIME: 30 MINUTES
COOKING TIME: 25 MINUTES
SERVINGS: 6 PINT-SIZED JARS (16 OUNCES EACH)

MAXIMUM STORAGE TIME: 1 YEAR (UNOPENED). ONCE OPENED, REFRIGERATE AND USE WITHIN 1 MONTH
RECOMMENDED HEADSPACE: 1/2 INCH (12 MM)

INGREDIENTS

- 4 cups diced fresh peaches (about 4 large peaches)
- 2 cups diced red bell pepper (about 300 grams)
- 1 cup diced red onion (about 1 large onion)
- 1 cup white wine vinegar (240 ml)
- 3/4 cup granulated sugar (150 grams)
- 1/2 cup water (120 ml)

- 1/4 cup finely chopped jalapeño peppers (seeds removed) (about 2 jalapeños or 50 grams)
- 2 teaspoons yellow mustard seeds (5 grams)
- 1 teaspoon salt (5 grams)
- 1/2 teaspoon ground black pepper (1 gram)
- 6 clean pint-sized canning jars with lids and bands

INSTRUCTIONS

1. In a large saucepan, mix peaches, red bell pepper, onion, vinegar, sugar, water, jalapeño peppers, mustard seeds, salt, and black pepper.
2. Bring the mixture to a boil over medium heat, then reduce to a simmer. Cook, stirring regularly, until thickened, about 25 minutes.
3. Boil jars, lids, and bands for 10 minutes to sterilize them. Keep jars warm.
4. Fill the jars with the hot relish, leaving 12 mm (1/2 inch) headspace. Remove air bubbles.
5. Clean the rims, secure lids, and tighten rings finger-tight.
6. Soak the jars in boiling water for 15 minutes.
7. Take out the jars and leave to cool down for 12 to 24 hours. Check seals.

PREPARATION TIPS: Warming the jars prior to filling helps prevent thermal shock.

NUTRITIONAL VALUE (PER SERVING - 1 TABLESPOON): Calories: 20, Carbohydrates: 5g, Fat: 0g, Protein: 0g, Sodium: 40mg, Sugar: 4g

SPICY FIG AND DATE CHUTNEY

PREPARATION TIME: 20 MINUTES
COOKING TIME: 40 MINUTES
SERVINGS: 6 PINT-SIZED JARS (16 OUNCES EACH)

MAXIMUM STORAGE TIME: 1 YEAR (UNOPENED). ONCE OPENED, REFRIGERATE AND USE WITHIN 1 MONTH
RECOMMENDED HEADSPACE: 1/2 INCH (12 MM)

INGREDIENTS

- 3 cups chopped dried figs (about 450 grams)
- 2 cups chopped dates (about 300 grams)
- 1 large red onion, finely chopped (150 grams)
- 1 1/2 cups apple cider vinegar (360 ml)
- 1 cup water (240 ml)
- 3/4 cup brown sugar (packed) (150 grams)

- 1/2 cup raisins (100 grams)
- 2 teaspoons minced fresh ginger (5 grams)
- 1 teaspoon ground cinnamon (2 grams)
- 1/2 teaspoon ground allspice (1 gram)
- 1/4 teaspoon cayenne pepper (optional, to taste)
- 6 clean pint-sized canning jars with lids and bands

INSTRUCTIONS

1. In a large saucepan, mix together figs, dates, onion, vinegar, water, brown sugar, raisins, ginger, cinnamon, allspice, and cayenne pepper.
2. Bring to a boil over medium heat, then reduce heat and simmer. Stir occasionally until the mixture thickens, about 40 minutes.
3. Boil jars, lids, and bands for 10 minutes to sterilize them. Keep jars warm.
4. Fill the jars with the hot chutney, leaving 12 mm (1/2 inch) headspace. Remove any air bubbles.
5. Clean the rims, secure lids, and tighten rings finger-tight.
6. Soak the jars in boiling water for 15 minutes.
7. Take out the jars and leave to cool down for 12 to 24 hours. Check seals.

PREPARATION TIPS:
- Chop the figs and dates into small, even pieces to ensure they cook evenly.
- Stir the chutney frequently during cooking to ovoid sticking to the pan.
- Fill and seal jars while they are still warm to ensure proper sealing.

NUTRITIONAL VALUE (PER SERVING - 1 TABLESPOON): Calories: 35, Carbohydrates: 9g, Fat: 0g, Protein: 0g, Sodium: 5mg, Sugar: 8g

BLUEBERRY-CUCUMBER RELISH

PREPARATION TIME: 20 MINUTES
COOKING TIME: 30 MINUTES
SERVINGS: 5 PINT-SIZED JARS (16 OUNCES EACH)

MAXIMUM STORAGE TIME: 1 YEAR (UNOPENED). ONCE OPENED, REFRIGERATE AND USE WITHIN 1 MONTH
RECOMMENDED HEADSPACE: 1/2 INCH (12 MM)

INGREDIENTS

- *3 cups fresh blueberries (about 360 grams)*
- *2 cups finely diced cucumber (about 300 grams)*
- *1 cup finely chopped red onion (about 200 grams)*
- *1 cup white vinegar (240 ml)*
- *3/4 cup granulated sugar (150 grams)*
- *1/2 cup finely chopped fresh mint leaves*

- *2 tablespoons grated lemon zest (about 2 lemons)*
- *1 teaspoon salt (5 grams)*
- *1/2 teaspoon ground black pepper (1 gram)*
- *1/4 teaspoon crushed red pepper flakes (optional)*
- *5 clean pint-sized canning jars with lids and bands*

INSTRUCTIONS

1. In a large saucepan, mix blueberries, cucumber, onion, vinegar, sugar, mint, lemon zest, salt, black pepper, and red pepper flakes.
2. Bring to a boil over medium heat, then reduce to a simmer. Cook, stirring regularly, until the mixture thickens and the berries begin to burst, about 30 minutes.
3. Boil jars, lids, and bands for 10 minutes to sterilize them. Keep jars warm.
4. Fill the jars with the hot relish, leaving 12 mm (1/2 inch) headspace. Remove air bubbles.
5. Clean the rims, secure lids, and tighten rings finger-tight.
6. Soak the jars in boiling water for 15 minutes, starting the timer once the water boils.
7. Take out the jars and leave to cool down for 12 to 24 hours. Check seals.

SHOPPING TIPS:

- Use fresh, plump blueberries for the best flavor.
- Choose crisp cucumbers with firm skin.

PREPARATION TIPS:

- Finely dice the cucumber and chop the onion for a uniform texture.

NUTRITIONAL VALUE (PER SERVING - 1 TABLESPOON): Calories: 15, Carbohydrates: 4g, Fat: 0g, Protein: 0g, Sodium: 20mg, Sugar: 3g

Chapter 7
Pressure Canning Recipes

VEGETABLES

CLASSIC HEARTY VEGETABLE SOUP

PREPARATION TIME: 30 MINUTES
COOKING TIME: 1 HOUR COOKING, 90 MINUTES PRESSURE CANNING
SERVINGS: ABOUT 6 QUART-SIZED JARS (32 OUNCES EACH)

MAXIMUM STORAGE TIME: 2 YEARS (UNOPENED). ONCE OPENED, REFRIGERATE AND USE WITHIN 1 WEEK
RECOMMENDED HEADSPACE: LEAVE 1 INCH (25 MM) HEADSPACE

INGREDIENTS

- 4 cups diced carrots (about 1 kg)
- 4 cups diced potatoes (about 1 kg)
- 3 cups diced celery (about 750 grams)
- 2 cups diced onions (about 500 grams)
- 2 cups frozen peas (about 300 grams)
- 2 cups frozen corn (about 300 grams)
- 2 cups chopped green beans (about 300 grams)

- 8 cups vegetable broth or water (about 2 liters)
- 2 teaspoons salt (10 grams)
- 1 teaspoon ground black pepper (2 grams)
- 1 tablespoon dried basil (5 grams)
- 1 tablespoon dried parsley (5 grams)
- 6 clean quart-sized canning jars with lids and bands

INSTRUCTIONS

1. Wash, peel, and dice carrots, potatoes, celery, and onions. Thaw peas and corn if necessary.
2. In a large pot, mix together all vegetables, vegetable broth or water, salt, pepper, basil, and parsley. Bring to a boil, then simmer for about 30 minutes.
3. Boil jars, lids, and bands for 10 minutes to sterilize them. Keep jars warm.
4. Ladle the hot soup into jars, leaving 25 mm (1 inch) headspace. Remove any air bubbles.
5. Clean the rims, secure lids, and tighten rings finger-tight.
6. Process jars in a pressure canner at 10 pounds of pressure (11 pounds for dial-gauge canner) for 90 minutes for quart-sized jars.
7. Turn off heat and let pressure drop naturally after processing. Then wait 2 minutes before opening the canner. Take out the jars and leave to cool down for 12 to 24 hours. Check seals.

PREPARATION TIPS:
- Cutting the vegetables into uniform pieces ensures even cooking.
- Simmering the soup before canning helps blend the flavors and soften the vegetables.
- Ensure that the pressure canner is properly vented and reaches the correct pressure before starting the processing time.

NUTRITIONAL VALUE (PER SERVING - 1 CUP): Calories: 90, Carbohydrates: 20g, Fat: 0.5g, Protein: 3g, Sodium: 300mg, Sugar: 4g

SPICY PICKLED MIXED VEGETABLES

PREPARATION TIME: 40 MINUTES
COOKING TIME: 30 MINUTES COOKING, 25 MINUTES PRESSURE CANNING
SERVINGS: ABOUT 6 QUART-SIZED JARS (32 OUNCES EACH)

MAXIMUM STORAGE TIME: 18 MONTHS (UNOPENED). ONCE OPENED, REFRIGERATE AND USE WITHIN 1 MONTH
RECOMMENDED HEADSPACE: LEAVE 1 INCH (25 MM) HEADSPACE

INGREDIENTS

- 4 cups cauliflower florets (about 1 kg)
- 4 cups sliced carrots (about 1 kg)
- 3 cups sliced cucumbers (about 750 grams)
- 2 cups sliced bell peppers (mix of colors, about 500 grams)
- 2 cups white vinegar (480 ml)
- 2 cups water (480 ml)

- 1/4 cup salt (60 grams)
- 2 tablespoons sugar (30 grams)
- 4 cloves garlic, minced
- 2 tablespoons mustard seeds (10 grams)
- 2 teaspoons crushed red pepper flakes (to taste)
- 6 clean quart-sized canning jars with lids and bands

INSTRUCTIONS

1. Wash and slice cauliflower, carrots, cucumbers, and bell peppers.
2. In a large pot, mix together vinegar, water, salt, sugar, garlic, mustard seeds, and red pepper flakes. Bring to a boil.
3. Add the vegetables to the brine and return to a boil, then simmer for 10 minutes.
4. Boil jars, lids, and bands for 10 minutes to sterilize them. Keep jars warm.
5. Ladle the hot vegetable mixture into jars, distributing the brine evenly and leaving 25 mm (1 inch) headspace. Remove any air bubbles.
6. Clean the rims, secure lids, and tighten rings finger-tight.
7. Process jars in a pressure canner at 10 pounds of pressure (11 pounds for dial-gauge canner) for 25 minutes for quart-sized jars.
8. Turn off heat and let pressure drop naturally after processing. Then wait 2 minutes before opening the canner. Take out the jars and leave to cool down for 12 to 24 hours. Check seals.

PREPARATION TIPS:
- The spicy brine can be adjusted to taste by changing the amount of red pepper flakes.
- Ensure the vegetables are completely submerged in the brine for even flavor absorption.

NUTRITIONAL VALUE (PER SERVING - 1/2 CUP): Calories: 25, Carbohydrates: 5g, Fat: 0g, Protein: 1g, Sodium: 480mg, Sugar: 3g

COUNTRY STYLE VEGETABLE STEW

PREPARATION TIME: 45 MINUTES
COOKING TIME: 1 HOUR COOKING, 90 MINUTES PRESSURE CANNING
SERVINGS: ABOUT 6 QUART-SIZED JARS (32 OUNCES EACH)

MAXIMUM STORAGE TIME: 2 YEARS (UNOPENED). ONCE OPENED, REFRIGERATE AND USE WITHIN 1 WEEK
RECOMMENDED HEADSPACE: LEAVE 1 INCH (25 MM) HEADSPACE

CONTINUED →

INGREDIENTS

- 4 cups diced potatoes (about 1 kg)
- 3 cups sliced carrots (about 750 grams)
- 2 cups diced celery (about 500 grams)
- 2 cups chopped onions (about 500 grams)
- 2 cups green peas (fresh or frozen, 300 grams)
- 2 cups chopped green beans (about 300 grams)
- 8 cups vegetable broth or water (about 2 liters)
- 1 tablespoon olive oil
- 2 cloves garlic, minced
- 2 teaspoons dried thyme (4 grams)
- 2 teaspoons dried rosemary (4 grams)
- Salt and black pepper to taste
- 6 clean quart-sized canning jars with lids and bands

INSTRUCTIONS

1. In a large pot, heat olive oil over medium heat. Add onions, garlic, thyme, and rosemary, and sauté until onions are translucent.
2. Add potatoes, carrots, celery, peas, and green beans to the pot. Pour in the vegetable broth or water. Season with salt and black pepper.
3. Bring to a boil, then reduce heat and simmer for about 1 hour.
4. Boil jars, lids, and bands for 10 minutes to sterilize them. Keep jars warm.
5. Ladle the hot stew into jars, leaving 25 mm (1 inch) headspace. Remove any air bubbles.
6. Clean the rims, secure lids, and tighten rings finger-tight.
7. Process jars in a pressure canner at 10 pounds of pressure (11 pounds for dial-gauge canner) for 90 minutes for quart-sized jars.
8. Turn off heat and let pressure drop naturally after processing. Then wait 2 minutes before opening the canner. Take out the jars and leave to cool down for 12 to 24 hours. Check seals.

NUTRITIONAL VALUE (PER SERVING - 1 CUP): Calories: 120, Carbohydrates: 25g, Fat: 1.5g, Protein: 3g, Sodium: 300mg, Sugar: 5g

---

SWEET AND SOUR BRUSSEL SPROUTS

PREPARATION TIME: 20 MINUTES
COOKING TIME: 10 MINUTES COOKING, 25 MINUTES PRESSURE CANNING
SERVINGS: ABOUT 6 QUART-SIZED JARS (32 OUNCES EACH)

MAXIMUM STORAGE TIME: 2 YEARS (UNOPENED). ONCE OPENED, REFRIGERATE AND USE WITHIN 1 MONTH
RECOMMENDED HEADSPACE: LEAVE 1 INCH (25 MM) HEADSPACE

INGREDIENTS

- 6 cups Brussel sprouts, trimmed and halved
- 2 cups white vinegar (480 ml)
- 1 cup water (240 ml)
- 1 cup sugar (200 grams)
- 2 teaspoons mustard seeds (10 grams)
- 1 teaspoon salt (5 grams)
- 1/2 teaspoon ground black pepper (1 gram)
- 6 clean quart-sized canning jars with lids and bands

INSTRUCTIONS

1. Wash and trim Brussel sprouts, cutting any large ones in half.
2. In a large pot, combine water, vinegar, mustard seeds, sugar, salt, and black pepper. Bring to a boil, stirring to ensure that the sugar is dissolved.
3. Add Brussel sprouts to the boiling brine and return to a boil. Reduce heat and simmer for about 5 minutes.
4. Boil jars, lids, and bands for 10 minutes to sterilize them. Keep jars warm.

5. Ladle the Brussel sprouts and brine into jars, leaving 25 mm (1 inch) headspace. Remove any air bubbles.
6. Clean the rims, secure lids, and tighten rings finger-tight.

7. Process jars in a pressure canner at 10 pounds of pressure (11 pounds for dial-gauge canner) for 25 minutes for quart-sized jars.
8. Turn off heat and let pressure drop naturally after processing. Then wait 2 minutes before opening the canner. Take out the jars and leave to cool down for 12 to 24 hours. Check seals.

PREPARATION TIPS:
- Blanching the Brussel sprouts in the sweet and sour brine helps to infuse them with flavor while maintaining a firm texture.
- Make sure to cut larger Brussel sprouts in half to ensure even cooking and flavor absorption.

NUTRITIONAL VALUE (PER SERVING - 1/2 CUP): Calories: 50, Carbohydrates: 10g, Fat: 0g, Protein: 2g, Sodium: 80mg, Sugar: 7g

RUSTIC POTATO AND LEEK SOUP

PREPARATION TIME: 25 MINUTES
COOKING TIME: 35 MINUTES COOKING, 75 MINUTES PRESSURE CANNING
SERVINGS: ABOUT 6 QUART-SIZED JARS (32 OUNCES EACH)

MAXIMUM STORAGE TIME: 2 YEARS (UNOPENED). ONCE OPENED, REFRIGERATE AND USE WITHIN 1 WEEK
RECOMMENDED HEADSPACE: LEAVE 1 INCH (25 MM) HEADSPACE

INGREDIENTS

- 6 cups diced potatoes (about 1.5 kg)
- 4 cups sliced leeks (white and light green parts only, about 4 large leeks or 1 kg)
- 2 cups chopped onions (about 500 grams)
- 2 cloves garlic, minced
- 8 cups chicken or vegetable broth (about 2 liters)

- 1 cup heavy cream (240 ml)
- 2 tablespoons butter
- 2 teaspoons salt (10 grams)
- 1 teaspoon ground black pepper (2 grams)
- 1 tablespoon chopped fresh thyme (5 grams)
- 6 clean quart-sized canning jars with lids and bands

INSTRUCTIONS

1. In a large pot, melt butter over medium heat. Add leeks, onions, and garlic, sautéing until they are soft and translucent.
2. Stir in diced potatoes and pour in the broth. Bring to a boil, then reduce heat and simmer for about 25 minutes.
3. Partially blend the soup using an immersion blender, leaving some chunks for consistency. Stir in heavy cream, salt, pepper, and thyme.
4. Boil jars, lids, and bands for 10 minutes to sterilize them. Keep jars warm.

5. Ladle the hot soup into jars, leaving 25 mm (1 inch) headspace. Remove any air bubbles.
6. Clean the rims, secure lids, and tighten rings finger-tight.
7. Process jars in a pressure canner at 10 pounds of pressure (11 pounds for dial-gauge canner) for 75 minutes for quart-sized jars.
8. Turn off heat and let pressure drop naturally after processing. Then wait 2 minutes before opening the canner. Take out the jars and leave to cool down for 12 to 24 hours. Check seals.

NUTRITIONAL VALUE (PER SERVING - 1 CUP): Calories: 180, Carbohydrates: 25g, Fat: 7g, Protein: 4g, Sodium: 600mg, Sugar: 4g

HERBED BABY CARROTS AND PEAS

PREPARATION TIME: 20 MINUTES
COOKING TIME: 5 MINUTES COOKING, 40 MINUTES
PRESSURE CANNING
SERVINGS: ABOUT 6 QUART-SIZED JARS (32
OUNCES EACH)

MAXIMUM STORAGE TIME: 18 MONTHS
(UNOPENED). ONCE OPENED, REFRIGERATE AND
USE WITHIN 1 MONTH
RECOMMENDED HEADSPACE: LEAVE 1 INCH (25
MM) HEADSPACE

INGREDIENTS

- 6 cups baby carrots (about 1.5 kg)
- 4 cups frozen peas (about 600 grams)
- 1 cup chopped fresh parsley (about 40 grams)
- 1/2 cup chopped fresh dill (about 20 grams)
- 6 cups water (for blanching)
- 2 teaspoons salt (for blanching)
- 6 cups water (or as needed for canning)
- 1 teaspoon salt (for canning)
- 6 clean quart-sized canning jars with lids and bands

INSTRUCTIONS

1. Bring a large pot of water to a boil with 2 teaspoons of salt. Add baby carrots and blanch for 3 minutes. Add peas and continue to blanch for an additional 2 minutes. Drain and put in ice water to halt cooking.
2. Finely chop parsley and dill.
3. In a large bowl, gently mix together blanched carrots and peas with chopped parsley and dill.
4. Boil jars, lids, and bands for 10 minutes to sterilize them. Keep jars warm.
5. Pack the vegetable and herb mixture into jars, leaving 25 mm (1 inch) headspace.

Maintaining 25 mm headspace, pour boiling water over vegetables. Add 1 teaspoon of salt per quart jar.
6. Clean the rims, secure lids, and tighten rings finger-tight.
7. Process jars in a pressure canner at 10 pounds of pressure (11 pounds for dial-gauge canner) for 40 minutes for quart-sized jars.
8. Turn off heat and let pressure drop naturally after processing. Then wait 2 minutes before opening the canner. Take out the jars and leave to cool down for 12 to 24 hours. Check seals.

PREPARATION TIPS: Blanching preserves the color and texture of the vegetables.

NUTRITIONAL VALUE (PER SERVING - 1/2 CUP): Calories: 60, Carbohydrates: 12g, Fat: 0.5g, Protein: 3g, Sodium: 300mg, Sugar: 5g

SAVORY MUSHROOM AND ONION MEDLEY

PREPARATION TIME: 30 MINUTES
COOKING TIME: 20 MINUTES COOKING, 90
MINUTES PRESSURE CANNING
SERVINGS: ABOUT 6 QUART-SIZED JARS (32
OUNCES EACH)

MAXIMUM STORAGE TIME: 2 YEARS (UNOPENED).
ONCE OPENED, REFRIGERATE AND USE WITHIN 1
WEEK
RECOMMENDED HEADSPACE: LEAVE 1 INCH (25
MM) HEADSPACE

INGREDIENTS

- 6 cups sliced mushrooms (mix of varieties like button, cremini, or portobello, about 1.5 kg)
- 4 cups chopped onions (about 1 kg)
- 2 cups beef or vegetable broth (480 ml)
- 1/4 cup soy sauce or tamari (60 ml)
- 1/4 cup balsamic vinegar (60 ml)
- 2 cloves garlic, minced
- 1 tablespoon dried thyme (5 grams)
- 1 tablespoon olive oil
- Salt and black pepper to taste
- 6 clean quart-sized canning jars with lids and bands

INSTRUCTIONS

1. In a large skillet, heat olive oil over medium heat. Add onions and garlic, sautéing until onions are translucent. Add mushrooms and continue to sauté until they dry out and brown.
2. Stir in beef or vegetable broth, soy sauce, balsamic vinegar, and thyme. Bring to a simmer and cook for about 10 minutes. Season with salt and black pepper to taste.
3. Boil jars, lids, and bands for 10 minutes to sterilize them. Keep jars warm.
4. Ladle the hot mushroom and onion mixture into jars, leaving 25 mm (1 inch) headspace. Remove any air bubbles.
5. Clean the rims, secure lids, and tighten rings finger-tight.
6. Process jars in a pressure canner at 10 pounds of pressure (11 pounds for dial-gauge canner) for 90 minutes for quart-sized jars.
7. Turn off heat and let pressure drop naturally after processing. Then wait 2 minutes before opening the canner. Take out the jars and leave to cool down for 12 to 24 hours. Check seals.

PREPARATION TIPS:
- Sautéing the mushrooms and onions before canning deepens their flavors.
- This savory mixture is perfect as a side dish, a topping for steaks or burgers, or as an addition to hearty stews.

NUTRITIONAL VALUE (PER SERVING - 1/2 CUP): Calories: 50, Carbohydrates: 7g, Fat: 1g, Protein: 2g, Sodium: 300mg, Sugar: 3g

SPICED CARROT AND LENTIL SOUP

PREPARATION TIME: 20 MINUTES
COOKING TIME: 35 MINUTES COOKING, 75 MINUTES PRESSURE CANNING
SERVINGS: ABOUT 6 QUART-SIZED JARS (32 OUNCES EACH)

MAXIMUM STORAGE TIME: 2 YEARS (UNOPENED). ONCE OPENED, REFRIGERATE AND USE WITHIN 1 WEEK
RECOMMENDED HEADSPACE: LEAVE 1 INCH (25 MM) HEADSPACE

INGREDIENTS

- 4 cups diced carrots (about 1 kg)
- 3 cups cooked lentils (about 600 grams, can be from canned lentils, rinsed and drained)
- 2 cups chopped onions (about 500 grams)
- 1 cup diced celery (about 250 grams)
- 8 cups vegetable broth or water (about 2 liters)
- 2 cloves garlic, minced
- 2 teaspoons ground cumin (4 grams)
- 1 teaspoon ground coriander (2 grams)
- 1/2 teaspoon ground turmeric (1 gram)
- Salt and black pepper to taste
- 1 tablespoon olive oil
- 6 clean quart-sized canning jars with lids and bands

CONTINUED →

INSTRUCTIONS

1. In a large pot, heat olive oil over medium heat. Add onions, garlic, cumin, coriander, and turmeric, sautéing until onions are translucent.
2. Add carrots, celery, and cooked lentils to the pot. Pour in the vegetable broth or water. Season with salt and black pepper. Bring to a boil, then reduce heat and simmer for about 30 minutes.
3. Boil jars, lids, and bands for 10 minutes to sterilize them. Keep jars warm.
4. Fill the jars with the hot soup, leaving 25 mm (1 inch) headspace. Remove any air bubbles.
5. Clean the rims, secure lids, and tighten rings finger-tight.
6. Process jars in a pressure canner at 10 pounds of pressure (11 pounds for dial-gauge canner) for 75 minutes for quart-sized jars.
7. Turn off heat and let pressure drop naturally after processing. Then wait 2 minutes before opening the canner. Take out the jars and leave to cool down for 12 to 24 hours. Check seals.

NUTRITIONAL VALUE (PER SERVING - 1 CUP): Calories: 120, Carbohydrates: 20g, Fat: 2g, Protein: 6g, Sodium: 300mg, Sugar: 5g

HEARTY BEAN AND VEGETABLE CHILI

PREPARATION TIME: 20 MINUTES
COOKING TIME: 40 MINUTES COOKING, 90 MINUTES PRESSURE CANNING
SERVINGS: ABOUT 6 QUART-SIZED JARS (32 OUNCES EACH)

MAXIMUM STORAGE TIME: 2 YEARS (UNOPENED). ONCE OPENED, REFRIGERATE AND USE WITHIN 1 WEEK
RECOMMENDED HEADSPACE: LEAVE 1 INCH (25 MM) HEADSPACE

INGREDIENTS

- *4 cups cooked kidney beans (about 800 grams, can use canned, rinsed, and drained)*
- *3 cups diced tomatoes (about 750 grams)*
- *2 cups diced bell peppers (about 500 grams)*
- *1 cup diced onion (about 200 grams)*
- *1 cup frozen corn (about 150 grams)*
- *1 jalapeño pepper, finely chopped (adjust to taste)*
- *3 cloves garlic, minced*
- *2 tablespoons chili powder (10 grams)*
- *1 teaspoon ground cumin (2 grams)*
- *1 teaspoon smoked paprika (2 grams)*
- *Salt and black pepper to taste*
- *6 clean quart-sized canning jars with lids and bands*

INSTRUCTIONS

1. In a large pot, mix together kidney beans, tomatoes, bell peppers, onion, corn, jalapeño, garlic, chili powder, cumin, smoked paprika, salt, and black pepper.
2. Bring the mixture to a boil, then reduce heat and simmer for about 40 minutes, or until the vegetables are tender and flavors are well combined.
3. Boil jars, lids, and bands for 10 minutes to sterilize them. Keep jars warm.
4. Ladle the hot chili into jars, leaving 25 mm (1 inch) headspace. Remove any air bubbles.
5. Clean the rims, secure lids, and tighten rings finger-tight.
6. Process jars in a pressure canner at 10 pounds of pressure (11 pounds for dial-gauge canner) for 90 minutes for quart-sized jars.
7. Turn off heat and let pressure drop naturally after processing. Then wait 2 minutes before opening the canner. Take out the jars and leave to cool down for 12 to 24 hours. Check seals.

TANGY TOMATO AND BASIL SAUCE

PREPARATION TIME: 30 MINUTES
COOKING TIME: 30 MINUTES COOKING, 25 MINUTES PRESSURE CANNING
SERVINGS: ABOUT 6 QUART-SIZED JARS (32 OUNCES EACH)

MAXIMUM STORAGE TIME: 18 MONTHS (UNOPENED). ONCE OPENED, REFRIGERATE AND USE WITHIN 1 MONTH
RECOMMENDED HEADSPACE: LEAVE 1 INCH (25 MM) HEADSPACE

INGREDIENTS

- 8 cups chopped ripe tomatoes (about 4 kg)
- 1 cup finely chopped onion (about 200 grams)
- 1/2 cup chopped fresh basil (about 20 grams)
- 4 cloves garlic, minced
- 2 tablespoons olive oil

- 1/4 cup balsamic vinegar (60 ml)
- 2 teaspoons salt (10 grams)
- 1 teaspoon ground black pepper (2 grams)
- 1 teaspoon sugar (optional) (2 grams)
- 6 clean quart-sized canning jars with lids and bands

INSTRUCTIONS

1. In a large pot, heat olive oil over medium heat. Add onions and garlic, sautéing until onions are translucent.
2. Stir in chopped tomatoes, basil, balsamic vinegar, salt, black pepper, and sugar (if using). Bring to a simmer and cook for about 30 minutes, or until the sauce thickens.
3. Boil jars, lids, and bands for 10 minutes to sterilize them. Keep jars warm.
4. Ladle the hot sauce into jars, leaving 25 mm (1 inch) headspace. Remove any air bubbles.
5. Clean the rims, secure lids, and tighten rings finger-tight.
6. Process jars in a pressure canner at 10 pounds of pressure (11 pounds for dial-gauge canner) for 25 minutes for quart-sized jars.
7. Turn off heat and let pressure drop naturally after processing. Then wait 2 minutes before opening the canner. Take out the jars and leave to cool down for 12 to 24 hours. Check seals.

SHOPPING TIPS:
- Choose ripe, flavorful tomatoes for the best taste.
- Fresh basil will enhance the flavor of the sauce compared to dried basil.

PREPARATION TIPS:
- This sauce is perfect as a condiment with grilled meats, a base for pizza, or for pasta dishes.

NUTRITIONAL VALUE (PER SERVING - 1/4 CUP): Calories: 20, Carbohydrates: 3g, Fat: 1g, Protein: 1g, Sodium: 80mg, Sugar: 2g

MEAT RECIPES

CLASSIC BEEF STEW FOR PRESSURE CANNING

PREPARATION TIME: 30 MINUTES
COOKING TIME: 2 HOURS COOKING, 90 MINUTES PRESSURE CANNING
SERVINGS: ABOUT 6 QUART-SIZED JARS (32 OUNCES EACH)

MAXIMUM STORAGE TIME: 3 YEARS (UNOPENED). ONCE OPENED, REFRIGERATE AND USE WITHIN 1 WEEK
RECOMMENDED HEADSPACE: LEAVE 1 INCH (25 MM) HEADSPACE

INGREDIENTS

- 4 lbs beef chuck roast, cut into 1-inch cubes
- 4 cups diced potatoes (about 1 kg)
- 3 cups sliced carrots (about 750 grams)
- 2 cups diced onions (about 500 grams)
- 2 cups sliced celery (about 500 grams)
- 6 cloves garlic, minced
- 1/4 cup tomato paste (60 ml)
- 8 cups beef broth (about 2 liters)
- 2 teaspoons salt (10 grams)
- 1 teaspoon ground black pepper (2 grams)
- 2 tablespoons Worcestershire sauce (30 ml)
- 2 tablespoons olive oil
- 6 clean quart-sized canning jars with lids and bands

INSTRUCTIONS

1. In a large skillet, heat olive oil over medium-high heat. Brown the beef cubes in batches, ensuring they're not crowded. Transfer to a large pot.
2. In the same skillet, sauté onions, garlic, celery, and tomato paste for about 5 minutes.
3. Add sautéed vegetables to the pot with beef. Add carrots, potatoes, beef broth, salt, pepper, and Worcestershire sauce. Bring to a boil, then simmer for 1.5 hours, or until the beef is tender.
4. Boil jars, lids, and bands for 10 minutes to sterilize them. Keep jars warm.
5. Ladle the hot stew into jars, leaving 25 mm (1 inch) headspace. Remove any air bubbles.
6. Clean the rims, secure lids, and tighten rings finger-tight.
7. Process jars in a pressure canner at 11 pounds of pressure (for weighted-gauge canner) or 10 pounds (for dial-gauge canner) for 90 minutes for quart-sized jars.
8. Turn off heat and let pressure drop naturally after processing. Then wait 2 minutes before opening the canner. Take out the jars and leave to cool down for 12 to 24 hours. Check seals.

PREPARATION TIPS:
- Browning the beef before canning adds depth to the flavor.
- Ensure proper browning by not overcrowding the pan and allowing each piece of meat to develop a rich color.
- Allow the stew to simmer until the beef and vegetables are tender but not overcooked, as they will continue to cook during the canning process.

NUTRITIONAL VALUE (PER SERVING - 1 CUP): Calories: 250, Carbohydrates: 15g, Fat: 10g, Protein: 25g, Sodium: 600mg, Sugar: 3g

BARBECUE BEEF BRISKET

PREPARATION TIME: 40 MINUTES (INCLUDING MARINATING TIME)
COOKING TIME: 3 HOURS COOKING, 90 MINUTES PRESSURE CANNING
SERVINGS: ABOUT 6 QUART-SIZED JARS (32 OUNCES EACH)

MAXIMUM STORAGE TIME: 3 YEARS (UNOPENED). ONCE OPENED, REFRIGERATE AND USE WITHIN 1 WEEK
RECOMMENDED HEADSPACE: LEAVE 1 INCH (25 MM) HEADSPACE

INGREDIENTS

- 4 lbs beef brisket, trimmed and cut into 2-inch chunks (about 1.8 kg)
- 1 cup barbecue sauce (240 ml)
- 2 cups beef broth (480 ml)
- 1 cup chopped onions (about 200 grams)
- 1/2 cup apple cider vinegar (120 ml)
- 1/4 cup brown sugar (50 grams)
- 2 tablespoons Worcestershire sauce (30 ml)
- 2 cloves garlic, minced
- 1 tablespoon smoked paprika (5 grams)
- 1 teaspoon ground cumin (2 grams)
- Salt and black pepper to taste
- 6 clean quart-sized canning jars with lids and bands

INSTRUCTIONS

1. In a large bowl, combine barbecue sauce, apple cider vinegar, brown sugar, Worcestershire sauce, garlic, smoked paprika, and cumin. Add beef brisket chunks and toss to coat. Let marinate for at least 30 minutes.
2. In a large pot, combine marinated beef, onions, and beef broth. Bring to a boil, then reduce heat and simmer for about 2.5 hours, or until the beef is very tender.
3. Boil jars, lids, and bands for 10 minutes to sterilize them. Keep jars warm.
4. Ladle the hot beef and sauce into jars, leaving 25 mm (1 inch) headspace. Remove any air bubbles.
5. Clean the rims, secure lids, and tighten rings finger-tight.
6. Process jars in a pressure canner at 11 pounds of pressure (for weighted-gauge canner) or 10 pounds (for dial-gauge canner) for 90 minutes for quart-sized jars.
7. Turn off heat and let pressure drop naturally after processing. Then wait 2 minutes before opening the canner. Take out the jars and leave to cool down for 12 to 24 hours. Check seals.

PREPARATION TIPS:
- Marinating the beef enhances its flavor and tenderness.
- Slow cooking the brisket until tender ensures it will be flavorful and succulent even after canning.

NUTRITIONAL VALUE (PER SERVING - 1/2 CUP): Calories: 300, Carbohydrates: 15g, Fat: 15g, Protein: 25g, Sodium: 650mg, Sugar: 10g

---

SAVORY BEEF GOULASH

PREPARATION TIME: 20 MINUTES
COOKING TIME: 1 HOUR COOKING, 90 MINUTES PRESSURE CANNING
SERVINGS: ABOUT 6 QUART-SIZED JARS (32 OUNCES EACH)

MAXIMUM STORAGE TIME: 3 YEARS (UNOPENED). ONCE OPENED, REFRIGERATE AND USE WITHIN 1 WEEK
RECOMMENDED HEADSPACE: LEAVE 1 INCH (25 MM) HEADSPACE

CONTINUED →

INGREDIENTS

- 4 lbs beef chuck, cut into 1-inch cubes (1.8 kg)
- 4 cups beef broth (about 1 liter)
- 2 cups diced onions (about 500 grams)
- 2 cups diced bell peppers (mixed colors, about 500 grams)
- 1 cup diced tomatoes (about 250 grams)
- 3 cloves garlic, minced
- 1/4 cup tomato paste (60 ml)
- 2 tablespoons paprika (10 grams)
- 1 teaspoon caraway seeds (2 grams)
- Salt and black pepper to taste
- 2 tablespoons olive oil
- 6 clean quart-sized canning jars with lids and bands

INSTRUCTIONS

1. In a large skillet, heat olive oil over medium-high heat. Brown the beef cubes in batches, then transfer to a large pot.
2. In the same skillet, sauté bell peppers, onions, and garlic until softened. Add to the pot with the beef.
3. Add diced tomatoes, tomato paste, caraway seeds, beef broth, paprika, salt, and black pepper to the pot. Bring to a boil, then reduce heat and simmer for about 1 hour, or until the beef is tender.
4. Boil jars, lids, and bands for 10 minutes to sterilize them. Keep jars warm.
5. Ladle the hot goulash into jars, leaving 25 mm (1 inch) headspace. Remove any air bubbles.
6. Clean the rims, secure lids, and tighten rings finger-tight.
7. Process jars in a pressure canner at 10 pounds of pressure (11 pounds for dial-gauge canner) for 90 minutes for quart-sized jars.
8. Turn off heat and let pressure drop naturally after processing. Then wait 2 minutes before opening the canner. Take out the jars and leave to cool down for 12 to 24 hours. Check seals.

PREPARATION TIPS:

- Browning the meat before simmering helps to seal in the flavors.
- This hearty goulash is perfect served over noodles, rice, or enjoyed on its own.

NUTRITIONAL VALUE (PER SERVING - 1 CUP): Calories: 300, Carbohydrates: 10g, Fat: 15g, Protein: 25g, Sodium: 700mg, Sugar: 4g

---

SOUTHWEST BEEF AND BEAN CHILI

PREPARATION TIME: 30 MINUTES
COOKING TIME: 1 HOUR COOKING, 90 MINUTES PRESSURE CANNING
SERVINGS: ABOUT 6 QUART-SIZED JARS (32 OUNCES EACH)

MAXIMUM STORAGE TIME: 3 YEARS (UNOPENED). ONCE OPENED, REFRIGERATE AND USE WITHIN 1 WEEK
RECOMMENDED HEADSPACE: LEAVE 1 INCH (25 MM) HEADSPACE

INGREDIENTS

- 4 lbs ground beef (about 1.8 kg)
- 4 cups cooked black beans (about 800 grams, can use canned, rinsed and drained)
- 2 cups diced onions (about 500 grams)
- 2 cups diced bell peppers (about 500 grams)
- 1 can (14.5 ounces) diced tomatoes with juice
- 3 cloves garlic, minced
- 1/4 cup chili powder (20 grams)
- 2 teaspoons ground cumin (4 grams)
- 1 teaspoon smoked paprika (2 grams)
- 1/2 teaspoon cayenne pepper (adjust to taste)
- Salt and black pepper to taste
- 6 cups beef broth or water (about 1.5 liters)
- 2 tablespoons olive oil

INSTRUCTIONS

1. In a large skillet, heat olive oil over medium-high heat. Add ground beef and cook until browned. Drain excess fat.
2. In a large pot, combine browned beef, black beans, onions, bell peppers, diced tomatoes, garlic, chili powder, cumin, smoked paprika, cayenne pepper, salt, black pepper, and beef broth or water.
3. Bring the mixture to a boil, then reduce heat and simmer for about 1 hour, stirring occasionally, until flavors are well combined and vegetables are tender.
4. Boil jars, lids, and bands for 10 minutes to sterilize them. Keep jars warm.
5. Ladle the hot chili into jars, leaving 25 mm (1 inch) headspace. Remove any air bubbles.
6. Clean the rims, secure lids, and tighten rings finger-tight.
7. Process jars in a pressure canner at 10 pounds of pressure (11 pounds for dial-gauge canner) for 90 minutes for quart-sized jars.
8. Turn off heat and let pressure drop naturally after processing. Then wait 2 minutes before opening the canner. Take out the jars and leave to cool down for 12 to 24 hours. Check seals.

PREPARATION TIPS: This Southwest Beef and Bean Chili is perfect for a hearty meal and can be served with rice, bread, or on its own.

NUTRITIONAL VALUE (PER SERVING - 1 CUP): Calories: 350, Carbohydrates: 20g, Fat: 15g, Protein: 30g, Sodium: 800mg, Sugar: 5g

---

SMOKY PORK AND BEANS

PREPARATION TIME: 30 MINUTES
COOKING TIME: 2 HOURS COOKING, 90 MINUTES PRESSURE CANNING
SERVINGS: ABOUT 6 QUART-SIZED JARS (32 OUNCES EACH)

MAXIMUM STORAGE TIME: 3 YEARS (UNOPENED). ONCE OPENED, REFRIGERATE AND USE WITHIN 1 WEEK
RECOMMENDED HEADSPACE: LEAVE 1 INCH (25 MM) HEADSPACE

INGREDIENTS

- 4 lbs pork shoulder, cut into 1-inch cubes (about 1.8 kg)
- 4 cups dry navy beans, soaked overnight and drained (about 800 grams)
- 1 large onion, chopped (about 200 grams)
- 3 cloves garlic, minced
- 1/4 cup molasses (60 ml)
- 1/4 cup brown sugar (50 grams)
- 1/4 cup apple cider vinegar (60 ml)
- 1 tablespoon Worcestershire sauce (15 ml)
- 1 tablespoon smoked paprika (5 grams)
- 2 teaspoons mustard powder (4 grams)
- Salt and black pepper to taste
- 6 cups water (or as needed)
- 2 tablespoons olive oil
- 6 clean quart-sized canning jars with lids and bands

INSTRUCTIONS

1. In a large skillet, heat olive oil over medium-high heat. Brown the pork cubes in batches, then transfer to a large pot.
2. Add soaked and drained navy beans, chopped onion, garlic, molasses, brown sugar, apple cider vinegar, Worcestershire sauce, smoked paprika, mustard powder, salt, and black pepper to the pot with pork. Add enough water to cover the ingredients.
3. Bring to a boil, then reduce heat and simmer for about 2 hours.
4. Boil jars, lids, and bands for 10 minutes to sterilize them. Keep jars warm.

CONTINUED →

5. Ladle the hot pork and beans mixture into jars, leaving 25 mm (1 inch) headspace. Remove any air bubbles.
6. Clean the rims, secure lids, and tighten rings finger-tight.
7. Process jars in a pressure canner at 10 pounds of pressure (11 pounds for dial-gauge canner) for 90 minutes for quart-sized jars.
8. Turn off heat and let pressure drop naturally after processing. Then wait 2 minutes before opening the canner. Take out the jars and leave to cool down for 12 to 24 hours. Check seals.

PREPARATION TIPS:

- Browning the pork enhances its flavor and adds depth to the dish.
- Adjust the amount of water as needed to ensure the beans are well-cooked and the pork is tender.

NUTRITIONAL VALUE (PER SERVING - 1 CUP): Calories: 350, Carbohydrates: 30g, Fat: 15g, Protein: 25g, Sodium: 500mg, Sugar: 10g

---

SPICED PORK STEW

PREPARATION TIME: 40 MINUTES
COOKING TIME: 1 HOUR 30 MINUTES COOKING, 90 MINUTES PRESSURE CANNING
SERVINGS: ABOUT 6 QUART-SIZED JARS (32 OUNCES EACH)

MAXIMUM STORAGE TIME: 3 YEARS (UNOPENED). ONCE OPENED, REFRIGERATE AND USE WITHIN 1 WEEK
RECOMMENDED HEADSPACE: LEAVE 1 INCH (25 MM) HEADSPACE

INGREDIENTS

- *4 lbs pork shoulder or butt, cut into 1-inch cubes (about 1.8 kg)*
- *4 cups diced potatoes (about 1 kg)*
- *3 cups sliced carrots (about 750 grams)*
- *2 cups chopped onions (about 500 grams)*
- *2 cups beef or chicken broth (about 480 ml)*
- *1 can (14.5 ounces) diced tomatoes with juice*
- *3 cloves garlic, minced*

- *2 tablespoons chili powder (10 grams)*
- *1 tablespoon ground cumin*
- *1 teaspoon dried oregano*
- *Salt and black pepper to taste*
- *2 tbsp vegetable oil*
- *6 clean quart-sized canning jars with lids and bands*

INSTRUCTIONS

1. In a large skillet, heat vegetable oil over medium-high heat. Brown the pork cubes in batches, then transfer to a large pot.
2. To the pot with pork, add potatoes, carrots, onions, garlic, diced tomatoes with juice, broth, chili powder, cumin, oregano, salt, and black pepper.
3. Bring to a boil, then reduce heat and simmer for about 1 hour 30 minutes, or until the pork is tender and vegetables are cooked through.
4. Boil jars, lids, and bands for 10 minutes to sterilize them. Keep jars warm.
5. Ladle the hot stew into jars, leaving 25 mm (1 inch) headspace. Remove any air bubbles.
6. Clean the rims, secure lids, and tighten rings finger-tight.
7. Process jars in a pressure canner at 10 pounds of pressure (11 pounds for dial-gauge canner) for 90 minutes for quart-sized jars.
8. Turn off heat and let pressure drop naturally after processing. Then wait 2 minutes before opening the canner. Take out the jars and leave to cool down for 12 to 24 hours. Check seals.

NUTRITIONAL VALUE (PER SERVING - 1 CUP): Calories: 300, Carbohydrates: 20g, Fat: 15g, Protein: 25g, Sodium: 600mg, Sugar: 5g

HONEY GARLIC PORK CHOPS

PREPARATION TIME: 20 MINUTES
COOKING TIME: 40 MINUTES COOKING, 75 MINUTES PRESSURE CANNING
SERVINGS: ABOUT 6 QUART-SIZED JARS (32 OUNCES EACH)

MAXIMUM STORAGE TIME: 3 YEARS (UNOPENED). ONCE OPENED, REFRIGERATE AND USE WITHIN 1 WEEK
RECOMMENDED HEADSPACE: LEAVE 1 INCH (25 MM) HEADSPACE

INGREDIENTS

- 4 lbs pork chops, boneless (about 1.8 kg)
- 1 cup honey (240 ml)
- 1/2 cup soy sauce (120 ml)
- 1/4 cup minced garlic (about 60 grams)
- 2 tablespoons apple cider vinegar (30 ml)

- 1 teaspoon ground ginger (2 grams)
- Salt and black pepper to taste
- 2 tablespoons vegetable oil
- 6 clean quart-sized canning jars with lids and bands

INSTRUCTIONS

1. In a large bowl, whisk together honey, soy sauce, garlic, apple cider vinegar, and ground ginger. Season pork chops with salt and black pepper. Add pork chops to the marinade and let sit for at least 15 minutes.
2. In a large skillet, heat vegetable oil over medium-high heat. Brown pork chops on all sides and place in a large pot.
3. Cover the pork chops in the pot with the leftover marinade.
4. Bring the mixture to a simmer and cook for about 40 minutes, or until the pork chops are tender.
5. Boil jars, lids, and bands for 10 minutes to sterilize them. Keep jars warm.
6. Place one pork chop in each jar, and then ladle the hot marinade over them, leaving 25 mm (1 inch) headspace. Remove any air bubbles.
7. Clean the rims, secure lids, and tighten rings finger-tight.
8. Process jars in a pressure canner at 10 pounds of pressure (11 pounds for dial-gauge canner) for 75 minutes for quart-sized jars.
9. Turn off heat and let pressure drop naturally after processing. Then wait 2 minutes before opening the canner. Take out the jars and leave to cool down for 12 to 24 hours. Check seals.

SHOPPING TIPS: Choose boneless pork chops of uniform thickness for even cooking.

PREPARATION TIPS: Allowing the pork chops to marinate for at least 15 minutes helps infuse them with the flavors of the sauce.

NUTRITIONAL VALUE (PER SERVING - 1 PORK CHOP WITH SAUCE): Calories: 350, Carbohydrates: 30g, Fat: 15g, Protein: 25g, Sodium: 800mg, Sugar: 25g

ZESTY PORK AND VEGETABLE MEDLEY

PREPARATION TIME: 25 MINUTES
COOKING TIME: 1 HOUR COOKING, 75 MINUTES PRESSURE CANNING
SERVINGS: ABOUT 6 QUART-SIZED JARS (32 OUNCES EACH)

MAXIMUM STORAGE TIME: 3 YEARS (UNOPENED). ONCE OPENED, REFRIGERATE AND USE WITHIN 1 WEEK
RECOMMENDED HEADSPACE: LEAVE 1 INCH (25 MM) HEADSPACE

CONTINUED →

INGREDIENTS

- 4 lbs pork loin, cut into 1-inch cubes (about 1.8 kg)
- 3 cups diced potatoes (about 750 grams)
- 2 cups diced carrots (about 500 grams)
- 2 cups green beans, trimmed and cut into 1-inch pieces (about 300 grams)
- 1 large onion, chopped (about 200 grams)
- 3 cloves garlic, minced
- 1 can (14.5 ounces) diced tomatoes with juice
- 2 teaspoons dried basil (4 grams)
- 2 teaspoons dried oregano (4 grams)
- Salt and black pepper to taste
- 6 cups chicken or vegetable broth (about 1.5 liters)
- 2 tablespoons olive oil
- 6 clean quart-sized canning jars with lids and bands

INSTRUCTIONS

1. In a large skillet, heat olive oil over medium-high heat. Brown the pork cubes in batches, then transfer to a large pot.
2. In the same skillet, sauté onions and garlic until translucent. Add to the pot with the pork.
3. Add diced potatoes, carrots, green beans, diced tomatoes with juice, basil, oregano, salt, pepper, and broth to the pot. Bring to a boil, then reduce heat and simmer for about 1 hour.
4. Boil jars, lids, and bands for 10 minutes to sterilize them. Keep jars warm.
5. Ladle the hot pork and vegetable medley into jars, leaving 25 mm (1 inch) headspace. Remove any air bubbles.
6. Clean the rims, secure lids, and tighten rings finger-tight.
7. Process jars in a pressure canner at 10 pounds of pressure (11 pounds for dial-gauge canner) for 75 minutes for quart-sized jars.
8. Turn off heat and let pressure drop naturally after processing. Then wait 2 minutes before opening the canner. Take out the jars and leave to cool down for 12 to 24 hours. Check seals.

PREPARATION TIPS:
- Cutting the pork and vegetables into uniform sizes ensures even cooking.
- This medley is a complete meal in a jar, full of protein and vegetables, and can be easily heated up for a quick, nutritious meal.

NUTRITIONAL VALUE (PER SERVING - 1 CUP): Calories: 260, Carbohydrates: 20g, Fat: 10g, Protein: 22g, Sodium: 600mg, Sugar: 4g

---

APPLE CIDER PORK WITH ROOT VEGETABLES

PREPARATION TIME: 30 MINUTES
COOKING TIME: 1 HOUR 30 MINUTES COOKING, 75 MINUTES PRESSURE CANNING
SERVINGS: ABOUT 6 QUART-SIZED JARS (32 OUNCES EACH)

MAXIMUM STORAGE TIME: 3 YEARS (UNOPENED). ONCE OPENED, REFRIGERATE AND USE WITHIN 1 WEEK
RECOMMENDED HEADSPACE: LEAVE 1 INCH (25 MM) HEADSPACE

INGREDIENTS

- 4 lbs pork shoulder, trimmed and cut into 1-inch chunks (about 1.8 kg)
- 3 cups diced sweet potatoes (about 750 grams)
- 2 cups diced parsnips (about 500 grams)
- 1 large onion, chopped (about 200 grams)
- 2 cups apple cider (about 480 ml)
- 1 cup chicken broth (about 240 ml)
- 2 tablespoons brown sugar (30 grams)
- 2 teaspoons ground cinnamon (4 grams)
- 1/2 teaspoon ground nutmeg (1 gram)
- Salt and black pepper to taste
- 2 tablespoons olive oil

INSTRUCTIONS

1. In a large skillet, heat olive oil over medium-high heat. Brown the pork chunks in batches, then transfer to a large pot.
2. To the pot with pork, add sweet potatoes, parsnips, onion, apple cider, chicken broth, brown sugar, cinnamon, nutmeg, salt, and black pepper.
3. Bring to a boil, then reduce heat and simmer for about 1 hour 30 minutes.
4. Boil jars, lids, and bands for 10 minutes to sterilize them. Keep jars warm.
5. Ladle the hot pork and vegetable mixture into jars, leaving 25 mm (1 inch) headspace. Remove any air bubbles. Clean the rims, secure lids, and tighten rings finger-tight.
6. Process jars in a pressure canner at 10 pounds of pressure (11 pounds for dial-gauge canner) for 75 minutes for quart-sized jars.
7. Turn off heat and let pressure drop naturally after processing. Then wait 2 minutes before opening the canner. Take out the jars and leave to cool down for 12 to 24 hours. Check seals.

SHOPPING TIPS:

- Choose a pork shoulder with some fat for tenderness and flavor.

PREPARATION TIPS:

- The combination of apple cider and spices gives a sweet and aromatic flavor to the dish.
- This comforting pork stew is ideal for a hearty meal, especially during colder months, and pairs well with crusty bread or over a bed of rice.

NUTRITIONAL VALUE (PER SERVING - 1 CUP): Calories: 320, Carbohydrates: 25g, Fat: 15g, Protein: 22g, Sodium: 400mg, Sugar: 10g

---

SUCCULENT PULLED PORK

PREPARATION TIME: 15 MINUTES
COOKING TIME: 75 MINUTES

SERVINGS: ABOUT 6 JARS (1 QUART EACH)
RECOMMENDED HEADSPACE: LEAVE 1 INCH (25 MM) HEADSPACE

INGREDIENTS

- *3 lbs (1.4 kg) pork shoulder, cut into chunks*
- *Salt and pepper to taste*
- *2 tablespoons (30 ml) vegetable oil*
- *1 large onion, diced*
- *4 cloves garlic, minced*
- *2 cups (480 ml) barbecue sauce*
- *1/2 cup (120 ml) apple cider vinegar*
- *1/2 cup (120 ml) chicken broth*

INSTRUCTIONS

1. Season pork with salt and pepper on all sides.
2. In a large pot, heat vegetable oil over medium-high heat. Add pork and brown on all sides.
3. Add onions and garlic, cook for an additional 2-3 minutes. Stir in barbecue sauce, apple cider vinegar, and chicken broth. Bring to a boil.
4. Reduce heat to low and simmer for about 45 minutes, or until pork is tender.
5. Use two forks to shred the pork into small pieces.
6. Ladle hot pulled pork into sterilized jars, leaving 1-inch (2.5 cm) headspace.
7. Wipe the rims, place lids, and screw on bands until fingertip-tight.
8. Place jars in the pressure canner, lock the lid, and bring to a boil on high heat. Let vent for 10 minutes, then close the vent and continue heating to achieve 10 pounds pressure. Process for 75 minutes.
9. Turn off heat and let pressure drop naturally before opening canner and removing jars to cool.

CLASSIC CHICKEN NOODLE SOUP

PREPARATION TIME: 20 MINUTES
COOKING TIME: 1 HOUR COOKING, 90 MINUTES PRESSURE CANNING
SERVINGS: ABOUT 6 QUART-SIZED JARS (32 OUNCES EACH)

MAXIMUM STORAGE TIME: 3 YEARS (UNOPENED). ONCE OPENED, REFRIGERATE AND USE WITHIN 1 WEEK
RECOMMENDED HEADSPACE: LEAVE 1 INCH (25 MM) HEADSPACE

INGREDIENTS

- *4 lbs chicken breast or thighs, cut into 1-inch pieces (about 1.8 kg)*
- *4 cups sliced carrots (about 1 kg)*
- *3 cups sliced celery (about 750 grams)*
- *2 cups chopped onions (about 500 grams)*
- *1 tablespoon minced garlic (about 15 grams)*
- *8 cups chicken broth (about 2 liters)*
- *2 teaspoons dried thyme (4 grams)*
- *2 teaspoons dried parsley (4 grams)*
- *Salt and black pepper to taste*
- *2 tablespoons olive oil*
- *6 cups egg noodles, uncooked (add when serving) (about 600 grams)*
- *6 clean quart-sized canning jars with lids and bands*

INSTRUCTIONS

1. In a large skillet, heat olive oil over medium-high heat. Brown the chicken pieces, then transfer to a large pot.
2. In the same skillet, sauté onions, garlic, celery, and carrots. Add to the pot with chicken.
3. Add chicken broth, thyme, parsley, salt, and pepper to the pot. Bring to a boil, then reduce heat and simmer for about 1 hour.
4. Boil jars, lids, and bands for 10 minutes to sterilize them. Keep jars warm.
5. Ladle the hot chicken and vegetable mixture into jars, leaving 25 mm (1 inch) headspace. Remove any air bubbles.
6. Clean the rims, secure lids, and tighten rings finger-tight.
7. Pressure Canning: Process jars in a pressure canner at 10 pounds of pressure (11 pounds for dial-gauge canner) for 90 minutes for quart-sized jars.
8. Turn off heat and let pressure drop naturally after processing. Then wait 2 minutes before opening the canner. Take out the jars and leave to cool down for 12 to 24 hours. Check seals.

PREPARATION TIPS:
- Add uncooked noodles when reheating the soup to avoid them becoming too soft or mushy.
- Serve it with a side of crackers or crusty bread for a complete experience.

NUTRITIONAL VALUE (PER SERVING - 1 CUP WITHOUT NOODLES): Calories: 200, Carbohydrates: 5g, Fat: 7g, Protein: 30g, Sodium: 600mg, Sugar: 2g

---

SOUTHWESTERN CHICKEN STEW

PREPARATION TIME: 25 MINUTES
COOKING TIME: 1 HOUR COOKING, 90 MINUTES PRESSURE CANNING
SERVINGS: ABOUT 6 QUART-SIZED JARS (32 OUNCES EACH)

MAXIMUM STORAGE TIME: 3 YEARS (UNOPENED). ONCE OPENED, REFRIGERATE AND USE WITHIN 1 WEEK
RECOMMENDED HEADSPACE: LEAVE 1 INCH (25 MM) HEADSPACE

INGREDIENTS

- 4 lbs boneless, skinless chicken thighs, cut into 1-inch pieces (about 1.8 kg)
- 3 cups black beans, cooked (about 600 grams)
- 2 cups frozen corn (about 300 grams)
- 2 large bell peppers, diced (about 500 grams)
- 1 large onion, chopped (about 200 grams)
- 3 cloves garlic, minced
- 1 can (14.5 ounces) diced tomatoes with juice
- 1 can (4 ounces) green chilies, chopped
- 2 teaspoons ground cumin (4 grams)
- 1 teaspoon smoked paprika (2 grams)
- 1/2 teaspoon chili powder (adjust to taste)
- Salt and black pepper to taste
- 8 cups chicken broth (about 2 liters)
- 2 tablespoons olive oil
- 6 clean quart-sized canning jars with lids and bands

INSTRUCTIONS

1. In a large skillet, heat olive oil over medium-high heat. Brown the chicken pieces, then transfer to a large pot.
2. Add black beans, corn, bell peppers, onion, garlic, diced tomatoes, green chilies, cumin, smoked paprika, chili powder, salt, pepper, and chicken broth to the pot.
3. Bring to a boil, then reduce heat and simmer for about 1 hour, or until the chicken is tender and flavors are well combined.
4. Boil jars, lids, and bands for 10 minutes to sterilize them. Keep jars warm.
5. Ladle the hot stew into jars, leaving 25 mm (1 inch) headspace. Remove any air bubbles.
6. Clean the rims, secure lids, and tighten rings finger-tight.
7. Process jars in a pressure canner at 10 pounds of pressure (11 pounds for dial-gauge canner) for 90 minutes for quart-sized jars.
8. Turn off heat and let pressure drop naturally after processing. Then wait 2 minutes before opening the canner. Take out the jars and leave to cool down for 12 to 24 hours. Check seals.

NUTRITIONAL VALUE (PER SERVING - 1 CUP): Calories: 220, Carbohydrates: 15g, Fat: 8g, Protein: 25g, Sodium: 700mg, Sugar: 3g

---

HOMESTYLE CHICKEN POT PIE FILLING

PREPARATION TIME: 30 MINUTES
COOKING TIME: 45 MINUTES COOKING, 75 MINUTES PRESSURE CANNING
SERVINGS: ABOUT 6 QUART-SIZED JARS (32 OUNCES EACH)

MAXIMUM STORAGE TIME: 3 YEARS (UNOPENED). ONCE OPENED, REFRIGERATE AND USE WITHIN 1 WEEK
RECOMMENDED HEADSPACE: LEAVE 1 INCH (25 MM) HEADSPACE

INGREDIENTS

- 4 lbs boneless, skinless chicken breasts, cut into cubes (about 1.8 kg)
- 3 cups diced potatoes (about 750 grams)
- 2 cups sliced carrots (about 500 grams)
- 1 cup diced onions (about 200 grams)
- 1 cup frozen peas (about 150 grams)
- 1 cup sliced celery (about 250 grams)
- 4 cups chicken broth (about 1 liter)
- 1 cup heavy cream (about 240 ml)
- 2 tblsp cornstarch mixed with 2 tblsp water
- 1 teaspoon dried thyme (2 grams)
- 1 teaspoon dried parsley (2 grams)
- Salt and black pepper to taste
- 2 tablespoons olive oil
- 6 clean quart-sized canning jars with lids and bands

CONTINUED →

INSTRUCTIONS

1. In a large pot, heat olive oil over medium heat. Add chicken, potatoes, carrots, onions, and celery. Cook until the chicken is no longer pink and vegetables begin to soften.
2. Pour in chicken broth, add thyme, parsley, salt, and pepper. Bring to a simmer and cook for about 30 minutes.
3. Mix cornstarch with water to create a slurry. Stir this into the pot along with the frozen peas. Cook until the mixture thickens slightly, then remove from heat and whisk in heavy cream.
4. Boil jars, lids, and bands for 10 minutes to sterilize them. Keep jars warm.
5. Ladle the hot chicken pot pie filling into jars, leaving 25 mm (1 inch) headspace. Remove any air bubbles.
6. Clean the rims, secure lids, and tighten rings finger-tight.
7. Process jars in a pressure canner at 11 pounds of pressure (for weighted-gauge canner) or 10 pounds (for dial-gauge canner) for 75 minutes for quart-sized jars.
8. Turn off heat and let pressure drop naturally after processing. Then wait 2 minutes before opening the canner. Take out the jars and leave to cool down for 12 to 24 hours. Check seals.

NUTRITIONAL VALUE (PER SERVING - 1 CUP): Calories: 220, Carbohydrates: 18g, Fat: 8g, Protein: 20g, Sodium: 400mg, Sugar: 3g

---

CREAMY CHICKEN AND MUSHROOM SOUP

PREPARATION TIME: 20 MINUTES
COOKING TIME: 1 HOUR COOKING, 90 MINUTES PRESSURE CANNING
SERVINGS: ABOUT 6 QUART-SIZED JARS (32 OUNCES EACH)

MAXIMUM STORAGE TIME: 3 YEARS (UNOPENED). ONCE OPENED, REFRIGERATE AND USE WITHIN 1 WEEK
RECOMMENDED HEADSPACE: LEAVE 1 INCH (25 MM) HEADSPACE

INGREDIENTS

- 4 lbs boneless, skinless chicken breast, cut into 1-inch pieces (about 1.8 kg)
- 4 cups sliced mushrooms (about 1 kg)
- 2 cups diced onions (about 500 grams)
- 1 cup diced celery (about 250 grams)
- 3 cloves garlic, minced
- 6 cups chicken broth (about 1.5 liters)

- 2 cups heavy cream (about 480 ml)
- 1 teaspoon dried thyme (2 grams)
- 1 teaspoon dried rosemary (2 grams)
- Salt and black pepper to taste
- 2 tablespoons butter
- 6 clean quart-sized canning jars with lids and bands

INSTRUCTIONS

1. In a large pot, melt butter over medium-high heat. Add chicken, mushrooms, onions, celery, and garlic. Sauté until the chicken is cooked through and vegetables are softened.
2. Pour in chicken broth, add thyme, rosemary, salt, and black pepper. Bring to a boil, then reduce heat and simmer for about 1 hour.
3. After simmering, add heavy cream to the soup, stirring well. Heat through, but do not boil.
4. Boil jars, lids, and bands for 10 minutes to sterilize them. Keep jars warm.
5. Ladle the hot soup into jars, leaving 25 mm (1 inch) headspace. Remove any air bubbles.
6. Clean the rims, secure lids, and tighten rings finger-tight.
7. Process jars in a pressure canner at 10 pounds of pressure (11 pounds for dial-gauge canner) for 90 minutes for quart-sized jars.
8. Turn off heat and let pressure drop naturally after processing. Then wait 2 minutes before opening the canner. Take out the jars and leave to cool down for 12 to 24 hours. Check seals.

TURKEY CHILI WITH BEANS

PREPARATION TIME: 25 MINUTES
COOKING TIME: 1 HOUR COOKING, 90 MINUTES PRESSURE CANNING
SERVINGS: ABOUT 6 QUART-SIZED JARS (32 OUNCES EACH)

MAXIMUM STORAGE TIME: 3 YEARS (UNOPENED). ONCE OPENED, REFRIGERATE AND USE WITHIN 1 WEEK
RECOMMENDED HEADSPACE: LEAVE 1 INCH (25 MM) HEADSPACE

INGREDIENTS

- 4 lbs ground turkey (about 1.8 kg)
- 3 cups cooked kidney beans (about 600 grams)
- 2 cups diced tomatoes (canned or fresh, about 500 grams)
- 2 large onions, chopped (about 400 grams)
- 1 bell pepper, diced (about 200 grams)
- 4 cloves garlic, minced
- 1/4 cup chili powder (20 grams)

- 2 teaspoons ground cumin (4 grams)
- 1 teaspoon smoked paprika (2 grams)
- 1/2 teaspoon cayenne pepper (adjust to taste)
- Salt and black pepper to taste
- 8 cups turkey or chicken broth (about 2 liters)
- 2 tablespoons olive oil
- 6 clean quart-sized canning jars with lids and bands

INSTRUCTIONS

1. In a large skillet, heat olive oil over medium-high heat. Add ground turkey and cook until browned, breaking it up as it cooks.
2. In a large pot, combine browned turkey, kidney beans, diced tomatoes, onions, bell pepper, garlic, chili powder, cumin, smoked paprika, cayenne pepper, salt, pepper, and broth.
3. Bring the mixture to a boil, then reduce heat and simmer for about 1 hour, stirring occasionally, until flavors are well combined and vegetables are tender.
4. Boil jars, lids, and bands for 10 minutes to sterilize them. Keep jars warm.
5. Ladle the hot chili into jars, leaving 25 mm (1 inch) headspace. Remove any air bubbles.
6. Clean the rims, secure lids, and tighten rings finger-tight.
7. Pressure Canning: Process jars in a pressure canner at 10 pounds of pressure (11 pounds for dial-gauge canner) for 90 minutes for quart-sized jars.
8. Turn off heat and let pressure drop naturally after processing. Then wait 2 minutes before opening the canner. Take out the jars and leave to cool down for 12 to 24 hours. Check seals.

PREPARATION TIPS:
- The chili can be customized with additional spices or ingredients like corn or other beans.

NUTRITIONAL VALUE (PER SERVING - 1 CUP): Calories: 260, Carbohydrates: 20g, Fat: 8g, Protein: 28g, Sodium: 500mg, Sugar: 4g

HEARTY TURKEY AND VEGETABLE SOUP

PREPARATION TIME: 30 MINUTES
COOKING TIME: 1 HOUR COOKING, 90 MINUTES PRESSURE CANNING
SERVINGS: ABOUT 6 QUART-SIZED JARS (32 OUNCES EACH)

MAXIMUM STORAGE TIME: 2-3 YEARS (UNOPENED). ONCE OPENED, REFRIGERATE AND USE WITHIN A WEEK
RECOMMENDED HEADSPACE: LEAVE 1 INCH (25 MM) HEADSPACE

INGREDIENTS

- 4 lbs turkey breast, cut into 1-inch cubes (1.8 kg)
- 4 cups diced carrots (about 1 kg)
- 3 cups diced potatoes (about 750 grams)
- 2 cups diced celery (about 500 grams)
- 2 cups chopped onions (about 500 grams)
- 4 cloves garlic, minced
- 8 cups turkey or chicken broth (about 2 liters)
- 2 teaspoons dried thyme (4 grams)
- 2 teaspoons dried rosemary (4 grams)
- Salt and black pepper to taste
- 2 tablespoons olive oil
- 6 clean quart-sized canning jars with lids and bands

INSTRUCTIONS

1. In a large pot, heat olive oil over medium heat. Add turkey cubes and brown slightly. Add onions, garlic, carrots, potatoes, and celery. Cook until vegetables are slightly softened.
2. Pour in turkey or chicken broth, add thyme, rosemary, salt, and black pepper. Bring to a boil, then reduce heat and simmer for about 1 hour, or until the turkey is cooked through and vegetables are tender.
3. Boil jars, lids, and bands for 10 minutes to sterilize them. Keep jars warm.
4. Ladle the hot soup into jars, leaving 1 inch (25 mm) headspace. Ensure you distribute the turkey and vegetables evenly among the jars. Remove air bubbles with a non-metallic spatula. 5. Sealing: Wipe the rims with a clean, damp cloth to remove any residue. Place the lids on the jars and screw on the bands until they are fingertip tight.
6. Process jars in a pressure canner at 10 pounds of pressure (11 pounds for dial-gauge canner) for 90 minutes for quart-sized jars.
7. Turn off the heat and let the canner depressurize naturally after processing. Wait for 2 minutes before opening the canner lid. Remove jars using a jar lifter and let them cool on a towel or wooden surface for 12-24 hours. Check seals.

NUTRITIONAL VALUE (PER SERVING - 1 CUP): Calories: 180, Carbohydrates: 15g, Fat: 4g, Protein: 20g, Sodium: 300mg, Sugar: 3g

---

TURKEY AND WILD RICE SOUP

PREPARATION TIME: 20 MINUTES
COOKING TIME: 1 HOUR COOKING, 90 MINUTES PRESSURE CANNING
SERVINGS: ABOUT 6 QUART-SIZED JARS (32 OUNCES EACH)

MAXIMUM STORAGE TIME: 2-3 YEARS (UNOPENED). ONCE OPENED, REFRIGERATE AND USE WITHIN A WEEK
RECOMMENDED HEADSPACE: LEAVE 1 INCH (25 MM) HEADSPACE

INGREDIENTS

- 4 lbs turkey breast, cut into 1-inch cubes (1.8 kg)
- 3 cups wild rice, rinsed (about 600 grams)

- 2 cups sliced mushrooms (about 500 grams)
- 2 cups chopped onions (about 500 grams)
- 1 cup chopped celery (about 250 grams)
- 1 cup chopped carrots (about 250 grams)
- 6 cloves garlic, minced
- 8 cups turkey or chicken broth (about 2 liters)

- 2 teaspoons dried thyme (4 grams)
- 2 teaspoons dried sage (4 grams)
- Salt and black pepper to taste
- 2 tablespoons olive oil
- 6 clean quart-sized canning jars with lids and bands

INSTRUCTIONS

1. In a large pot, heat olive oil over medium heat. Add turkey cubes and sauté until lightly browned. Add onions, celery, carrots, garlic, and mushrooms, cooking until vegetables are softened.
2. Stir in wild rice, then pour in turkey or chicken broth. Season with sage, thyme, salt, and black pepper.
3. Bring the mixture to a boil, then reduce heat and simmer for about 1 hour.
4. Boil jars, lids, and bands for 10 minutes to sterilize them. Keep jars warm.
5. Ladle the hot soup into jars, leaving 25 mm (1 inch) headspace. Remove any air bubbles.
6. Wipe the rims with a clean, damp cloth to remove any residue. Place the lids on the jars and screw on the bands until they are fingertip tight.
7. Process jars in a pressure canner at 11 pounds of pressure (for weighted-gauge canner) or 10 pounds (for dial-gauge canner) for 90 minutes for quart-sized jars.
8. Turn off the heat and let the canner depressurize naturally after processing. Wait for 2 minutes before opening the canner lid. Remove jars using a jar lifter and leave to cool down for 12 to 24 hours. Check seals.

PREPARATION TIPS:
- Wild rice adds a nutty flavor and hearty texture to the soup, making it satisfying and nutritious.
- This soup is perfect for a warm, comforting meal and pairs well with crusty bread or a green salad.

NUTRITIONAL VALUE (PER SERVING - 1 CUP): Calories: 220, Carbohydrates: 25g, Fat: 4g, Protein: 25g, Sodium: 500mg, Sugar: 3g

SAVORY TURKEY STEW WITH HERBS

PREPARATION TIME: 30 MINUTES
COOKING TIME: 1 HOUR 15 MINUTES COOKING, 90 MINUTES PRESSURE CANNING
SERVINGS: ABOUT 6 QUART-SIZED JARS (32 OUNCES EACH)

MAXIMUM STORAGE TIME: 2-3 YEARS (UNOPENED). ONCE OPENED, REFRIGERATE AND USE WITHIN 1 WEEK
RECOMMENDED HEADSPACE: LEAVE 1 INCH (25 MM) HEADSPACE

INGREDIENTS

- 4 lbs turkey thighs, deboned and cut into 1-inch pieces (about 1.8 kg)
- 3 cups quartered baby potatoes (about 750 grams)
- 2 cups chopped carrots (about 500 grams)
- 2 cups chopped parsnips (about 500 grams)
- 1 large onion, diced (about 200 grams)
- 3 cloves garlic, minced

- 8 cups chicken or turkey broth (about 2 liters)
- 1 teaspoon dried rosemary (2 grams)
- 1 teaspoon dried thyme (2 grams)
- 1/2 teaspoon dried sage (1 gram)
- Salt and black pepper to taste
- 2 tablespoons olive oil
- 6 clean quart-sized canning jars with lids and bands

CONTINUED

INSTRUCTIONS

1. In a large skillet, heat olive oil over medium-high heat. Brown the turkey pieces, then transfer to a large pot.
2. Add potatoes, carrots, parsnips, onion, and garlic to the pot.
3. Pour in chicken or turkey broth. Stir in sage, thyme, rosemary, salt, and black pepper.
4. Bring the mixture to a boil, then reduce heat and simmer for about 1 hour 15 minutes, or until the turkey is tender and the vegetables are cooked through.
5. Boil jars, lids, and bands for 10 minutes to sterilize them. Keep jars warm.
6. Ladle the hot stew into jars, leaving 25 mm (1 inch) headspace. Remove any air bubbles.
7. Clean the rims, secure lids, and tighten rings finger-tight.
8. Process jars in a pressure canner at 10 pounds of pressure (11 pounds for dial-gauge canner) for 90 minutes for quart-sized jars.
9. Turn off heat and let pressure drop naturally after processing. Then wait 2 minutes before opening the canner. Take out the jars and leave to cool down for 12 to 24 hours. Check seals.

SHOPPING TIPS:
- Select turkey thighs for more flavor; they tend to be juicier and more tender than breast meat.
- Look for fresh, firm vegetables for the stew, as they hold up better during canning.

PREPARATION TIPS:
- Browning the turkey before simmering adds depth to the stew's flavor.
- Serve with crusty bread or over rice for a complete meal.

NUTRITIONAL VALUE (PER SERVING - 1 CUP): Calories: 230, Carbohydrates: 18g, Fat: 6g, Protein: 28g, Sodium: 500mg, Sugar: 5g

---

FISH AND SEAFOOD

LEMON-DILL SALMON

PREPARATION TIME: 20 MINUTES
COOKING TIME: 1 HOUR COOKING, 100 MINUTES PRESSURE CANNING
SERVINGS: YIELDS ABOUT 6 PINT-SIZED JARS (16 OUNCES EACH)

MAXIMUM STORAGE TIME: 2 YEARS (UNOPENED). ONCE OPENED, REFRIGERATE AND USE WITHIN 3 DAYS
RECOMMENDED HEADSPACE: LEAVE 1 INCH (25 MM) HEADSPACE

INGREDIENTS

- 4 lbs fresh salmon fillets, skin removed (1.8 kg)
- 2 lemons, thinly sliced
- Fresh dill, roughly chopped (about 40 grams)
- 1 teaspoon salt (5 grams) per jar
- 1/2 teaspoon black pepper (1 gram) per jar
- 6 clean pint-sized canning jars with lids and bands

INSTRUCTIONS

1. Cut the salmon into pieces that will fit into your jars, leaving 1 inch (25 mm) headspace at the top.
2. Place a layer of lemon slices and a sprinkle of dill at the bottom of each jar. Add the salmon pieces, then

top with more lemon slices and dill. Sprinkle salt and pepper into each jar.
3. Boil jars, lids, and bands for 10 minutes to sterilize them. Keep jars warm.
4. Pack the salmon into jars, ensuring you maintain the 25 mm (1 inch) headspace. Remove any air bubbles by gently tapping the jars.
5. Clean the rims, secure lids, and tighten rings finger-tight.
6. Process jars in a pressure canner at 11 pounds of pressure (for weighted-gauge canner) or 10 pounds (for dial-gauge canner) for 100 minutes for pint-sized jars.
7. Turn off heat and let pressure drop naturally after processing. Then wait 2 minutes before opening the canner. Take out the jars and leave to cool down for 12 to 24 hours. Check seals.

PREPARATION TIPS:
- This lemon-dill salmon is versatile and can be used in salads, as a main dish, or in sandwiches.
- Ensure that the salmon is packed tightly in the jars to prevent it from breaking apart during canning.

NUTRITIONAL VALUE (PER SERVING - 1/2 JAR): Calories: 280, Carbohydrates: 0g, Fat: 13g, Protein: 38g, Sodium: 500mg, Sugar: 0g

---

SPICY TUNA CAKES

PREPARATION TIME: 30 MINUTES
COOKING TIME: 45 MINUTES COOKING, 100 MINUTES PRESSURE CANNING
SERVINGS: 6 PINT-SIZED JARS (16 OUNCES EACH)

MAXIMUM STORAGE TIME: 18 MONTHS (UNOPENED). ONCE OPENED, REFRIGERATE AND USE WITHIN 3 DAYS
RECOMMENDED HEADSPACE: LEAVE 1 INCH (25 MM) HEADSPACE

INGREDIENTS

- *4 lbs canned tuna in water, drained (about 1.8 kg)*
- *1 cup finely chopped onions (about 200 grams)*
- *1 cup finely chopped red bell peppers (200 grams)*
- *1/2 cup chopped fresh parsley (about 20 grams)*
- *2 tablespoons hot sauce (adjust to taste) (30 ml)*
- *2 teaspoons garlic powder (4 grams)*
- *Salt and black pepper to taste*
- *6 clean pint-sized canning jars with lids and bands*

INSTRUCTIONS

1. In a large bowl, mix together the drained tuna, onions, bell peppers, parsley, hot sauce, garlic powder, salt, and black pepper. Form the mixture into small patties that will fit into the jars.
2. Boil jars, lids, and bands for 10 minutes to sterilize them. Keep jars warm.
3. Place tuna patties into jars, leaving 1 inch (25 mm) headspace.
4. Clean the rims, secure lids, and tighten rings finger-tight.
5. Process jars in a pressure canner at 11 pounds of pressure (for weighted-gauge canner) or 10 pounds (for dial-gauge canner) for 100 minutes for pint-sized jars.
6. Turn off heat and let pressure drop naturally after processing. Then wait 2 minutes before opening the canner. Take out the jars and leave to cool down for 12 to 24 hours. Check seals.

PREPARATION TIPS: These spicy tuna cakes can be used as a quick protein addition to salads, sandwiches, or served with a side of vegetables.

NUTRITIONAL VALUE (PER SERVING - 1/2 JAR): Calories: 210, Carbohydrates: 4g, Fat: 5g, Protein: 35g, Sodium: 500mg, Sugar: 2g

MEDITERRANEAN SARDINE SPREAD

PREPARATION TIME: 20 MINUTES
COOKING TIME: NO COOKING REQUIRED, 100 MINUTES PRESSURE CANNING
SERVINGS: ABOUT 6 PINT-SIZED JARS (16 OUNCES EACH)

MAXIMUM STORAGE TIME: 2 YEARS (UNOPENED). ONCE OPENED, REFRIGERATE AND USE WITHIN 3 DAYS
RECOMMENDED HEADSPACE: LEAVE 1 INCH (25 MM) HEADSPACE

INGREDIENTS

- 4 lbs sardines, fresh or pre-canned and drained (about 1.8 kg)
- 1 cup chopped Kalamata olives (about 150 grams)
- 1/2 cup capers, drained (about 60 grams)
- 1/2 cup chopped fresh parsley (about 20 grams)
- 1/4 cup extra virgin olive oil (60 ml)
- 2 lemons, zested and juiced
- 2 teaspoons dried oregano (4 grams)
- Salt and black pepper to taste
- 6 clean pint-sized canning jars with lids and bands

INSTRUCTIONS

1. In a large bowl, combine sardines, Kalamata olives, capers, olive oil, parsley, oregano, lemon juice, lemon zest, salt, and black pepper. Gently mix to combine without breaking the sardines too much.
2. Boil jars, lids, and bands for 10 minutes to sterilize them. Keep jars warm.
3. Pack the sardine mixture into jars, leaving 1 inch (25 mm) headspace.
4. Clean the rims, secure lids, and tighten rings finger-tight.
5. Process jars in a pressure canner at 11 pounds of pressure (for weighted-gauge canner) or 10 pounds (for dial-gauge canner) for 100 minutes for pint-sized jars.
6. Turn off heat and let pressure drop naturally after processing. Then wait 2 minutes before opening the canner. Take out the jars and leave to cool down for 12 to 24 hours. Check seals.

PREPARATION TIPS:
- This Mediterranean sardine spread is versatile and can be used on toast, as part of an appetizer platter, or as a filling for sandwiches.
- The combination of olives, capers, and lemon gives a fresh and tangy flavor to the sardines, making it a delightful Mediterranean treat.

NUTRITIONAL VALUE (PER SERVING - 1/4 JAR): Calories: 190, Carbohydrates: 3g, Fat: 12g, Protein: 18g, Sodium: 650mg, Sugar: 1g

---

HERB-INFUSED TROUT FILLETS

PREPARATION TIME: 15 MINUTES
COOKING TIME: NO COOKING REQUIRED, 100 MINUTES PRESSURE CANNING
SERVINGS: ABOUT 6 PINT-SIZED JARS (16 OUNCES EACH)

MAXIMUM STORAGE TIME: 2 YEARS (UNOPENED). ONCE OPENED, REFRIGERATE AND USE WITHIN 3 DAYS
RECOMMENDED HEADSPACE: LEAVE 1 INCH (25 MM) HEADSPACE

INGREDIENTS

- 4 lbs trout fillets, skin removed (about 1.8 kg)
- 2 lemons, thinly sliced
- 1 bunch fresh dill, roughly chopped (40 grams)
- 1 bunch fresh parsley, roughly chopped (40 grams)
- 1 tablespoon black peppercorns (15 grams)
- 2 teaspoons sea salt (10 grams) per jar
- 6 clean pint-sized canning jars with lids and bands

INSTRUCTIONS

1. Cut the trout fillets into pieces that will fit into your jars, leaving 1 inch (25 mm) headspace at the top.
2. Place a layer of lemon slices at the bottom of each jar. Add the trout pieces, and top with more lemon slices, dill, parsley, peppercorns, and sea salt.
3. Boil jars, lids, and bands for 10 minutes to sterilize them. Keep jars warm.
4. Ensure the trout is packed well into the jars, maintaining the 25 mm (1 inch) headspace.
5. Clean the rims, secure lids, and tighten rings finger-tight.
6. Process jars in a pressure canner at 11 pounds of pressure (for weighted-gauge canner) or 10 pounds (for dial-gauge canner) for 100 minutes for pint-sized jars.
7. Turn off heat and let pressure drop naturally after processing. Then wait 2 minutes before opening the canner. Take out the jars and leave to cool down for 12 to 24 hours. Check seals.

PREPARATION TIPS:

- This herb-infused trout is perfect for a light meal or as a gourmet addition to salads and pasta dishes.
- The lemon and herbs provide a fresh and aromatic flavor, complementing the trout's natural taste.

NUTRITIONAL VALUE (PER SERVING - 1/4 JAR): Calories: 210, Carbohydrates: 1g, Fat: 8g, Protein: 32g, Sodium: 500mg, Sugar: 0g

---

CURRIED MACKEREL IN TOMATO SAUCE

PREPARATION TIME: 25 MINUTES
COOKING TIME: 30 MINUTES COOKING, 100 MINUTES PRESSURE CANNING
SERVINGS: ABOUT 6 PINT-SIZED JARS (16 OUNCES EACH)

MAXIMUM STORAGE TIME: 2 YEARS (UNOPENED). ONCE OPENED, REFRIGERATE AND USE WITHIN 3 DAYS
RECOMMENDED HEADSPACE: LEAVE 1 INCH (25 MM) HEADSPACE

INGREDIENTS

- 4 lbs mackerel fillets, cut into pieces (about 1.8 kg)
- 2 cups diced tomatoes (fresh or canned)
- 1 large onion, finely chopped (about 200 grams)
- 3 cloves garlic, minced
- 2 tablespoons curry powder (10 grams)
- 1 teaspoon ground cumin (2 grams)
- 1/2 teaspoon ground turmeric (1 gram)
- 1/2 teaspoon cayenne pepper (adjust to taste)

- Salt and black pepper to taste
- 2 tablespoons vegetable oil
- 1/4 cup fresh cilantro, chopped (for garnish)
- 6 clean pint-sized canning jars with lids and bands

CONTINUED →

INSTRUCTIONS

1. In a large skillet, heat vegetable oil over medium heat. Add onions and garlic, sautéing until softened. Stir in curry powder, cumin, turmeric, cayenne pepper, salt, and black pepper. Cook until thickened adding diced tomatoes.
2. Place the mackerel pieces into the curry mixture, and gently coat them with the sauce. Cook for about 10 minutes, or until the fish is cooked through.
3. Boil jars, lids, and bands for 10 minutes to sterilize them. Keep jars warm.
4. Spoon the mackerel and tomato curry into jars, leaving 1 inch (25 mm) headspace. Ensure even distribution of fish and sauce.
5. Clean the rims, secure lids, and tighten rings finger-tight.
6. Process jars in a pressure canner at 11 pounds of pressure (for weighted-gauge canner) or 10 pounds (for dial-gauge canner) for 100 minutes for pint-sized jars.
7. Turn off heat and let pressure drop naturally after processing. Then wait 2 minutes before opening the canner. Take out the jars and leave to cool down for 12 to 24 hours. Check seals.

PREPARATION TIPS:

- Gently simmering the mackerel in the curry sauce helps infuse the fish with the aromatic spices.
- This curried mackerel can be served with flatbreads or over rice.
- Garnish with fresh cilantro before serving.

NUTRITIONAL VALUE (PER SERVING - 1/4 JAR): Calories: 230, Carbohydrates: 5g, Fat: 15g, Protein: 20g, Sodium: 400mg, Sugar: 2g

CLASSIC NEW ENGLAND CLAM CHOWDER

PREPARATION TIME: 35 MINUTES
COOKING TIME: 45 MINUTES COOKING, 100 MINUTES PRESSURE CANNING
SERVINGS: ABOUT 6 QUART-SIZED JARS (32 OUNCES EACH)

MAXIMUM STORAGE TIME: 18 MONTHS (UNOPENED). ONCE OPENED, REFRIGERATE AND USE WITHIN 1 WEEK
RECOMMENDED HEADSPACE: LEAVE 1 INCH (25 MM) HEADSPACE

INGREDIENTS

- *4 lbs fresh clams, shucked, with juice reserved (about 1.8 kg)*
- *4 cups diced potatoes (about 1 kg)*
- *2 cups diced onions (about 500 grams)*
- *2 cups diced celery (about 500 grams)*
- *4 cloves garlic, minced*
- *6 cups fish or seafood broth (about 1.5 liters)*

- *2 cups heavy cream (about 480 ml)*
- *1/4 cup unsalted butter (about 60 grams)*
- *2 tablespoons all-purpose flour (30 grams)*
- *1 teaspoon dried thyme (2 grams)*
- *Salt and black pepper to taste*
- *6 clean quart-sized canning jars with lids and bands*

INSTRUCTIONS

1. In a large pot, melt butter over medium heat. Add onions, celery, and garlic, sautéing until softened. Sprinkle flour over the vegetables and cook for 2 minutes.
2. Stir in fish or seafood broth, diced potatoes, thyme, salt, and black pepper. Bring to a simmer and cook for about 20 minutes.
3. Stir in the clams and their juice, and cook for an additional 10 minutes.

4. Boil jars, lids, and bands for 10 minutes to sterilize them. Keep jars warm.
5. Turn off the heat and stir in the heavy cream.
6. Ladle the hot chowder into jars, leaving 25 mm (1 inch) headspace. Remove any air bubbles.
7. Clean the rims, secure lids, and tighten rings finger-tight.
8. Process jars in a pressure canner at 11 pounds of pressure (for weighted-gauge canner) or 10 pounds (for dial-gauge canner) for 100 minutes for quart-sized jars.
9. Turn off heat and let pressure drop naturally after processing. Then wait 2 minutes before opening the canner. Take out the jars and leave to cool down for 12 to 24 hours. Check seals.

PREPARATION TIPS:
- This classic clam chowder is perfect for a comforting and hearty meal, especially during colder months.
- Serve with oyster crackers or crusty bread for a complete dining experience.

NUTRITIONAL VALUE (PER SERVING - 1 CUP): Calories: 250, Carbohydrates: 20g, Fat: 15g, Protein: 10g, Sodium: 400mg, Sugar: 3g

SPICY SHRIMP CREOLE

PREPARATION TIME: 30 MINUTES
COOKING TIME: 30 MINUTES COOKING, 100 MINUTES PRESSURE CANNING
SERVINGS: ABOUT 6 QUART-SIZED JARS (32 OUNCES EACH)

MAXIMUM STORAGE TIME: 2 YEARS (UNOPENED). ONCE OPENED, REFRIGERATE AND USE WITHIN 3 DAYS
RECOMMENDED HEADSPACE: LEAVE 1 INCH (25 MM) HEADSPACE

INGREDIENTS

- 4 lbs large shrimp, peeled and deveined (1.8 kg)
- 2 cups diced tomatoes (fresh or canned)
- 1 large onion, chopped (about 200 grams)
- 1 green bell pepper, chopped (about 200 grams)
- 1 red bell pepper, chopped (about 200 grams)
- 3 cloves garlic, minced
- 1/4 cup tomato paste (60 ml)
- 2 tablespoons Cajun seasoning (10 grams)
- 1 teaspoon smoked paprika (2 grams)
- 1/2 teaspoon cayenne pepper (adjust to taste)
- Salt and black pepper to taste
- 2 tablespoons vegetable oil

INSTRUCTIONS

1. In a large skillet, heat vegetable oil over medium heat. Add onions, bell peppers, and garlic, cooking until softened.
2. Stir in diced tomatoes, Cajun seasoning, tomato paste, cayenne pepper, smoked paprika, salt, and black pepper. Cook for about 10 minutes, until the mixture thickens slightly.
3. Add shrimp to the skillet and cook until just pink, about 5 minutes.
4. Boil jars, lids, and bands for 10 minutes to sterilize them. Keep jars warm.
5. Spoon the shrimp mixture into jars, leaving 25 mm (1 inch) headspace. Remove any air bubbles.
6. Clean the rims, secure lids, and tighten rings finger-tight.
7. Process jars in a pressure canner at 11 pounds of pressure (for weighted-gauge canner) or 10 pounds (for dial-gauge canner) for 100 minutes for quart-sized jars.
8. Turn off heat and let pressure drop naturally after processing. Then wait 2 minutes before opening the canner. Take out the jars and leave to cool down for 12 to 24 hours. Check seals.

NUTRITIONAL VALUE (PER SERVING - 1 CUP): Calories: 200, Carbohydrates: 10g, Fat: 6g, Protein: 25g, Sodium: 500mg, Sugar: 5g

GARLIC BUTTER SCALLOPS

PREPARATION TIME: 20 MINUTES
COOKING TIME: NO COOKING REQUIRED, 100 MINUTES PRESSURE CANNING
SERVINGS: ABOUT 6 PINT-SIZED JARS (16 OUNCES EACH)

MAXIMUM STORAGE TIME: 2 YEARS (UNOPENED). ONCE OPENED, REFRIGERATE AND USE WITHIN 3 DAYS
RECOMMENDED HEADSPACE: LEAVE 1 INCH (25 MM) HEADSPACE

INGREDIENTS

- *4 lbs sea scallops (about 1.8 kg)*
- *1 cup unsalted butter, melted (about 240 grams)*
- *4 cloves garlic, minced*
- *2 tablespoons fresh lemon juice (30 ml)*
- *2 tablespoons chopped fresh parsley (10 grams)*
- *1 teaspoon salt (5 grams)*
- *1/2 teaspoon black pepper (1 gram)*
- *6 clean pint-sized canning jars with lids and bands*

INSTRUCTIONS

1. Rinse the scallops and pat them dry.
2. In a bowl, mix together melted butter, garlic, lemon juice, parsley, salt, and black pepper.
3. Place scallops into jars, leaving 25 mm (1 inch) headspace. Pour the garlic butter mixture over the scallops, ensuring each jar has an even distribution.
4. Boil jars, lids, and bands for 10 minutes to sterilize them. Keep jars warm.
5. Clean the rims, secure lids, and tighten rings finger-tight.
6. Process jars in a pressure canner at 11 pounds of pressure (for weighted-gauge canner) or 10 pounds (for dial-gauge canner) for 100 minutes for pint-sized jars.
7. Turn off heat and let pressure drop naturally after processing. Then wait 2 minutes before opening the canner. Take out the jars and leave to cool down for 12 to 24 hours. Check seals.

PREPARATION TIPS:
- These garlic butter scallops are perfect for a luxurious appetizer or main course.
- Serve with pasta, crusty bread, or over a bed of fresh greens.

NUTRITIONAL VALUE (PER SERVING - 1/2 JAR): Calories: 300, Carbohydrates: 2g, Fat: 22g, Protein: 24g, Sodium: 600mg, Sugar: 0g

TOMATO BASIL MUSSELS

PREPARATION TIME: 25 MINUTES
COOKING TIME: NO COOKING REQUIRED, 100 MINUTES PRESSURE CANNING
SERVINGS: ABOUT 6 PINT-SIZED JARS (16 OUNCES EACH)

MAXIMUM STORAGE TIME: 18 MONTHS (UNOPENED). ONCE OPENED, REFRIGERATE AND USE WITHIN 3 DAYS
RECOMMENDED HEADSPACE: LEAVE 1 INCH (25 MM) HEADSPACE

INGREDIENTS

- *4 lbs fresh mussels, cleaned and debearded (about 1.8 kg)*
- *2 cups diced tomatoes (fresh or canned) (about 500 grams)*

146

- *1 cup dry white wine (about 240 ml)*
- *1/2 cup chopped fresh basil (about 20 grams)*
- *4 cloves garlic, minced*
- *2 tablespoons olive oil*
- *1 teaspoon salt (5 grams)*
- *1/2 teaspoon black pepper (1 gram)*
- *6 clean pint-sized canning jars with lids and bands*

INSTRUCTIONS

1. Ensure the mussels are thoroughly cleaned and debearded.
2. In a bowl, combine diced tomatoes, olive oil, white wine, garlic, basil, salt, and black pepper.
3. Place mussels into jars, leaving 25 mm (1 inch) headspace. Pour the tomato basil mixture over the mussels, making sure each jar has an even distribution.
4. Boil jars, lids, and bands for 10 minutes to sterilize them. Keep jars warm.
5. Clean the rims, secure lids, and tighten rings finger-tight.
6. Process jars in a pressure canner at 11 pounds of pressure (for weighted-gauge canner) or 10 pounds (for dial-gauge canner) for 100 minutes for pint-sized jars.
7. Turn off heat and let pressure drop naturally after processing. Then wait 2 minutes before opening the canner. Take out the jars and leave to cool down for 12 to 24 hours. Check seals.

PREPARATION TIPS: These tomato basil mussels are a delightful treat, perfect served over pasta or with crusty bread to soak up the flavorful sauce.

NUTRITIONAL VALUE (PER SERVING - 1/2 JAR): Calories: 210, Carbohydrates: 6g, Fat: 8g, Protein: 25g, Sodium: 500mg, Sugar: 2g

---

ZESTY LEMON PEPPER CRAB

PREPARATION TIME: 20 MINUTES
COOKING TIME: NO COOKING REQUIRED, 100 MINUTES PRESSURE CANNING
SERVINGS: 6 PINT-SIZED JARS (16 OUNCES EACH)

MAXIMUM STORAGE TIME: 2 YEARS (UNOPENED). ONCE OPENED, REFRIGERATE AND USE WITHIN 3 DAYS
RECOMMENDED HEADSPACE: 1 INCH (25 MM)

INGREDIENTS

- *4 lbs crab meat, fresh or canned and drained (about 1.8 kg)*
- *2 lemons, zested and juiced*
- *1/4 cup chopped fresh dill (about 15 grams)*
- *2 tablespoons black peppercorns (10 grams)*
- *2 teaspoons sea salt (10 grams)*
- *2 tablespoons olive oil*
- *6 clean pint-sized canning jars with lids and bands*

INSTRUCTIONS

1. If using fresh crab, cook, clean, and separate the meat. If using canned, drain and set aside.
2. In a bowl, mix together lemon zest, lemon juice, fresh dill, black peppercorns, sea salt, and olive oil.
3. Place crab meat into jars, leaving 1 inch (25 mm) headspace. Pour the lemon pepper mixture over the crab meat, ensuring each jar has an even distribution.
4. Boil jars, lids, and bands for 10 minutes to sterilize them. Keep jars warm.
5. Clean the rims, secure lids, and tighten rings finger-tight.
6. Process jars in a pressure canner at 11 pounds of pressure (for weighted-gauge canner) or 10 pounds (for dial-gauge canner) for 100 minutes for pint-sized jars.
7. Turn off heat and let pressure drop naturally after processing. Then wait 2 minutes before opening the canner. Take out the jars and leave to cool down for 12 to 24 hours. Check seals.

BEANS AND LEGUMES

SMOKY BARBECUE BAKED BEANS

PREPARATION TIME: 30 MINUTES
SOAKING TIME FOR BEANS: 12 HOURS
COOKING TIME: 2 HOURS COOKING, 75 MINUTES PRESSURE CANNING
SERVINGS: ABOUT 6 QUART-SIZED JARS (32 OUNCES EACH)

MAXIMUM STORAGE TIME: 2-3 YEARS (UNOPENED). ONCE OPENED, REFRIGERATE AND USE WITHIN 1 WEEK
RECOMMENDED HEADSPACE: LEAVE 1 INCH (25 MM) HEADSPACE

INGREDIENTS

- 4 lbs dry navy beans (about 1.8 kg)
- 1 large onion, chopped (about 200 grams)
- 3 cloves garlic, minced
- 1 cup barbecue sauce (240 ml)
- 1/2 cup molasses (120 ml)
- 1/3 cup brown sugar (70 grams)
- 1/4 cup apple cider vinegar (60 ml)
- 2 tablespoons Worcestershire sauce (30 ml)

- 1 tablespoon smoked paprika
- 1 teaspoon ground mustard
- 1 teaspoon chili powder
- 6 cups water (or as needed) (about 1.5 liters)
- Salt and black pepper to taste
- 6 clean quart-sized canning jars with lids and bands

INSTRUCTIONS

1. Rinse the navy beans and soak them overnight in a large pot of water.
2. Drain and rinse the beans, then return them to the pot. Cover with fresh water and bring to a boil. Reduce heat and simmer for about 1-1.5 hours.
3. In a separate bowl, mix together barbecue sauce, molasses, brown sugar, Worcestershire sauce, smoked paprika, ground mustard, apple cider vinegar, chili powder, salt, and black pepper.
4. Once beans are cooked, drain them and return to the pot. Add the chopped onion, minced garlic, and prepared sauce. Stir well and cook for an additional 30 minutes.
5. Boil jars, lids, and bands for 10 minutes to sterilize them. Keep jars warm.
6. Ladle the beans and sauce mixture into jars, leaving 25 mm (1 inch) headspace. Remove any air bubbles.
7. Clean the rims, secure lids, and tighten rings finger-tight.
8. Process jars in a pressure canner at 10 pounds of pressure (11 pounds for dial-gauge canner) for 75 minutes for quart-sized jars.
9. Turn off heat and let pressure drop naturally after processing. Then wait 2 minutes before opening the canner. Remove jars and let them cool on a towel or wooden surface for 12-24 hours. Check seals; the lid should not flex when pressed.

PREPARATION TIPS:
- Soaking the beans overnight helps reduce cooking time and improve digestibility.
- These smoky barbecue baked beans are perfect as a side dish for barbecues, picnics, or as a hearty meal on their own.

NUTRITIONAL VALUE (PER SERVING - 1 CUP): Calories: 220, Carbohydrates: 40g, Fat: 2g, Protein: 12g, Sodium: 400mg, Sugar: 15g

SPICY CHILI BEANS

PREPARATION TIME: 30 MINUTES
SOAKING TIME FOR BEANS: 12 HOURS
COOKING TIME: 1 HOUR 30 MINUTES COOKING, 75 MINUTES PRESSURE CANNING
SERVINGS: ABOUT 6 QUART-SIZED JARS (32 OUNCES EACH)

MAXIMUM STORAGE TIME: 2-3 YEARS (UNOPENED). ONCE OPENED, REFRIGERATE AND USE WITHIN 1 WEEK
RECOMMENDED HEADSPACE: LEAVE 1 INCH (25 MM) HEADSPACE

INGREDIENTS

- 4 lbs dry kidney beans (about 1.8 kg)
- 1 large onion, diced (about 200 grams)
- 2 bell peppers (one red, one green), diced
- 4 cloves garlic, minced
- 2 cans (14.5 ounces each) diced tomatoes with juice
- 3 tablespoons chili powder (15 grams)
- 2 teaspoons cumin powder (4 grams)
- 1 teaspoon smoked paprika (2 grams)
- 1/2 teaspoon cayenne pepper (adjust to taste)
- 6 cups beef or vegetable broth (about 1.5 liters)
- Salt and black pepper to taste
- 6 clean quart-sized canning jars with lids and bands

INSTRUCTIONS

1. Rinse the kidney beans and soak them overnight in a large pot of water.
2. Drain and rinse the beans, then return them to the pot. Add fresh water and bring to a boil. Reduce heat and simmer for about 1 hour.
3. In a separate pan, sauté onions, bell peppers, and garlic until softened. Add diced tomatoes with juice, chili powder, cumin, smoked paprika, cayenne pepper, salt, and black pepper. Simmer for 10 minutes.
4. Drain the cooked beans and mix them with the chili mixture. Add beef or vegetable broth and bring to a simmer.
5. Boil jars, lids, and bands for 10 minutes to sterilize them. Keep jars warm.
6. Ladle the bean mixture into jars, leaving 25 mm (1 inch) headspace. Remove any air bubbles.
7. Clean the rims, secure lids, and tighten rings finger-tight.
8. Process jars in a pressure canner at 10 pounds of pressure (11 pounds for dial-gauge canner) for 75 minutes for quart-sized jars.
9. Turn off heat and let pressure drop naturally after processing. Then wait 2 minutes before opening the canner. Take out the jars and leave to cool down for 12 to 24 hours. Check seals.

NUTRITIONAL VALUE (PER SERVING - 1 CUP): Calories: 250, Carbohydrates: 45g, Fat: 2g, Protein: 15g, Sodium: 500mg, Sugar: 5g

SWEET AND TANGY BOSTON BAKED BEANS

PREPARATION TIME: 45 MINUTES
SOAKING TIME FOR BEANS: 12 HOURS
COOKING TIME: 2 HOURS COOKING, 75 MINUTES PRESSURE CANNING
SERVINGS: ABOUT 6 QUART-SIZED JARS (32 OUNCES EACH)

MAXIMUM STORAGE TIME: 2-3 YEARS (UNOPENED). ONCE OPENED, REFRIGERATE AND USE WITHIN 1 WEEK
RECOMMENDED HEADSPACE: LEAVE 1 INCH (25 MM) HEADSPACE

CONTINUED →

INGREDIENTS

- 4 lbs dry navy beans (about 1.8 kg)
- 1 large onion, finely chopped (about 200 grams)
- 1/2 cup molasses (120 ml)
- 1/3 cup brown sugar (70 grams)
- 1/4 cup apple cider vinegar (60 ml)
- 1/4 cup tomato ketchup (60 ml)
- 1 tablespoon dry mustard powder (5 grams)
- 1 teaspoon salt (5 grams)
- 1/2 teaspoon ground black pepper (1 gram)
- 8 cups water (or as needed) (about 2 liters)
- 6 clean quart-sized canning jars with lids and bands

INSTRUCTIONS

1. Rinse the navy beans and soak them overnight in a large pot of water.
2. Drain and rinse the beans, then return them to the pot. Cover with fresh water and bring to a boil. Reduce heat and simmer for about 1.5-2 hours.
3. In a separate bowl, mix together molasses, brown sugar, apple cider vinegar, tomato ketchup, mustard powder, salt, and black pepper.
4. Once beans are cooked, drain them and return to the pot. Add the chopped onion and prepared sauce. Stir well and cook for an additional 30 minutes.
5. Boil jars, lids, and bands for 10 minutes to sterilize them. Keep jars warm.
6. Ladle the beans and sauce mixture into jars, leaving 25 mm (1 inch) headspace. Remove any air bubbles.
7. Clean the rims, secure lids, and tighten rings finger-tight.
8. Process jars in a pressure canner at 10 pounds of pressure (11 pounds for dial-gauge canner) for 75 minutes for quart-sized jars.
9. Turn off heat and let pressure drop naturally after processing. Then wait 2 minutes before opening the canner. Take out the jars and leave to cool down for 12 to 24 hours. Check seals.

NUTRITIONAL VALUE (PER SERVING - 1 CUP): Calories: 260, Carbohydrates: 50g, Fat: 1g, Protein: 14g, Sodium: 300mg, Sugar: 20g

---

HEARTY MIXED BEAN SOUP

PREPARATION TIME: 30 MINUTES
SOAKING TIME FOR BEANS: 12 HOURS
COOKING TIME: 1 HOUR 30 MINUTES COOKING, 75 MINUTES PRESSURE CANNING
SERVINGS: ABOUT 6 QUART-SIZED JARS (32 OUNCES EACH)

MAXIMUM STORAGE TIME: 2-3 YEARS (UNOPENED). ONCE OPENED, REFRIGERATE AND USE WITHIN 1 WEEK
RECOMMENDED HEADSPACE: LEAVE 1 INCH (25 MM) HEADSPACE

INGREDIENTS

- 2 lbs dry mixed beans (navy, kidney, black, pinto, etc.) (about 900 grams)
- 1 large carrot, diced (about 200 grams)
- 2 stalks celery, diced (about 200 grams)
- 1 large onion, diced (about 200 grams)
- 3 cloves garlic, minced
- 1 can (14.5 ounces) diced tomatoes with juice
- 8 cups vegetable or chicken broth (about 2 liters)
- 2 teaspoons dried thyme (4 grams)
- 2 teaspoons dried basil (4 grams)
- 1 teaspoon smoked paprika (2 grams)
- Salt and black pepper to taste
- 2 tablespoons olive oil
- 6 clean quart-sized canning jars with lids and bands

INSTRUCTIONS

1. Rinse the mixed beans and soak them overnight in a large pot of water.
2. Drain and rinse the beans, then return them to the pot. Add fresh water and bring to a boil. Reduce heat and simmer for about 1 hour.
3. In a separate pan, heat olive oil over medium heat. Sauté carrots, celery, onion, and garlic until softened.
4. Add the sautéed vegetables, diced tomatoes, broth, thyme, basil, smoked paprika, salt, and pepper to the pot with beans. Bring to a simmer and cook for 30 minutes.
5. Boil jars, lids, and bands for 10 minutes to sterilize them. Keep jars warm.
6. Ladle the soup mixture into jars, leaving 25 mm (1 inch) headspace. Remove any air bubbles.
7. Clean the rims, secure lids, and tighten rings finger-tight.
8. Process jars in a pressure canner at 10 pounds of pressure (11 pounds for dial-gauge canner) for 75 minutes for quart-sized jars.
9. Turn off heat and let pressure drop naturally after processing. Then wait 2 minutes before opening the canner. Take out the jars and leave to cool down for 12 to 24 hours. Check seals.

NUTRITIONAL VALUE (PER SERVING - 1 CUP): Calories: 180, Carbohydrates: 30g, Fat: 3g, Protein: 10g, Sodium: 300mg, Sugar: 5g

---

SPICY BLACK BEAN AND CORN SALSA

PREPARATION TIME: 15 MINUTES
COOKING TIME: NO COOKING REQUIRED, 75 MINUTES PRESSURE CANNING
SERVINGS: ABOUT 6 QUART-SIZED JARS (32 OUNCES EACH)

MAXIMUM STORAGE TIME: 2 YEARS (UNOPENED). ONCE OPENED, REFRIGERATE AND USE WITHIN 1 WEEK
RECOMMENDED HEADSPACE: LEAVE 1 INCH (25 MM) HEADSPACE

INGREDIENTS

- 4 lbs canned black beans, rinsed and drained
- 4 cups frozen corn, thawed (about 1 kg)
- 2 large red bell peppers, diced (about 400 grams)
- 2 jalapeño peppers, finely chopped (adjust to taste)
- 1 large red onion, finely chopped (200 grams)
- 1 cup chopped fresh cilantro (about 40 grams)
- 1/2 cup lime juice (about 120 ml)
- 1/4 cup olive oil (60 ml)
- 2 tablespoons ground cumin (10 grams)
- 1 tablespoon chili powder (5 grams)
- Salt and black pepper to taste
- 6 clean quart-sized canning jars with lids and bands

INSTRUCTIONS

1. In a large mixing bowl, combine black beans, corn, red bell peppers, jalapeño peppers, red onion, cilantro, lime juice, olive oil, cumin, chili powder, salt, and black pepper. Mix ingredients well for equal distribution.
2. Boil jars, lids, and bands for 10 minutes to sterilize them. Keep jars warm.
3. Spoon the salsa mixture into jars, leaving 25 mm (1 inch) headspace. Remove any air bubbles.
4. Clean the rims, secure lids, and tighten rings finger-tight.
5. Process jars in a pressure canner at 10 pounds of pressure (11 pounds for dial-gauge canner) for 75 minutes for quart-sized jars.
6. Turn off heat and let pressure drop naturally after processing. Then wait 2 minutes before opening the canner. Take out the jars and leave to cool down for 12 to 24 hours. Check seals.

NUTRITIONAL VALUE (PER SERVING - 1 CUP): Calories: 150, Carbohydrates: 25g, Fat: 4g, Protein: 6g, Sodium: 200mg, Sugar: 4g

SMOKY LENTIL STEW

PREPARATION TIME: 30 MINUTES
COOKING TIME: 1 HOUR COOKING, 75 MINUTES PRESSURE CANNING
SERVINGS: ABOUT 6 QUART-SIZED JARS (32 OUNCES EACH)

MAXIMUM STORAGE TIME: 2-3 YEARS (UNOPENED). ONCE OPENED, REFRIGERATE AND USE WITHIN 1 WEEK
RECOMMENDED HEADSPACE: LEAVE 1 INCH (25 MM) HEADSPACE

INGREDIENTS

- 4 lbs green or brown lentils, rinsed (about 1.8 kg)
- 2 large carrots, diced (about 400 grams)
- 2 stalks celery, diced (about 200 grams)
- 1 large onion, diced (about 200 grams)
- 4 cloves garlic, minced
- 8 cups vegetable broth (about 2 liters)
- 2 cans (14.5 ounces each) diced tomatoes with juice

- 2 tablespoons smoked paprika (10 grams)
- 1 tablespoon ground cumin (5 grams)
- 1 teaspoon dried thyme (2 grams)
- Salt and black pepper to taste
- 2 tablespoons olive oil
- 6 clean quart-sized canning jars with lids and bands

INSTRUCTIONS

1. In a large pot, cook lentils in vegetable broth until just tender, about 20-25 minutes. Do not overcook as they will continue cooking during canning.
2. In a separate pan, heat olive oil over medium heat. Sauté carrots, celery, onion, and garlic until softened.
3. Add the sautéed vegetables to the pot with lentils. Stir in diced tomatoes, smoked paprika, cumin, thyme, salt, and black pepper. Simmer the stew for 10-15 minutes.
4. Boil jars, lids, and bands for 10 minutes to sterilize them. Keep jars warm.
5. Ladle the stew into jars, leaving 25 mm (1 inch) headspace. Remove any air bubbles.
6. Clean the rims, secure lids, and tighten rings finger-tight.
7. Process jars in a pressure canner at 10 pounds of pressure (11 pounds for dial-gauge canner) for 75 minutes for quart-sized jars.
8. Turn off heat and let pressure drop naturally after processing. Then wait 2 minutes before opening the canner. Take out the jars and leave to cool down for 12 to 24 hours. Check seals.

PREPARATION TIPS:

- This hearty lentil stew is perfect as a standalone meal or served over rice or with crusty bread.

NUTRITIONAL VALUE (PER SERVING - 1 CUP): Calories: 220, Carbohydrates: 38g, Fat: 3g, Protein: 14g, Sodium: 300mg, Sugar: 4g

---

SOUTHWEST BLACK BEAN SOUP

PREPARATION TIME: 30 MINUTES
COOKING TIME: 1 HOUR COOKING, 75 MINUTES PRESSURE CANNING
SERVINGS: ABOUT 6 QUART-SIZED JARS (32 OUNCES EACH)

MAXIMUM STORAGE TIME: 2-3 YEARS (UNOPENED). ONCE OPENED, REFRIGERATE AND USE WITHIN 1 WEEK
RECOMMENDED HEADSPACE: LEAVE 1 INCH (25 MM) HEADSPACE

INGREDIENTS

- 4 lbs dried black beans, rinsed and soaked overnight (about 1.8 kg)
- 2 large onions, chopped (about 400 grams)
- 2 red bell peppers, diced (about 400 grams)
- 4 cloves garlic, minced
- 1 jalapeño pepper, finely chopped (adjust to taste)
- 8 cups chicken or vegetable broth (about 2 liters)
- 2 cans (14.5 ounces each) diced tomatoes with juice
- 2 tablespoons ground cumin (10 grams)
- 1 tablespoon chili powder (5 grams)
- 1 teaspoon smoked paprika (2 grams)
- Salt and black pepper to taste
- 2 tablespoons olive oil
- 1/2 cup chopped fresh cilantro (for garnish) (about 20 grams)
- 6 clean quart-sized canning jars with lids and bands

INSTRUCTIONS

1. In a large pot, cook soaked black beans in water until tender, about 45-60 minutes. Drain and set aside.
2. In another pot, heat olive oil over medium heat. Sauté onions, bell peppers, garlic, and jalapeño until softened.
3. Add cooked black beans to the pot with sautéed vegetables. Stir in broth, diced tomatoes, cumin, chili powder, smoked paprika, salt, and black pepper. Bring to a simmer and cook for 15 minutes.
4. Boil jars, lids, and bands for 10 minutes to sterilize them. Keep jars warm.
5. Ladle the soup into jars, leaving 25 mm (1 inch) headspace. Remove any air bubbles.
6. Clean the rims, secure lids, and tighten rings finger-tight.
7. Process jars in a pressure canner at 10 pounds of pressure (11 pounds for dial-gauge canner) for 75 minutes for quart-sized jars.
8. Turn off heat and let pressure drop naturally after processing. Then wait 2 minutes before opening the canner. Take out the jars and leave to cool down for 12 to 24 hours. Check seals.

NUTRITIONAL VALUE (PER SERVING - 1 CUP): Calories: 230, Carbohydrates: 40g, Fat: 4g, Protein: 15g, Sodium: 400mg, Sugar: 5g

---

CLASSIC CHICKPEA CURRY

PREPARATION TIME: 40 MINUTES
SOAKING TIME FOR CHICKPEAS: 12 HOURS
COOKING TIME: 1 HOUR 30 MINUTES COOKING, 75 MINUTES PRESSURE CANNING
SERVINGS: ABOUT 6 QUART-SIZED JARS (32 OUNCES EACH)

MAXIMUM STORAGE TIME: 2-3 YEARS (UNOPENED). ONCE OPENED, REFRIGERATE AND USE WITHIN 1 WEEK
RECOMMENDED HEADSPACE: LEAVE 1 INCH (25 MM) HEADSPACE

INGREDIENTS

- 4 lbs dried chickpeas, soaked overnight (1.8 kg)
- 2 large onions, finely chopped (about 400 grams)
- 4 cloves garlic, minced
- 1-inch piece ginger, grated (about 2.5 cm)
- 2 cans (14.5 ounces each) diced tomatoes
- 3 tablespoons curry powder (15 grams)
- 1 teaspoon turmeric powder (2 grams)
- 1/2 teaspoon cayenne pepper (adjust to taste)
- 1 teaspoon garam masala (2 grams)
- 8 cups vegetable broth (about 2 liters)
- Salt and black pepper to taste
- 2 tablespoons vegetable oil
- 1/2 cup chopped fresh cilantro (for garnish)
- 6 clean quart-sized canning jars with lids and bands

CONTINUED ➡

INSTRUCTIONS

1. In a large pot, cook the soaked chickpeas in water until tender, about 1 hour. Drain and set aside.
2. In a separate large pot, heat vegetable oil over medium heat. Sauté onions, garlic, and ginger until the onions are translucent. Add curry powder, turmeric, cayenne pepper, and garam masala, cooking for another minute.
3. Add cooked chickpeas, diced tomatoes, and vegetable broth to the pot. Season with salt and black pepper. Bring to a simmer and cook for 30 minutes.
4. Boil jars, lids, and bands for 10 minutes to sterilize them. Keep jars warm.
5. Filling Jars Ladle the chickpea curry into jars, leaving 25 mm (1 inch) headspace. Remove any air bubbles.
6. Clean the rims, secure lids, and tighten rings finger-tight.
7. Process jars in a pressure canner at 10 pounds of pressure (11 pounds for dial-gauge canner) for 75 minutes for quart-sized jars.
8. Turn off heat and let pressure drop naturally after processing. Then wait 2 minutes before opening the canner. Take out the jars and leave to cool down for 12 to 24 hours. Check seals.

NUTRITIONAL VALUE (PER SERVING - 1 CUP): Calories: 260, Carbohydrates: 45g, Fat: 5g, Protein: 15g, Sodium: 400mg, Sugar: 7g

---

SAVORY WHITE BEAN AND ROSEMARY STEW

PREPARATION TIME: 35 MINUTES
SOAKING TIME FOR BEANS: 12 HOURS
COOKING TIME: 1 HOUR 30 MINUTES COOKING, 75 MINUTES PRESSURE CANNING
SERVINGS: ABOUT 6 QUART-SIZED JARS (32 OUNCES EACH)

MAXIMUM STORAGE TIME: 2-3 YEARS (UNOPENED). ONCE OPENED, REFRIGERATE AND USE WITHIN 1 WEEK
RECOMMENDED HEADSPACE: LEAVE 1 INCH (25 MM) HEADSPACE

INGREDIENTS

- 4 lbs dried Great Northern beans, soaked overnight
- 2 large onions, chopped (about 400 grams)
- 4 carrots, diced (about 400 grams)
- 4 stalks celery, diced (about 400 grams)
- 4 cloves garlic, minced
- 8 cups vegetable broth (about 2 liters)
- 1/4 cup fresh rosemary, chopped (about 10 grams)
- 2 bay leaves
- 2 teaspoons salt (10 grams)
- 1 teaspoon black pepper (2 grams)
- 2 tablespoons olive oil
- 6 clean quart-sized canning jars with lids and bands

INSTRUCTIONS

1. In a large pot, cook the soaked Great Northern beans in water until tender, about 1 hour. Drain and set aside. In another pot, heat olive oil over medium heat. Sauté onions, carrots, celery, and garlic until softened.
2. Add the cooked beans to the pot with sautéed vegetables. Stir in vegetable broth, rosemary, bay leaves, salt, and black pepper. Bring to a simmer and cook for 30 minutes.
3. Boil jars, lids, and bands for 10 minutes to sterilize them. Keep jars warm.
4. Ladle the stew into jars, leaving 25 mm (1 inch) headspace. Remove any air bubbles.
5. Clean the rims, secure lids, and tighten rings finger-tight.
6. Process jars in a pressure canner at 10 pounds of pressure (11 pounds for dial-gauge canner) for 75 minutes for quart-sized jars.
7. Turn off heat and let pressure drop naturally after processing. Then wait 2 minutes before opening the canner. Take out the jars and leave to cool down for 12 to 24 hours. Check seals.

SOUPS, STEWS, AND BROTH

HARVEST VEGETABLE SOUP

PREPARATION TIME: 30 MINUTES
COOKING TIME: 45 MINUTES COOKING, 75 MINUTES PRESSURE CANNING
SERVINGS: ABOUT 6 QUART-SIZED JARS (32 OUNCES EACH)

MAXIMUM STORAGE TIME: 2 YEARS (UNOPENED). ONCE OPENED, REFRIGERATE AND USE WITHIN 1 WEEK
RECOMMENDED HEADSPACE: LEAVE 1 INCH (25 MM) HEADSPACE

INGREDIENTS

- 2 lbs potatoes, diced (about 900 grams)
- 1 lb carrots, diced (about 450 grams)
- 1 lb green beans, cut into 1-inch pieces (about 450 grams)
- 2 cups corn kernels, fresh or frozen (300 grams)
- 1 large onion, chopped (about 200 grams)
- 3 cloves garlic, minced

- 1 lb tomatoes, diced (about 450 grams)
- 8 cups vegetable broth (about 2 liters)
- 2 teaspoons dried thyme (4 grams)
- 1 teaspoon dried basil (2 grams)
- Salt and black pepper to taste
- 2 tablespoons olive oil
- 6 clean quart-sized canning jars with lids and bands

INSTRUCTIONS

1. In a large pot, heat olive oil over medium heat. Sauté onions and garlic until translucent. Add carrots and potatoes, cook for 10 minutes.
2. Stir in green beans, corn, tomatoes, vegetable broth, thyme, basil, salt, and pepper. Bring to a boil, then simmer for 30 minutes.
3. Boil jars, lids, and bands for 10 minutes to sterilize them. Keep jars warm.
4. Fill the jars with the soup, leaving 25 mm (1 inch) headspace. Remove any air bubbles.
5. Clean the rims, secure lids, and tighten rings finger-tight.
6. Process jars in a pressure canner at 10 pounds of pressure (11 pounds for dial-gauge canner) for 75 minutes for quart-sized jars.
7. Turn off the heat, let the pressure return to zero naturally, and then wait 2 minutes before opening the canner. Take out the jars and leave to cool down for 12 to 24 hours. Check seals.

NUTRITIONAL VALUE (PER SERVING - 1 CUP): Calories: 120, Carbohydrates: 25g, Fat: 2g, Protein: 3g, Sodium: 300mg, Sugar: 4g

---

HEARTY VEGETABLE AND BARLEY SOUP

PREPARATION TIME: 20 MINUTES
COOKING TIME: 1 HOUR COOKING, 75 MINUTES PRESSURE CANNING
SERVINGS: ABOUT 6 QUART-SIZED JARS (32 OUNCES EACH)

MAXIMUM STORAGE TIME: 2-3 YEARS (UNOPENED). ONCE OPENED, REFRIGERATE AND USE WITHIN 1 WEEK
RECOMMENDED HEADSPACE: LEAVE 1 INCH (25 MM) HEADSPACE

CONTINUED →

INGREDIENTS

- 2 cups pearl barley (about 400 grams)
- 4 large carrots, diced (about 600 grams)
- 3 celery stalks, diced (about 300 grams)
- 2 large onions, chopped (about 400 grams)
- 4 cloves garlic, minced
- 1 cup frozen peas (about 150 grams)
- 1 cup frozen corn (about 150 grams)
- 1 can (14.5 ounces) diced tomatoes (410 grams)
- 8 cups vegetable broth (about 2 liters)
- 1 teaspoon dried thyme (2 grams)
- 1 teaspoon dried basil (2 grams)
- Salt and black pepper to taste
- 2 tablespoons olive oil
- 6 clean quart-sized canning jars with lids and bands

INSTRUCTIONS

1. In a large pot, heat olive oil over medium heat. Add onions, carrots, celery, and garlic. Sauté for about 10 minutes.
2. Stir in pearl barley, then add vegetable broth. Bring the mixture to a boil.
3. Reduce heat and add thyme, basil, salt, and black pepper. Simmer for 40 minutes.
4. Stir in frozen peas, corn, and canned tomatoes. Cook for an additional 10 minutes.
5. Boil jars, lids, and bands for 10 minutes to sterilize them. Keep jars warm.
6. Fill the jars with the hot soup, leaving 25 mm (1 inch) headspace. Remove any air bubbles.
7. Clean the rims, secure lids, and tighten rings finger-tight.
8. Process jars in a pressure canner at 10 pounds of pressure (11 pounds for dial-gauge canner) for 75 minutes for quart-sized jars.
9. Turn off heat and let pressure drop naturally after processing. Then wait 2 minutes before opening the canner. Take out the jars and leave to cool down for 12 to 24 hours. Check seals.

NUTRITIONAL VALUE (PER SERVING - 1 CUP): Calories: 180, Carbohydrates: 35g, Fat: 3g, Protein: 5g, Sodium: 300mg, Sugar: 4g

---

TUSCAN WHITE BEAN AND KALE SOUP

PREPARATION TIME: 15 MINUTES
COOKING TIME: 45 MINUTES COOKING, 75 MINUTES PRESSURE CANNING
SERVINGS: ABOUT 6 QUART-SIZED JARS (32 OUNCES EACH)

MAXIMUM STORAGE TIME: 2-3 YEARS (UNOPENED). ONCE OPENED, REFRIGERATE AND USE WITHIN 1 WEEK
RECOMMENDED HEADSPACE: LEAVE 1 INCH (25 MM) HEADSPACE

INGREDIENTS

- 4 cups white beans (like cannellini or Great Northern), pre-soaked (about 800 grams)
- 6 cups chopped kale (about 1 kg)
- 3 large carrots, diced (about 600 grams)
- 2 medium onions, chopped (about 400 grams)
- 4 cloves garlic, minced
- 1 can (14.5 ounces) diced tomatoes, with juice (about 410 grams)
- 8 cups vegetable broth (about 2 liters)
- 2 teaspoons dried Italian seasoning (4 grams)
- 1/2 teaspoon red pepper flakes (adjust to taste)
- Salt and black pepper to taste
- 2 tablespoons olive oil
- 6 clean quart-sized canning jars with lids and bands

INSTRUCTIONS

1. In a large pot, heat olive oil over medium heat. Add onions, carrots, and garlic. Sauté for about 10 minutes.
2. Stir in pre-soaked white beans and vegetable broth. Bring the mixture to a boil.
3. Reduce heat, add Italian seasoning, red pepper flakes, salt, and black pepper. Simmer for 30 minutes, or until beans are tender.
4. Stir in chopped kale and canned tomatoes with juice. Cook for an additional 15 minutes, until kale is wilted but still vibrant.
5. Boil jars, lids, and bands for 10 minutes to sterilize them. Keep jars warm.
6. Fill the jars with the hot soup, leaving 25 mm (1 inch) headspace. Remove any air bubbles.
7. Clean the rims, secure lids, and tighten rings finger-tight.
8. Process jars in a pressure canner at 10 pounds of pressure (11 pounds for dial-gauge canner) for 75 minutes for quart-sized jars.
9. Turn off heat and let pressure drop naturally after processing. Then wait 2 minutes before opening the canner. Take out the jars and leave to cool down for 12 to 24 hours. Check seals.

SHOPPING TIPS: Choose dry white beans such as cannellini or Great Northern, and remember to soak them overnight before use.

NUTRITIONAL VALUE (PER SERVING - 1 CUP): Calories: 190, Carbohydrates: 30g, Fat: 4g, Protein: 10g, Sodium: 400mg, Sugar: 5g

---

BEEF BARLEY AND MUSHROOM SOUP

PREPARATION TIME: 25 MINUTES
COOKING TIME: 1 HOUR 15 MINUTES COOKING, 90 MINUTES PRESSURE CANNING
SERVINGS: ABOUT 6 QUART-SIZED JARS (32 OUNCES EACH)

MAXIMUM STORAGE TIME: 2-3 YEARS (UNOPENED). ONCE OPENED, REFRIGERATE AND USE WITHIN 1 WEEK
RECOMMENDED HEADSPACE: LEAVE 1 INCH (25 MM) HEADSPACE

INGREDIENTS

- 4 lbs stewing beef, cut into 1-inch pieces (1.8 kg)
- 2 cups pearl barley (about 400 grams)
- 3 cups sliced mushrooms (about 750 grams)
- 2 large onions, chopped (about 400 grams)
- 4 cloves garlic, minced
- 8 cups beef broth (about 2 liters)
- 2 tablespoons tomato paste (30 ml)
- 2 teaspoons dried rosemary (4 grams)
- 1 teaspoon dried thyme (2 grams)
- Salt and black pepper to taste
- 2 tablespoons olive oil
- 6 clean quart-sized canning jars with lids and bands

INSTRUCTIONS

1. In a large skillet, heat 1 tablespoon of olive oil over medium-high heat. Brown the beef pieces in batches, then transfer to a large soup pot.
2. In the same skillet, add another tablespoon of olive oil. Sauté onions, garlic, and mushrooms.
3. Add the sautéed vegetables to the beef along with pearl barley, beef broth, tomato paste, rosemary, thyme, salt, and black pepper. Stir well.
4. Bring the mixture to a boil, then reduce heat and simmer for about 1 hour, or until the flavors have melded together.
5. Boil jars, lids, and bands for 10 minutes to sterilize them. Keep jars warm.
6. Fill the jars with the hot soup, leaving 25 mm (1 inch) headspace. Remove any air bubbles.
7. Clean the rims, secure lids, and tighten rings finger-tight.

157

CONTINUED →

8. Process jars in a pressure canner at 11 pounds of pressure (for weighted-gauge canner) or 10 pounds (for dial-gauge canner) for 90 minutes for quart-sized jars.

9. Turn off heat and let pressure drop naturally after processing. Then wait 2 minutes before opening the canner. Take out the jars and leave to cool down for 12 to 24 hours. Check seals.

SHOPPING TIPS:

*   Opt for high-quality stewing beef with a good balance of meat and fat for flavor.

PREPARATION TIPS:

*   This Beef Barley and Mushroom Soup is hearty and filling, perfect for cold days.

NUTRITIONAL VALUE (PER SERVING - 1 CUP): Calories: 260, Carbohydrates: 30g, Fat: 8g, Protein: 20g, Sodium: 400mg, Sugar: 3g

---

SPICY BEEF AND VEGETABLE GUMBO

PREPARATION TIME: 20 MINUTES
COOKING TIME: 1 HOUR COOKING, 90 MINUTES PRESSURE CANNING
SERVINGS: ABOUT 6 QUART-SIZED JARS (32 OUNCES EACH)

MAXIMUM STORAGE TIME: 2-3 YEARS (UNOPENED). ONCE OPENED, REFRIGERATE AND USE WITHIN 1 WEEK
RECOMMENDED HEADSPACE: LEAVE 1 INCH (25 MM) HEADSPACE

INGREDIENTS

*   4 lbs beef chuck, cut into 1-inch cubes (1.8 kg)
*   3 cups okra, sliced (about 750 grams)
*   2 bell peppers (one red, one green), diced (about 400 grams total)
*   2 large onions, chopped (about 400 grams)
*   4 stalks celery, chopped (about 400 grams)
*   4 cloves garlic, minced
*   1 can (14.5 ounces) diced tomatoes, with juice (about 410 grams)
*   8 cups beef broth (about 2 liters)
*   2 tablespoons Cajun seasoning (10 grams)
*   1 teaspoon smoked paprika (2 grams)
*   1/2 teaspoon cayenne pepper (adjust to taste)
*   1/2 cup all-purpose flour (about 60 grams)
*   1/2 cup vegetable oil (about 120 ml)
*   Salt and black pepper to taste
*   6 clean quart-sized canning jars with lids and bands

INSTRUCTIONS

1. In a large pot, heat vegetable oil over medium heat. Gradually add flour, stirring constantly until the mixture becomes a dark brown color, about 10-15 minutes.
2. Add onions, bell peppers, celery, garlic, and beef to the roux. Cook until the beef is browned and vegetables are softened.
3. Stir in beef broth, diced tomatoes with juice, smoked paprika, Cajun seasoning, cayenne pepper, salt, and black pepper. Bring to a boil, then reduce heat and simmer for about 45 minutes.
4. Stir in okra and cook for an additional 15 minutes.
5. Boil jars, lids, and bands for 10 minutes to sterilize them. Keep jars warm.
6. Ladle the hot gumbo into jars, leaving 25 mm (1 inch) headspace. Remove any air bubbles.
7. Clean the rims, secure lids, and tighten rings finger-tight.
8. Process jars in a pressure canner at 11 pounds of pressure (for weighted-gauge canner) or 10 pounds (for dial-gauge canner) for 90 minutes for quart-sized jars.
9. Turn off heat and let pressure drop naturally after processing. Then wait 2 minutes before opening the canner. Take out the jars and leave to cool down for 12 to 24 hours. Check seals.

CLASSIC CHICKEN NOODLE SOUP

PREPARATION TIME: 20 MINUTES
COOKING TIME: 1 HOUR COOKING, 90 MINUTES PRESSURE CANNING
SERVINGS: ABOUT 6 QUART-SIZED JARS (32 OUNCES EACH)

MAXIMUM STORAGE TIME: 2-3 YEARS (UNOPENED). ONCE OPENED, REFRIGERATE AND USE WITHIN 1 WEEK
RECOMMENDED HEADSPACE: LEAVE 1 INCH (25 MM) HEADSPACE

INGREDIENTS

- 4 lbs chicken breast, cut into bite-sized pieces (about 1.8 kg)
- 4 large carrots, sliced (about 800 grams)
- 3 celery stalks, sliced (about 300 grams)
- 2 large onions, chopped (about 400 grams)
- 4 cloves garlic, minced
- 10 cups chicken broth (about 2.5 liters)

- 2 cups egg noodles (about 200 grams)
- 1 teaspoon dried thyme (2 grams)
- 1 teaspoon dried oregano (2 grams)
- Salt and black pepper to taste
- 2 tablespoons olive oil
- 6 clean quart-sized canning jars with lids and bands

INSTRUCTIONS

1. In a large pot, heat olive oil over medium heat. Add chicken pieces and cook until browned. Remove chicken and set aside.
2. In the same pot, add onions, carrots, celery, and garlic. Sauté until the vegetables are slightly softened.
3. Return the chicken to the pot. Add chicken broth, thyme, oregano, salt, and black pepper. Bring to a boil, then reduce heat and simmer for about 30 minutes.
4. Stir in egg noodles and cook for another 10 minutes.
5. Boil jars, lids, and bands for 10 minutes to sterilize them. Keep jars warm.
6. Fill the jars with the hot soup, leaving 25 mm (1 inch) headspace. Remember, the noodles will expand, so ensure there's enough liquid to cover them. Remove any air bubbles.
7. Clean the rims, secure lids, and tighten rings finger-tight.
8. Process jars in a pressure canner at 11 pounds of pressure (for weighted-gauge canner) or 10 pounds (for dial-gauge canner) for 90 minutes for quart-sized jars.
9. Turn off heat and let pressure drop naturally after processing. Then wait 2 minutes before opening the canner. Take out the jars and leave to cool down for 12 to 24 hours. Check seals.

NUTRITIONAL VALUE (PER SERVING - 1 CUP): Calories: 150, Carbohydrates: 12g, Fat: 4g, Protein: 18g, Sodium: 500mg, Sugar: 3g

---

CREAMY CHICKEN AND WILD RICE SOUP

PREPARATION TIME: 20 MINUTES
COOKING TIME: 1 HOUR COOKING, 90 MINUTES PRESSURE CANNING
SERVINGS: ABOUT 6 QUART-SIZED JARS (32 OUNCES EACH)

MAXIMUM STORAGE TIME: 2-3 YEARS (UNOPENED). ONCE OPENED, REFRIGERATE AND USE WITHIN 1 WEEK
RECOMMENDED HEADSPACE: LEAVE 1 INCH (25 MM) HEADSPACE

CONTINUED →

INGREDIENTS

- 4 lbs chicken thighs, boneless and skinless, cut into bite-sized pieces (about 1.8 kg)
- 2 cups wild rice, rinsed (about 400 grams)
- 3 large carrots, diced (about 600 grams)
- 2 onions, diced (about 400 grams)
- 3 celery stalks, diced (about 300 grams)
- 4 cloves garlic, minced
- 10 cups chicken broth (about 2.5 liters)
- 1 cup heavy cream (about 240 ml)
- 2 teaspoons dried parsley (4 grams)
- 1 teaspoon dried thyme (2 grams)
- Salt and black pepper to taste
- 2 tablespoons olive oil
- 6 clean quart-sized canning jars with lids and bands

INSTRUCTIONS

1. In a large pot, heat olive oil over medium heat. Add chicken and cook until lightly browned. Remove chicken and set aside.
2. In the same pot, add onions, carrots, celery, and garlic. Sauté until the vegetables are softened.
3. Return the chicken to the pot. Stir in wild rice and chicken broth. Add parsley, thyme, salt, and black pepper. Bring to a boil, then reduce heat and simmer for about 45 minutes, or until the rice is tender.
4. Stir in heavy cream and cook for an additional 10 minutes.
5. Boil jars, lids, and bands for 10 minutes to sterilize them. Keep jars warm.
6. Fill the jars with the hot soup, leaving 25 mm (1 inch) headspace. Remove any air bubbles.
7. Clean the rims, secure lids, and tighten rings finger-tight.
8. Process jars in a pressure canner at 11 pounds of pressure (for weighted-gauge canner) or 10 pounds (for dial-gauge canner) for 90 minutes for quart-sized jars.
9. Turn off heat and let pressure drop naturally after processing. Then wait 2 minutes before opening the canner. Take out the jars and leave to cool down for 12 to 24 hours. Check seals.

NUTRITIONAL VALUE (PER SERVING - 1 CUP): Calories: 200, Carbohydrates: 18g, Fat: 9g, Protein: 15g, Sodium: 450mg, Sugar: 3g

---

SPICY CHICKEN TORTILLA SOUP

PREPARATION TIME: 25 MINUTES
COOKING TIME: 45 MINUTES COOKING, 90 MINUTES PRESSURE CANNING
SERVINGS: ABOUT 6 QUART-SIZED JARS (32 OUNCES EACH)

MAXIMUM STORAGE TIME: 2-3 YEARS (UNOPENED). ONCE OPENED, REFRIGERATE AND USE WITHIN 1 WEEK
RECOMMENDED HEADSPACE: LEAVE 1 INCH (25 MM) HEADSPACE

INGREDIENTS

- 4 lbs boneless, skinless chicken breasts, chopped
- 2 large onions, chopped (about 400 grams)
- 3 bell peppers (assorted colors), diced (600 grams)
- 4 cloves garlic, minced
- 2 cans (14.5 ounces each) diced tomatoes, with juice (about 800 grams total)
- 2 cans (4 ounces each) diced green chilies (about 225 grams total)
- 10 cups chicken broth (about 2.5 liters)
- 2 tablespoons chili powder (10 grams)
- 1 tablespoon ground cumin (5 grams)
- 1 teaspoon smoked paprika (2 grams)
- 1/2 teaspoon cayenne pepper (adjust to taste)
- Salt and black pepper to taste
- 2 tablespoons olive oil
- 2 cups frozen corn kernels (about 400 grams)
- 1/2 cup chopped fresh cilantro (about 20 grams)

INSTRUCTIONS

1. In a large pot, heat olive oil over medium heat. Add chicken and cook until browned. Remove chicken and set aside.
2. In the same pot, add onions, bell peppers, and garlic. Sauté until the vegetables are softened.
3. Return the chicken to the pot. Stir in diced tomatoes with juice, green chilies, chicken broth, chili powder, cumin, smoked paprika, cayenne pepper, salt, and black pepper. Bring to a boil, then reduce heat and simmer for about 30 minutes.
4. Cook 5 more minutes with frozen corn. Remove from heat and stir in fresh cilantro.
5. Boil jars, lids, and bands for 10 minutes to sterilize them. Keep jars warm.
6. Fill the jars with the hot soup, leaving 25 mm (1 inch) headspace. Remove any air bubbles.
7. Clean the rims, secure lids, and tighten rings finger-tight.
8. Process jars in a pressure canner at 11 pounds of pressure (for weighted-gauge canner) or 10 pounds (for dial-gauge canner) for 90 minutes for quart-sized jars.
9. Turn off heat and let pressure drop naturally after processing. Then wait 2 minutes before opening the canner. Take out the jars and leave to cool down for 12 to 24 hours. Check seals.

NUTRITIONAL VALUE (PER SERVING - 1 CUP): Calories: 190, Carbohydrates: 15g, Fat: 5g, Protein: 20g, Sodium: 450mg, Sugar: 4g

---

CLASSIC BEEF STEW

PREPARATION TIME: 30 MINUTES
COOKING TIME: 2 HOURS COOKING, 90 MINUTES PRESSURE CANNING
SERVINGS: ABOUT 6 QUART-SIZED JARS (32 OUNCES EACH)

MAXIMUM STORAGE TIME: 2-3 YEARS (UNOPENED). ONCE OPENED, REFRIGERATE AND USE WITHIN 1 WEEK
RECOMMENDED HEADSPACE: LEAVE 1 INCH (25 MM) HEADSPACE

INGREDIENTS

- *4 lbs beef stew meat, cut into 1-inch cubes (1.8 kg)*
- *4 cups potatoes, peeled and cubed (about 1 kg)*
- *3 cups carrots, sliced (about 750 grams)*
- *2 cups onions, chopped (about 500 grams)*
- *1 cup celery, chopped (about 250 grams)*
- *4 cloves garlic, minced*
- *6 cups beef broth (about 1.5 liters)*
- *1 can (6 ounces) tomato paste (170 grams)*
- *2 tablespoons Worcestershire sauce (30 ml)*
- *1 teaspoon dried thyme (2 grams)*
- *1 teaspoon dried rosemary (2 grams)*
- *Salt and black pepper to taste*
- *3 tablespoons all-purpose flour*
- *3 tablespoons vegetable oil*
- *6 clean quart-sized canning jars with lids and bands*

INSTRUCTIONS

1. In a large skillet, heat 1 tablespoon of oil over medium-high heat. Brown the beef cubes in batches, then transfer to a large soup pot.
2. In the same skillet, add remaining oil. Sauté onions, garlic, carrots, and celery until slightly softened.
3. Add sautéed vegetables to the pot with beef. Stir in potatoes, beef broth, thyme, tomato paste, rosemary, Worcestershire sauce, salt, and black pepper.
4. In a small bowl, mix flour with a little water to make a paste. Stir into the stew to thicken.
5. Bring to a boil, then reduce heat and simmer for about 1.5 hours, or until beef is tender.
6. Boil jars, lids, and bands for 10 minutes to sterilize them. Keep jars warm.

CONTINUED →

7. Ladle the hot stew into jars, leaving 25 mm (1 inch) headspace. Remove any air bubbles.
8. Clean the rims, secure lids, and tighten rings finger-tight.
9. Process jars in a pressure canner at 11 pounds of pressure (for weighted-gauge canner) or 10 pounds (for dial-gauge canner) for 90 minutes for quart-sized jars.
10. Turn off heat and let pressure drop naturally after processing. Then wait 2 minutes before opening the canner. Take out the jars and leave to cool down for 12 to 24 hours. Check seals.

NUTRITIONAL VALUE (PER SERVING - 1 CUP): Calories: 250, Carbohydrates: 20g, Fat: 10g, Protein: 20g, Sodium: 400mg, Sugar: 5g

HEARTY WHITE FISH AND CORN CHOWDER

PREPARATION TIME: 20 MINUTES
COOKING TIME: 1 HOUR COOKING, 90 MINUTES PRESSURE CANNING
SERVINGS: ABOUT 6 QUART-SIZED JARS (32 OUNCES EACH)

MAXIMUM STORAGE TIME: 2-3 YEARS (UNOPENED). ONCE OPENED, REFRIGERATE AND USE WITHIN 1 WEEK
RECOMMENDED HEADSPACE: LEAVE 1 INCH (25 MM) HEADSPACE

INGREDIENTS

- *4 lbs white fish fillets, such as cod or halibut, cut into 1-inch pieces (about 1.8 kg)*
- *4 cups potatoes, peeled and cubed (about 1 kg)*
- *2 cups sweet corn kernels, fresh or frozen (about 500 grams)*
- *2 large onions, chopped (about 400 grams)*
- *4 cloves garlic, minced*
- *2 bell peppers, diced (about 400 grams)*

- *6 cups fish or vegetable broth (about 1.5 liters)*
- *2 cups heavy cream (about 480 ml)*
- *2 teaspoons dried thyme (4 grams)*
- *1 teaspoon smoked paprika (2 grams)*
- *Salt and black pepper to taste*
- *2 tablespoons butter or olive oil*
- *6 clean quart-sized canning jars with lids and bands*

INSTRUCTIONS

1. In a large pot, melt butter or heat olive oil over medium heat. Add onions, garlic, bell peppers, and potatoes. Cook for about 10 minutes.
2. Pour in fish or vegetable broth. Stir in thyme, smoked paprika, salt, and black pepper. Bring to a boil, then reduce heat and simmer until potatoes are almost tender, about 20 minutes.
3. Stir in fish fillets and corn. Continue to simmer for another 10 minutes, or until fish is cooked through and flakes easily.
4. Reduce heat to low and stir in heavy cream. Cook for an additional 5 minutes, being careful not to let it boil.
5. Boil jars, lids, and bands for 10 minutes to sterilize them. Keep jars warm.
6. Ladle the hot chowder into jars, leaving 25 mm (1 inch) headspace. Remove any air bubbles.
7. Clean the rims, secure lids, and tighten rings finger-tight.
8. Process jars in a pressure canner at 11 pounds of pressure (for weighted-gauge canner) or 10 pounds (for dial-gauge canner) for 90 minutes for quart-sized jars.
9. Turn off heat and let pressure drop naturally after processing. Then wait 2 minutes before opening the canner. Take out the jars and leave to cool down for 12 to 24 hours. Check seals.

NUTRITIONAL VALUE (PER SERVING - 1 CUP): Calories: 280, Carbohydrates: 25g, Fat: 14g, Protein: 20g, Sodium: 350mg, Sugar: 5g

HEARTY CHICKEN AND VEGETABLE STEW

PREPARATION TIME: 25 MINUTES
COOKING TIME: 1 HOUR COOKING, 90 MINUTES PRESSURE CANNING
SERVINGS: ABOUT 6 QUART-SIZED JARS (32 OUNCES EACH)

MAXIMUM STORAGE TIME: 2-3 YEARS (UNOPENED). ONCE OPENED, REFRIGERATE AND USE WITHIN 1 WEEK
RECOMMENDED HEADSPACE: LEAVE 1 INCH (25 MM) HEADSPACE

INGREDIENTS

- 4 lbs chicken thighs, boneless and skinless, cut into 1-inch pieces (about 1.8 kg)
- 3 cups potatoes, diced (about 750 grams)
- 2 cups carrots, sliced (about 500 grams)
- 2 cups celery, chopped (about 500 grams)
- 2 onions, diced (about 400 grams)
- 4 cloves garlic, minced
- 8 cups chicken broth (about 2 liters)
- 1 can (14.5 ounces) diced tomatoes, with juice (about 410 grams)
- 2 teaspoons dried thyme (4 grams)
- 1 teaspoon dried rosemary (2 grams)
- Salt and black pepper to taste
- 2 tablespoons olive oil
- 6 clean quart-sized canning jars with lids and bands

INSTRUCTIONS

1. In a large pot, heat 1 tablespoon of olive oil over medium-high heat. Brown the chicken pieces, then set them aside.
2. In the same pot, add the remaining oil and sauté onions, garlic, carrots, and celery until slightly softened.
3. Return the chicken to the pot. Add potatoes, chicken broth, diced tomatoes with juice, thyme, rosemary, salt, and black pepper.
4. Bring to a boil, then reduce heat and simmer for about 45 minutes.
5. Boil jars, lids, and bands for 10 minutes to sterilize them. Keep jars warm.
6. Ladle the hot stew into jars, leaving 25 mm (1 inch) headspace. Remove any air bubbles.
7. Clean the rims, secure lids, and tighten rings finger-tight.
8. Process jars in a pressure canner at 11 pounds of pressure (for weighted-gauge canner) or 10 pounds (for dial-gauge canner) for 90 minutes for quart-sized jars.
9. Turn off heat and let pressure drop naturally after processing. Then wait 2 minutes before opening the canner. Take out the jars and leave to cool down for 12 to 24 hours. Check seals.

NUTRITIONAL VALUE (PER SERVING - 1 CUP): Calories: 210, Carbohydrates: 20g, Fat: 7g, Protein: 18g, Sodium: 400mg, Sugar: 5g

RUSTIC PORK AND WHITE BEAN STEW

PREPARATION TIME: 20 MINUTES
COOKING TIME: 1 HOUR 30 MINUTES COOKING, 90 MINUTES PRESSURE CANNING
SERVINGS: ABOUT 6 QUART-SIZED JARS (32 OUNCES EACH)

MAXIMUM STORAGE TIME: 2-3 YEARS (UNOPENED). ONCE OPENED, REFRIGERATE AND USE WITHIN 1 WEEK
RECOMMENDED HEADSPACE: LEAVE 1 INCH (25 MM) HEADSPACE

CONTINUED →

INGREDIENTS

- 4 lbs pork shoulder, cut into 1-inch cubes (1.8 kg)
- 4 cups white beans, soaked overnight and drained (about 1 kg)
- 3 large carrots, diced (about 600 grams)
- 2 onions, chopped (about 400 grams)
- 4 cloves garlic, minced
- 8 cups chicken or pork broth (about 2 liters)
- 1 can (14.5 ounces) diced tomatoes, with juice (about 410 grams)
- 2 tablespoons tomato paste (30 ml)
- 2 teaspoons dried sage (4 grams)
- 1 teaspoon dried thyme (2 grams)
- Salt and black pepper to taste
- 2 tablespoons olive oil
- 6 clean quart-sized canning jars with lids and bands

INSTRUCTIONS

1. In a large pot, heat 1 tablespoon of olive oil over medium-high heat. Brown the pork cubes in batches, then set aside.
2. In the same pot, add the remaining oil and sauté onions, garlic, and carrots until softened.
3. Return the pork to the pot. Add white beans, chicken or pork broth, diced tomatoes with juice, tomato paste, sage, thyme, salt, and black pepper.
4. Bring to a boil, then reduce heat and simmer for about 1 hour 30 minutes, or until pork and beans are tender.
5. Boil jars, lids, and bands for 10 minutes to sterilize them. Keep jars warm.
6. Ladle the hot stew into jars, leaving 25 mm (1 inch) headspace. Remove any air bubbles.
7. Clean the rims, secure lids, and tighten rings finger-tight.
8. Process jars in a pressure canner at 11 pounds of pressure (for weighted-gauge canner) or 10 pounds (for dial-gauge canner) for 90 minutes for quart-sized jars.
9. Turn off heat and let pressure drop naturally after processing. Then wait 2 minutes before opening the canner. Take out the jars and leave to cool down for 12 to 24 hours. Check seals.

NUTRITIONAL VALUE (PER SERVING - 1 CUP): Calories: 300, Carbohydrates: 25g, Fat: 12g, Protein: 22g, Sodium: 500mg, Sugar: 4g

---

SPICY TOMATO AND LENTIL STEW

PREPARATION TIME: 15 MINUTES
COOKING TIME: 45 MINUTES COOKING, 90 MINUTES PRESSURE CANNING
SERVINGS: ABOUT 6 QUART-SIZED JARS (32 OUNCES EACH)

MAXIMUM STORAGE TIME: 2-3 YEARS (UNOPENED). ONCE OPENED, REFRIGERATE AND USE WITHIN 1 WEEK
RECOMMENDED HEADSPACE: LEAVE 1 INCH (25 MM) HEADSPACE

INGREDIENTS

- 4 cups red lentils, rinsed (about 800 grams)
- 3 large tomatoes, diced (about 600 grams)
- 2 onions, chopped (about 400 grams)
- 4 cloves garlic, minced
- 2 carrots, diced (about 400 grams)
- 2 bell peppers (one red, one green), diced (about 400 grams)
- 8 cups vegetable broth (about 2 liters)
- 2 tablespoons tomato paste (30 ml)
- 2 teaspoons ground cumin (4 grams)
- 1 teaspoon smoked paprika (2 grams)
- 1/2 teaspoon red chili flakes (adjust to taste)
- Salt and black pepper to taste
- 2 tablespoons olive oil
- 6 clean quart-sized canning jars with lids and bands

INSTRUCTIONS

1. In a large pot, heat olive oil over medium heat. Add onions, garlic, carrots, and bell peppers. Sauté until the vegetables are softened.
2. Stir in red lentils, vegetable broth, diced tomatoes, tomato paste, cumin, smoked paprika, chili flakes, salt, and black pepper.
3. Bring the mixture to a boil, then reduce heat and simmer for about 30-35 minutes, or until lentils are tender.
4. Boil jars, lids, and bands for 10 minutes to sterilize them. Keep jars warm.
5. Ladle the hot stew into jars, leaving 25 mm (1 inch) headspace. Remove any air bubbles.
6. Clean the rims, secure lids, and tighten rings finger-tight.
7. Process jars in a pressure canner at 11 pounds of pressure (for weighted-gauge canner) or 10 pounds (for dial-gauge canner) for 90 minutes for quart-sized jars.
8. Turn off heat and let pressure drop naturally after processing. Then wait 2 minutes before opening the canner. Take out the jars and leave to cool down for 12 to 24 hours. Check seals; the lid should not flex when pressed.

PREPARATION TIPS:

- This spicy tomato and lentil stew is a hearty, vegetarian-friendly dish, perfect for those who enjoy a bit of heat.
- Serve with a dollop of yogurt or sour cream to balance the spice, and pair it with crusty bread for a complete meal.

NUTRITIONAL VALUE (PER SERVING - 1 CUP): Calories: 220, Carbohydrates: 35g, Fat: 4g, Protein: 15g, Sodium: 300mg, Sugar: 6g

---

CLASSIC CHICKEN BONE BROTH

PREPARATION TIME: 20 MINUTES
COOKING TIME: 12 HOURS COOKING, 90 MINUTES PRESSURE CANNING
SERVINGS: ABOUT 6 QUART-SIZED JARS (32 OUNCES EACH)

MAXIMUM STORAGE TIME: 2-3 YEARS (UNOPENED). ONCE OPENED, REFRIGERATE AND USE WITHIN 1 WEEK
RECOMMENDED HEADSPACE: 1 INCH (25 MM) HEADSPACE

INGREDIENTS

- *4 lbs chicken bones, including necks, backs, and wings (about 1.8 kg)*
- *3 carrots, roughly chopped*
- *2 onions, quartered*
- *4 cloves garlic, smashed*
- *3 celery stalks, roughly chopped*
- *2 bay leaves*
- *1 tablespoon whole black peppercorns (5 grams)*
- *1 small bunch of fresh thyme*

- *1 small bunch of fresh parsley*
- *12 cups water (about 2.8 liters)*
- *2 tablespoons apple cider vinegar (30 ml)*
- *Salt to taste (optional)*
- *6 clean quart-sized canning jars with lids and bands*

INSTRUCTIONS

1. In a large stockpot, combine chicken bones, carrots, onions, garlic, celery, bay leaves, peppercorns, thyme, parsley, and water. Add apple cider vinegar (helps extract nutrients from bones).

CONTINUED →

2. Bring to a boil, then reduce heat to a low simmer. Let the broth simmer gently for 12 hours, removing foams or impurities from the top.
3. After simmering, strain the broth through a fine-mesh sieve. Optionally, season with salt to taste.
4. Boil jars, lids, and bands for 10 minutes to sterilize them. Keep jars warm.
5. Fill the jars with the hot broth, leaving 25 mm (1 inch) headspace. Remove any air bubbles.

6. Clean the rims, secure lids, and tighten rings finger-tight.
7. Process jars in a pressure canner at 11 pounds of pressure (for weighted-gauge canner) or 10 pounds (for dial-gauge canner) for 90 minutes for quart-sized jars.
8. Turn off heat and let pressure drop naturally after processing. Then wait 2 minutes before opening the canner. Take out the jars and leave to cool down for 12 to 24 hours. Check seals.

SHOPPING TIPS:

- Choose a variety of chicken bones for a richer flavor, including some meaty pieces like backs or wings.

NUTRITIONAL VALUE (PER SERVING - 1 CUP): Calories: 40, Carbohydrates: 2g, Fat: 0g, Protein: 5g

---

RICH BEEF BONE BROTH

PREPARATION TIME: 20 MINUTES
COOKING TIME: 12 HOURS COOKING, 90 MINUTES PRESSURE CANNING
SERVINGS: ABOUT 6 QUART-SIZED JARS (32 OUNCES EACH)

MAXIMUM STORAGE TIME: 2-3 YEARS (UNOPENED). ONCE OPENED, REFRIGERATE AND USE WITHIN 1 WEEK
RECOMMENDED HEADSPACE: LEAVE 1 INCH (25 MM) HEADSPACE

INGREDIENTS

- *4 lbs beef bones (a mix of marrow bones and bones with a little meat, like ribs) (about 1.8 kg)*
- *3 carrots, roughly chopped*
- *3 celery stalks, roughly chopped*
- *2 onions, quartered*
- *1 head of garlic, halved horizontally*
- *2 bay leaves*

- *1 teaspoon whole black peppercorns (2 grams)*
- *A few sprigs of fresh thyme*
- *A handful of fresh parsley*
- *12 cups water (about 2.8 liters)*
- *2 tablespoons apple cider vinegar (30 ml)*
- *Salt to taste (optional)*
- *6 clean quart-sized canning jars with lids and bands*

INSTRUCTIONS

1. Preheat the oven to 425°F (220°C). Roast beef bones on a baking sheet for 30 minutes, turning once, until browned.
2. Transfer the roasted bones to a large stockpot. Add carrots, celery, onions, garlic, bay leaves, peppercorns, thyme, parsley, water, and apple cider vinegar.
3. Bring to a boil, then reduce heat to low and simmer gently, uncovered, for 12 hours. Skim off any foam or impurities.
4. Use a fine-mesh sieve to strain the broth, discarding solids. Optionally season with salt.
5. Boil jars, lids, and bands for 10 minutes to sterilize them. Keep jars warm.

6. Carefully fill the jars with the hot broth, leaving 25 mm (1 inch) headspace.
7. Clean the rims, secure lids, and tighten rings finger-tight.
8. Process jars in a pressure canner at 11 pounds of pressure (for weighted-gauge canner) or 10 pounds (for dial-gauge canner) for 90 minutes for quart-sized jars.
9. Turn off heat and let pressure drop naturally after processing. Then wait 2 minutes before opening the canner. Take out the jars and leave to cool down for 12 to 24 hours. Check seals.

VEGETABLE BROTH

PREPARATION TIME: 15 MINUTES
COOKING TIME: 2 HOURS COOKING, 90 MINUTES PRESSURE CANNING
SERVINGS: ABOUT 6 QUART-SIZED JARS (32 OUNCES EACH)

MAXIMUM STORAGE TIME: 2-3 YEARS (UNOPENED). ONCE OPENED, REFRIGERATE AND USE WITHIN 1 WEEK
RECOMMENDED HEADSPACE: LEAVE 1 INCH (25 MM) HEADSPACE

INGREDIENTS

- 4 cups carrots, chopped (about 1 kg)
- 4 cups celery, chopped (about 1 kg)
- 3 large onions, chopped (about 600 grams)
- 1 head of garlic, halved
- 2 large tomatoes, quartered (about 500 grams)
- 2 bell peppers (any color), chopped (500 grams)
- 1 small bunch of fresh parsley

- 1 small bunch of fresh thyme
- 2 bay leaves
- 1 tablespoon black peppercorns (5 grams)
- 12 cups water (about 2.8 liters)
- Salt to taste (optional)
- 6 clean quart-sized canning jars with lids and bands

INSTRUCTIONS

1. In a large stockpot, add carrots, celery, onions, garlic, tomatoes, bell peppers, parsley, thyme, bay leaves, and peppercorns. Cover with water.
2. Bring to a boil, then reduce heat to low and simmer for 2 hours, allowing flavors to meld.
3. Use a fine-mesh sieve to strain the broth, discarding the solids. Optionally season with salt.
4. Boil jars, lids, and bands for 10 minutes to sterilize them. Keep jars warm.
5. Carefully fill the jars with the hot, leaving 25 mm (1 inch) headspace.
6. Clean the rims, secure lids, and tighten rings finger-tight.
7. Process jars in a pressure canner at 11 pounds of pressure (for weighted-gauge canner) or 10 pounds (for dial-gauge canner) for 90 minutes for quart-sized jars.
8. Turn off heat and let pressure drop naturally after processing. Then wait 2 minutes before opening the canner. Take out the jars and leave to cool down for 12 to 24 hours. Check seals.

NUTRITIONAL VALUE (PER SERVING - 1 CUP): Calories: 20, Carbohydrates: 4g, Protein: 1g

---

SPICY ASIAN-INSPIRED CHICKEN BROTH

PREPARATION TIME: 20 MINUTES
COOKING TIME: 3 HOURS COOKING, 90 MINUTES PRESSURE CANNING
SERVINGS: ABOUT 6 QUART-SIZED JARS (32 OUNCES EACH)

MAXIMUM STORAGE TIME: 2-3 YEARS (UNOPENED). ONCE OPENED, REFRIGERATE AND USE WITHIN 1 WEEK
RECOMMENDED HEADSPACE: LEAVE 1 INCH (25 MM) HEADSPACE

INGREDIENTS

- 4 lbs chicken bones, including necks and wings (about 1.8 kg)

- 6 cups water (about 1.4 liters)
- 2 onions, quartered

CONTINUED →

- 4 cloves garlic, smashed
- 1 large piece of ginger, sliced (about 100 grams)
- 2 stalks lemongrass, bruised and cut into large pieces
- 2 hot chili peppers, halved (adjust to taste)
- 1 tablespoon whole black peppercorns (5 grams)
- 1 bunch fresh cilantro
- 2 bay leaves
- 2 tablespoons soy sauce (30 ml)
- 1 tablespoon fish sauce (15 ml)
- Salt to taste (optional)
- 6 clean quart-sized canning jars with lids and bands

INSTRUCTIONS

1. In a large stockpot, combine chicken bones with water. Bring to a boil and then simmer for about 30 minutes, skimming off any impurities.
2. Add onions, garlic, ginger, lemongrass, chili peppers, peppercorns, cilantro, and bay leaves to the pot.
3. Reduce heat and simmer gently for about 2.5 hours, allowing flavors to infuse.
4. Stir in soy sauce and fish sauce. Optionally season with salt.
5. Use a fine-mesh sieve to strain the broth, discarding solids.
6. Boil jars, lids, and bands for 10 minutes to sterilize them. Keep jars warm.
7. Fill the jars with the hot broth, leaving 25 mm (1 inch) headspace.
8. Clean the rims, secure lids, and tighten rings finger-tight.
9. Process jars in a pressure canner at 11 pounds of pressure (for weighted-gauge canner) or 10 pounds (for dial-gauge canner) for 90 minutes for quart-sized jars.
10. Turn off heat and let pressure drop naturally after processing. Then wait 2 minutes before opening the canner. Take out the jars and leave to cool down for 12 to 24 hours. Check seals.

NUTRITIONAL VALUE (PER SERVING - 1 CUP): Calories: 30, Carbohydrates: 3g, Protein: 4g, Sodium: 300mg

---

HERB-INFUSED VEGETABLE BROTH

PREPARATION TIME: 15 MINUTES
COOKING TIME: 1 HOUR 30 MINUTES COOKING, 90 MINUTES PRESSURE CANNING
SERVINGS: ABOUT 6 QUART-SIZED JARS (32 OUNCES EACH)

MAXIMUM STORAGE TIME: 2-3 YEARS (UNOPENED). ONCE OPENED, REFRIGERATE AND USE WITHIN 1 WEEK
RECOMMENDED HEADSPACE: LEAVE 1 INCH (25 MM) HEADSPACE

INGREDIENTS

- 3 cups carrots, chopped (about 750 grams)
- 3 cups celery, chopped (about 750 grams)
- 4 onions, chopped (about 1 kg)
- 1 head of garlic, halved
- 2 large potatoes, cubed (about 500 grams)
- 1 bunch fresh parsley
- 1 bunch fresh dill
- 2 bay leaves
- 1 tablespoon whole black peppercorns (5 grams)
- 12 cups water (about 2.8 liters)
- Salt to taste (optional)
- 6 clean quart-sized canning jars with lids and bands

INSTRUCTIONS

1. In a large stockpot, add carrots, celery, onions, garlic, potatoes, parsley, dill, bay leaves, and peppercorns. Cover with water.
2. Bring to a boil, then reduce heat to low and let it simmer for about 1 hour 30 minutes.
3. Use a fine-mesh sieve to strain the broth, discarding the solids. Optionally season with salt.

4. Boil jars, lids, and bands for 10 minutes to sterilize them. Keep jars warm.
5. Carefully Fill the jars with the hot broth, leaving 25 mm (1 inch) headspace.
6. Clean the rims, secure lids, and tighten rings finger-tight.
7. Process jars in a pressure canner at 11 pounds of pressure (for weighted-gauge canner) or 10 pounds (for dial-gauge canner) for 90 minutes for quart-sized jars.
8. Turn off heat and let pressure drop naturally after processing. Then wait 2 minutes before opening the canner. Take out the jars and leave to cool down for 12 to 24 hours. Check seals.

SHOPPING TIPS:

• Use a variety of fresh vegetables for a rich and aromatic broth.

PREPARATION TIPS:

• This herb-infused vegetable broth serves as a delicious base for soups and stews or can be used in place of water to add flavor to grains and legumes.

NUTRITIONAL VALUE (PER SERVING - 1 CUP): Calories: 25, Carbohydrates: 6g, Fat: 0g, Protein: 1g